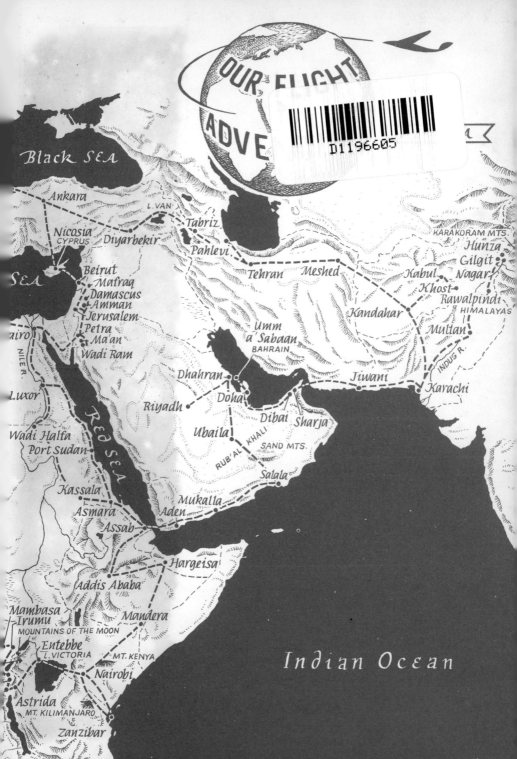

OUR FLIGHT TO ADVENTURE

To Edward Otero, whose
hospitality and help made
a great difference in the
enjoyment and success of
our journey.

Best wishes —

Tay and   Lowell Thomas Jr.
Dec. 13, '56

TAY
AND LOWELL
THOMAS
JR.

DOUBLEDAY & COMPANY, INC., GARDEN CITY, NEW YORK, 1956

OUR
FLIGHT
TO
ADVENTURE

DOUBLEDAY & COMPANY, INC., GARDEN CITY, NEW YORK, 1956

LIBRARY OF CONGRESS CATALOG CARD NUMBER 56–7532

COPYRIGHT © 1956 BY MARY THOMAS
AND LOWELL THOMAS, JR.

PRINTED IN THE UNITED STATES OF AMERICA

FIRST EDITION

To
our daughter ANNE

may her travels take her
beyond our limited horizons, and perhaps even to
other planets.

A Word of Appreciation

My WIFE AND I owe a large debt of gratitude to the many whose faith, encouragement, and assistance enabled us to make our flight to adventure. For their enthusiastic support, we owe especial thanks to Ken McCormick of Doubleday, Davidson Taylor and Donald Hyatt of N.B.C. Television, Ernest Heyn of the *American Weekly*, and DeWitt Wallace of the *Reader's Digest*.

But, most of all, we wish to thank Hawthorne Daniel, whose contribution to this book, by way of organization and editing, has been invaluable.

CONTENTS

OUR FLIGHT TO ADVENTURE

Flight Plan

ANY AIRPLANE FLIGHT MUST BE-
gin long before the plane leaves the ground. That is true even
for the average air-line passenger, but it was far more so for Tay
and me when, on a clear, cool morning in March 1954, we took
off from the airfield of Toussus-le-Noble in our own small, single-
engine plane on the first leg of a flight that turned out to be a
fabulous adventure.

In a certain sense, of course, this take-off was the actual beginning of our aerial Odyssey. Still, we were already 3000 miles from
home, and five busy months of preparation were behind us. In
fact, we had talked ever since our marriage in 1950 about some
such expedition, and much had already been accomplished when,
at last, our overladen little plane rose from the runway and began
its climb into the French sky.

Off to the north were the crowded roof tops of Paris, with the
Eiffel Tower standing tall and slender against the horizon some
eight or nine miles away, and with the Seine River looping back
and forth through the city and across the countryside. Our course,
however, lay in the opposite direction, for in the year or more we
planned to be away we intended to fly this plane of ours first to
Spain and then to equatorial Africa, after which we would go on

to Ethiopia and the Middle East, to the lands about the Persian Gulf, and then to India and other distant lands as well.

No such journey could have been justified without a serious purpose. From the very start, as we repeatedly told our families, our friends, and even ourselves, it was our aim to fly far from the beaten path wherever that was possible. We hoped to meet and spend a good deal of time among some of the world's more remote peoples. We wanted to learn what we could about them and, having done so, to make some kind of a report of our findings in the belief that the more knowledge there is of other peoples and other lands, the less misunderstanding there will be and the greater chance for international co-operation and world peace.

In a world that is so heavily burdened by difficulties and misunderstandings, this reason, when we gave it, was almost always accepted at face value. I must admit, however, that though we were entirely sincere in offering it as our controlling purpose, another reason—and a powerful one—was the wonderful opportunity this aerial journey offered for doing what both of us most enjoy—to travel to new places, to meet new peoples, to cross new horizons, and to pit ourselves and our ability—and even perhaps our luck—against such unexpected situations as we might come upon.

From the time the idea first occurred to us there was no question as to our mode of travel. It had to be in our own airplane. But more than that, the airplane had to be small. This was not only for financial reasons but also because we fully intended to push into regions where airfields and landing strips would leave much to be desired, or where, now and then, they might not exist at all.

This decision to fly was based, primarily, on our love of flying. Tay's father is an air-line executive and she had been born to aviation. I, on the other hand, had served as an Air Force pilot during World War II and still retain my enthusiasm for "the wild blue yonder." Both of us, in fact, were so "sold" on the air that we bought a secondhand Stinson shortly after we were married and flew it all over the country both on business and for fun. But the Stinson was not quite what our aerial expedition called for. We needed a plane with better take-off performance, more carrying capacity and range. And, we thought, it would be pleasant to have more speed than the Stinson's 110 miles per hour. Still, we hoped to find a ship that would require a minimum of maintenance and, of course, that would not cost too much. One engine, we decided, was all we wanted—or at least was all we wanted to pay for. We would watch it carefully and would catch any trouble on the ground before it had a chance to develop into anything serious aloft—or so we hoped.

From the first, our plan was to give a full year to the expedition. That naturally meant plenty of financing to cover expenses—hotel and gas bills, landing fees, insurance, and all the rest. What we really needed was a generous financial angel. In fact, more than one might come in handy, and in order to find them it occurred to us that it would be a good idea to have something concrete in hand—something like the new airplane, for instance—to show that we weren't just pipe-dreaming.

It was with this in mind that I left Tay at home in the autumn of 1953 and began calling on a number of airplane manufacturers. I naturally assumed that as a potential purchaser of a new airplane I would be welcomed with open arms, and that was usually the case, though one manufacturer frowned on the idea of being connected with the expedition in any way. The publicity for his company, he pointed out, would be bad if we ended up by killing ourselves in his plane.

With this exception, however, the manufacturers I saw were a considerate, optimistic lot, and those with whom I talked at the Cessna plant in Wichita, Kansas, were especially constructive and helpful. This pleased me particularly, too, for Cessna's latest single-engine model—"the 180"—impressed me very favorably. It was a "four-place" ship with sturdy, fixed landing gear, and a test flight over Wichita with Cessna's Bill Norris convinced me that the company's claims for the plane were, if anything, understatements. The little ship leaped into the air even before the throttle was fully opened. Its rate of climb exceeded a thousand

feet a minute, and it handled much more solidly than our old
Stinson—more like a big ship. Furthermore, the visibility over the
nose and out the side windows was excellent, the cabin was well
soundproofed, and the plane raced along at better than 160 miles
an hour!

I decided that the Cessna 180 was "it," and Tay promptly flew
to Wichita when I sent her a wire reporting "mission completed."
She was as impressed with the sturdiness and efficiency of our
fresh-off-the-line little ship as I was, and we promptly dubbed it
"Charlie" in honor of the final letter of its registration number.
This number, which was painted on the wing in letters two feet
high, was N2343C, and airport operators everywhere we went
always knew us as "Four Three Charlie." So the three of us—
Charlie and Tay and I—formed a *very* happy trio when we took
off from Wichita on the flight back home to New Jersey.

I had gone straight to the airplane manufacturers for more reasons than one. Because we were planning to visit so many remote
corners of the world, I wanted to make doubly sure of the strength
and reliability of the plane that was to take us there. And I also
wanted to make certain that such spare parts as we might require
from time to time would reach us quickly wherever we might
be. But I must admit that I hoped to get some kind of a financial
break as well. Even at this stage, the enterprise we had launched
was putting a heavy strain upon our budget, and anything we
could save in the purchase price of the plane would surely come
in handy later in the game. In this regard, however, my hopes
proved vain, though the Cessna Company gave me the factory
price and even agreed to repurchase the plane overseas at the
end of our flight. That agreement, in a way, gave us a kind of
financial anchor to windward, and the fact we never took advantage of it in no way lessened the psychological comfort it gave
us.

But now, with Charlie tucked away in a hangar not far from
home, our projected expedition began to appear in a new light.
Even brand-new, red and silver Cessnas, of course, do not fly on

air alone, and when we went seriously into the matter of costs we began to see that what we needed next was a good-sized barrel of dollars! We had been right about the plane, though. The very fact that Charlie was now a member of the family made our plans sound much more convincing. We naturally had to knock on a good many doors, and had to outline our plans over and over again, sometimes to listeners who were highly skeptical, but in a couple of months of concentrated effort, we managed to sell story and film rights, and other rights as well, and so raked up the funds we so urgently required.

Our expedition, by now, was well beyond the prospective stage, and occasional trips to Washington were necessary to enlist the aid of the State Department. We had to have all sorts of papers. Passports were essential, of course, and so were foreign flight permits. But more surprising was the "export license" from the State Department's Office of Munitions. This unexpected necessity, we learned, had come into existence because, in Latin America, at least, and possibly elsewhere, too, light planes such as ours had, on occasion, undergone enough conversion at the hands of revolutionists to reappear as "bombers" and "strafers" during local outbreaks. Neither the Cessna Company nor we ourselves had considered any such possibility for Charlie, but the State Department had. Hence our visit to the Office of Munitions, which took down all sorts of information about our ship, ourselves, and our plans, before arming us with the license their rulings made necessary.

There were embassies and consulates to see, as well. Our passports had to be stamped with endless visas. Maps and charts had to be collected, and—most important—we had to obtain an international *Carnet de Passage en Douane,* which would enable us to take our plane from country to country without putting up a customs bond at each frontier, just as these documents also enable motorists to take their cars.

While all these documents were being assembled, the equipment we were to take had to be assembled, too. We decided to use an Auricon 16-millimeter sound camera; a Bell & Howell 16-milli-meter camera; a two-unit Magnecorder; a smaller recorder; and a heavy electrical converter for running the sound equipment on the airplane battery. We were certain to need a considerable quantity of film and many cartons of flash bulbs. There was a typewriter and a tripod. And the spare parts and emergency sup-plies we dared not go without ultimately grew into proportions that appeared really formidable in view of the limited size of our plane.

Tay, meanwhile, had tackled the problem of what clothing and personal effects to take for the year we planned to be away. At first glance that might not seem to present much of a problem, but the itinerary we had in mind would lead us within twelve months not merely from winter to summer and back again, but actually through climates that would range from the fiery heat of African and Asiatic deserts to the dripping humidity of equatorial jungles and the cutting cold of the towering Himalayas in mid-winter.

"What we really need," Tay remarked, and with some reason, I thought, "is a DC-3!"

Certainly the problem looked hopeless, and as we continued to gather together what we simply "had" to take, Charlie, sitting silently and motionless in his hangar, seemed to be shrinking to even smaller dimensions at the very thought of the impossible load we were assembling for him. Ultimately, of course, we got to the point where we began to boil our requirements down a bit, and when, on February 22, 1954, we sailed from New York aboard the S.S. *America,* we had cut the total a great deal, though even the steamship may have shuddered a bit at our thirty foot lockers, suitcases, and packages.

Charlie, I should explain, had preceded us to France by ship, his wings pulled off and packed beside his red and silver fuselage in a sturdy packing case. And Jean Avot, an affluent Paris busi-nessman who tinkers with aviation more or less as a hobby and is Cessna's representative in Europe, had him all assembled again when we reached his hangar at the little airfield of Toussus-le-Noble outside Versailles.

We took the plane up on a test flight that same day, for we wanted to see if it had been properly put together again. Monsieur Avot and his headman came along, too, which gave us confidence in the job they had done—gave us confidence, that is, until Monsieur Avot dropped what he seemed to think was just a casual remark.

"The rigging may be a trifle off," he announced as we were taxiing to the runway. "Ribon, the mechanic, had to use his imagination a little in fixing on the right wing."

"Oho!" I thought. "Now what?"

Some mark or other, Monsieur Avot went on to explain, should have indicated the wing's exact positioning, and it had not been put on the main structure of the airplane when the wings had been dismantled. Still, the mechanic must have used his imagination well, for when we took off a few minutes later Charlie flew as well as ever.

We were still troubled, of course, by the contents of our thirty pieces of luggage—far more than Charlie would ever be able to handle properly. Something, obviously, had to go.

For one thing, we decided to send home all our dress clothing. Of course, we were not planning to drop in at many spots where we would miss such belongings, and, as Tay remarked when she reluctantly put aside her golden evening slippers, "A little more emergency water will be worth far more over the Sahara."

Out went a thermos jug and a spare flashlight. We'd miss them more than our evening clothes, but we could get along without them. Out went a carton of books, too, for they were heavy things, from Charlie's point of view at least. We even discarded our Mae West life vests, which, except as we crossed the eight or ten miles of open water in the Strait of Gibraltar, could serve no possible purpose for months. Why, we thought, should we carry Mae Wests when we had never even considered the idea of carrying parachutes?

It is surprising how many "absolutely essential" belongings aren't essential at all when one has to get rid of them. Larger and larger grew our pile of discards. Smaller and smaller grew the load we hoped to make Charlie carry. Time after time, when we had eliminated "absolutely everything" we could, we found that what remained still weighed too much, and we were forced to begin again on the task of cutting down. Finally, however, we reached the irreducible minimum—the absolute limit—and still our total load amounted to 525 pounds, which was 250 pounds more than the CAA had licensed the plane to carry. But now I remembered having been told at the factory that the load limit had been held down not by what the plane could lift, but by the strength of the main wheels. Something about them might give way—they might get flat arches, so to speak—if asked to hold up too much weight. But the landing gear on a plane—and that includes the wheels—must be built to withstand hard, "dropped-in" landings, so all a 250-pound overload would require of us was smooth, "greased-in" landings as well as the normal precaution of slowing down in rough air.

Consequently, with this in mind, we began to experiment with Charlie's weight-lifting capabilities, and we soon learned that a 250-pound overload made little difference. The take-off took a bit more room, but not as much as our Stinson had always needed. And the climb was not so fast. Oddly enough, however, the loss in cruising speed was hardly noticeable, and because of the high-wing design, the added weight gave even more stability.

Up to the last, our friend Jean Avot urged us to eliminate that extra eighth of a ton. Twice he told us of a pilot who had flown away from Paris in a similarly overloaded light plane, only to crash later on while taking off from a short African airstrip.

"The airfields are too high in Africa," he insisted, "and the air is too hot. You won't be able to get off with such a load." And Tay was inclined to believe him.

Once more we went over the list of what we were carrying and once more found nothing to leave behind. Already we had

removed the two-place rear seat, and the space it normally occupied was filled from side to side and from floor to ceiling. Just
fitting all that stuff in had taken hours of experimenting with
every conceivable arrangement. We had placed the heaviest ob-
jects—the sound camera and the two-unit Magnecorder—as near
the center of gravity as possible. Then we had lashed them down
as tightly as we could a few inches behind our sliding seats, which
hardly slid any more.

Crammed between these and the backs of our seats were other
pieces of photographic and sound equipment. Three suitcases,
which now contained what we hoped would prove to be a full
year's supply of clothing for the two of us, were tightly bound in
place between the sound camera and the ceiling. And jammed
in throughout all the rest of the baggage compartment, as well
as the space that was normally occupied by the rear seat, were
supplies of film and flash bulbs, and an almost unbelievable list
of other necessities which ended at last with our carefully labeled
spare parts, and our emergency food and water.

Altogether this amounted to almost twice the load Charlie
should have been asked to carry, but not an ounce of it—or so
we were convinced—could be left behind. And, among the more
important items of our load, was one thing more. It was a poem
that Tay had found sometime before and had pasted on the instrument panel. We never learned who wrote it, but we carried
it before us throughout every mile of the aerial journey we were
now about to begin.

> *Peace be in thy home,*
> *And in thy heart,*
> *Or if thou roam*
> *Earth's highways wide,*
> *The Lord be at thy side*
> *To bless and guide.*

When we taxied out to the runway I am sure that Jean Avot
was still doubtful, and Tay, too, a bit, but I had no doubts. Swing-

ing onto the runway I stopped the plane and my eyes fell on the
six lines of the poem as I listened carefully to the even cadence
of the engine. "Earth's highways wide," I realized, lay everywhere
before us.

"The Lord be at thy side to bless and guide," I read again, and
with that thought I opened the throttle.

Charlie hurried eagerly down the runway, and in another moment, despite our heavy load, we were in the air.

After years of dreaming and months of preparation our flight
to adventure had begun.

I. Paris to Gibraltar

O FF AT LAST, AND ON OUR WAY! Paris, though still visible behind us, was disappearing. Spain and Africa, the Middle East and Asia all lay ahead.

Charlie continued to climb on a course that led us well to the west of south. In less than half an hour we would be over the valley of the Loire near Orléans, and sixty miles or so farther on we would approach Tours and change our course for Toulouse, Perpignan, and the Spanish border.

"Can you believe that we're really on our way?" Tay asked with a touch of wonder in her voice.

It wasn't easy. After so many months of wrestling with preparations both of us now felt a little bewildered, as sometimes happens when one goes into action after a long period of hope and of delay. Tay, sitting in her right-hand seat, map in hand, was supposed to watch for check points as we headed toward the château country of the Loire at 150 miles an hour. Before long she would get around to it, too, and would do the job well, but at the moment she was marveling at the great good fortune that had made it possible for us to turn a dream into a reality, so I leaned forward over the control wheel and kept my eyes on the glinting rails of the Orléans Railway as it made its way toward Etampes.

As yet we had not really settled into place, though we would do so shortly, for we had flown together enough to be fully at home in the air. We were confident of our plane and of our preparations and were dressed for almost anything. Tay had pulled a blue cap over her brown hair and wore a dark green windbreaker over a wool shirt. Her plaid woolen slacks were predominantly red, and she had very sensibly chosen to wear a sturdy pair of hiking boots against the possibility of our being forced down. I wore a green jacket, too, but was much more conservative than Tay in the matter of slacks. Mine were khaki. My boots, too, were much heavier than hers and were just the kind I would want if I were to be called upon to hike over any rough section of French or Spanish countryside during these early days of March.

Several villages on the Orléans Railway appeared one after another below us, but the polished rails turned toward the south after fifty miles or so while we continued on our course. Thus we saw Orléans only as a blur on the horizon and did not even pick the railway out again until we saw it running beside the river Loire as we made our way downstream. At Blois and Amboise, Charlie buzzed us around the two magnificent châteaux for which these towns are famous, but as we approached Tours we climbed through a layer of haze into blue sky at 6000 feet and then dead-reckoned south toward Limoges over rolling, wooded farm land not unlike that of southern New England. Quaint and tightly clustered old-world villages that were utterly unlike any we knew at home appeared now and then below us, and here and there a spire stood high above the crowding roof tops.

Limoges, as we flew above it, traced a pattern of narrow streets all across its hilltop above the Vienne River, and running on to the south we now found the railroad that would help guide us to Toulouse. We were to land there in order to refuel and to clear the French customs, but the railroad was not easy to follow. It ran through Brive and Cahors—both towns of consequence even before Caesar conquered Gaul—but it played hide-and-seek all the way, vanishing frequently into long tunnels in that hilly country, and reappearing, sometimes, in unexpected places.

Just before we found Brive among its hills and beside its little river we caught a glimpse through the haze of snowy summits far away on our left. The map showed them to be the mountains of Auvergne, a part of the extensive Massif Central in which two peaks surpass 6000 feet. That is about the altitude of our old friend, Mount Washington, in our own White Mountains, but is little more than half as high as the greatest peaks of the Pyrenees, which, once we reached Toulouse, would make it advisable for us to change our course to the east so as to fly around their Mediterranean end as we crossed the border into Spain.

The railroad we were following continued to disappear into tunnels now and then as we flew on to the south over Cahors and Montauban. And as we approached Toulouse, we radioed for landing instructions. We knew that our call had been heard, for it was acknowledged, but an agonizingly long pause followed. Finally the reply came through very slowly word by word, as if the operator, uncertain of his English, were carefully reading an English translation.

"Sharlie aircraft," he said. "You—laanda—one—five."

We followed instructions, and the tower then guided us to the ramp.

"Tourn on ze left," we were told. "Come on. Come on. Come on. Well!"

That final "Well" was amusing and we guessed it to be a literal translation of the French *Eh bien,* but it gave us a little additional notice that we were far from home.

Customs formalities were simple at the Toulouse airport. In fact, the inspector did not even bother to look inside the plane, and with that task accomplished I got the Shell gas truck to fill our two wing tanks. Meanwhile, Tay bought a couple of ham and cheese sandwiches at the airport restaurant—really delicious sandwiches made with the kind of excellent French bread that has so much more character than ours. And when I had used our

international credit card in settling for the gasoline, we climbed
aboard Charlie again and took off with just enough time before
dark to reach Barcelona.

Our way from Toulouse as far as the medieval fortress town of
Carcassonne was plainly marked by a railroad, a highway, and
by the Canal du Midi. The distance is all of sixty miles, but we
were there in hardly more than twenty minutes and had to stop
munching Tay's sandwiches to get out our camera and photograph
the famous double ramparts of the Cité. Perched on top of an
abrupt hill on the right bank of the river Aude, this older portion
of Carcassonne traces its beginnings to pre-Roman times, and for
completeness and strength, its medieval fortifications are unique
in France and probably in Europe. From the air this strongly
walled old city still looks alive, and it is easy to believe that its
powerful towers and crenelated walls were never breached by an
enemy.

Less than an hour out of Toulouse we were over Perpignan,
and I radioed the airport there for the latest weather report
from Barcelona. Fortunately the French tower operator spoke
English, for neither Tay's French nor mine was good enough for
the rather technical reply we were given. Barcelona, we learned,
had a ceiling of 600 meters and a visibility of fifteen kilometers.
Translated into more familiar terms, these measurements came
to about 2000 feet and ten miles. This was good news, especially
when it was followed by the Perpignan operator's cheery addition: "Not much cloud Barcelona—not much cloud."

We shaped our course well to the east of south in order to
follow the railroad that leads from Perpignan to where the border
between France and Spain touches the Mediterranean, but as we
did so a low mat of gray cloud forced us down to 700 feet and
rain began to ping against the windshield. Tay, the map spread
out in her lap, watched closely for check points as we sped over
this final corner of France at 150 miles an hour. According to the
report we had just received, Barcelona's weather was confidently
saying, "Come on. Come on. You can make it." But the low clouds

and the rain were sounding a warning. The warning was more
for us, of course, than for air-line pilots, because our policy, which
we sometimes found difficult to follow, was to stay out of any
overcast or other blind flying conditions.

We might have avoided the dilemma we were in if we had
listened to a French flying friend in Paris.

"I wouldn't go that way," he had said when we had explained
how we proposed to enter Spain. "The mountains march right
into the sea."

He had then advised us to fly west of the Pyrenees, and to
enter Spain by way of Biarritz and San Sebastián, but we paid
no attention and stuck to our idea of rounding the Mediterranean
Costa Brava. Our aeronautical planning chart plainly showed that
the Pyrenees came to an end well short of the Mediterranean,
and we had somehow gained the notion that a belt of farm land
lay between the last of the icy summits and the beautiful silvery
beaches that we felt sure this portion of the coast would have.
And we had also assumed that throughout this belt of farm land,
level fields would everywhere permit us to land if we were forced
to do so.

But now, with the dull clouds pressing down upon us from
above, and with the rain still pinging on the windshield, we found
it advisable to leave the railroad for the nearby coast line and
began to regret having chosen this route. There was no area of
farm land. There was no level land at all—not even any beaches.
The Mediterranean was pounding with frothy fists against abrupt
and barren cliffs behind which, on our right, the broken terrain
rose steeply, disappearing almost at once into the clouds. It would
be impossible to land anywhere in this vicinity without a smashup,
and I was forcefully reminded of some advice General Charles
Lindbergh had given us when we had told him of the expedition
we had in mind. In a single-engine airplane, he had said, we
should avoid flying over any terrain where we could not land.
Inwardly, at least, that had made us smile, for it had come from
a flyer who certainly had had no such thought in mind when he

had become the first solo flyer to cross the North Atlantic. Further-more, the mono-motored plane in which he had flown over so many miles of open ocean had been measurably more primitive than Charlie.

As I thought General Lindbergh's advice over now, however, I had no inclination to smile. I was still convinced that there was mighty little chance of our being forced down. Charlie, though small, was a sturdy plane, and, compared to any commercial air liner, was simplicity plus. He had no complicated electrical and hydraulic systems to go on the bum, and his simple six-cylinder engine was remarkably reliable. Nevertheless, it now came home to me with a bang that when you are flying with only one propeller you can't just pull over to the side of the road if something goes wrong. You may have to go from wings to wheels in a hurry.

I looked down at the rocks and cliffs below and considered the disconcerting fact that Charlie's minimum power-off landing speed was about fifty-five miles an hour. I naturally wondered just how we would fare if we should be forced to land among those rocks and boulders at any such speed. Our shoulder straps would probably hold, and in doing so might save us from major injury. But out of the corner of my eye I caught a glimpse of the 525 pounds of baggage and equipment that was stacked behind us. It was lashed down, of course, but in any really bad landing it would surely tear loose, squashing us against the instrument panel and the engine just beyond.

Tay had her nose pressed against her side window as she studied pockets of mist that were visible here and there at the base of the cliffs that now lay beneath our starboard wing tip.

"Isn't that fog?" she asked.

"Oh no," I replied lightly. "There's too much wind for fog."

But I was less confident than I sounded, and I began to won-der. I was willing to keep on for Barcelona as long as we could fly "contact." If the visibility worsened with increasing rain, of course, or if fog really began to form, it would be wise to turn around and return to Perpignan. I didn't want to make such a suggestion yet, however, for if I did, Tay might vote to turn back at once.

In a situation like that, when there is any chance of suddenly "going on the gauges," it is reassuring to tune in a station ahead on the radio compass and watch the needle point confidently toward it through the murk. I tuned in on the Barcelona range, and the needle swung toward it, but then drifted away to starboard, homing on some Pyrenees thunderstorm.

I switched the radio compass off, for I hadn't found it reassuring after all.

The cliffs, the rocks, and the frothy green surf were still flashing by, too close for comfort beneath our starboard wing. Now and again I made out a patch of green where some tiny pasture, big enough, perhaps, for a goat or two, occupied some more or less level place above where the salt spray could be carried by the wind. I carefully examined each one I saw, but none of them was large enough for Charlie. Still, the weather got no worse, and soon we sped past a chain of white forts that ran inland a little way from the sea. They marked the Spanish frontier—the first of many frontiers we were to cross—but on our map this corner of Spain was a prohibited area, and we half imagined we might see orange flashes from guns directed at us, though nothing happened, and in a few moments we were beyond their range, inside Spain for the first time.

For quite a while our windshield had been growing harder to see through, and at last I had learned why. I was careful not to tell Tay, but I had to admit to myself that the rain on the windshield was mixed with engine oil. For some minutes I had been watching golden droplets as they danced across the access door on top of the engine nacelle. Reaching the edge of the door, they popped off in the propeller blast to spatter against the windshield, and I wondered if, by any chance, the oil filler cap had worked loose. It never had before, but I would have given a good deal for a reach under the hood to check it. I had heard that if that cap ever really came off, the rush of air would suck all the oil from the crankcase, and in that event, burned-out bearings and engine failure would quickly follow.

I glanced at the right side of the instrument panel and found that both the oil pressure and the oil temperature were normal. No trouble yet, and since we were now rounding Cabo Creus and in a few more minutes would be halfway from Perpignan to Barcelona, I felt justified in going on.

In another fifteen minutes the cliffs and rocks began to give way to a narrow ribbon of beach which soon came to be flanked by green fields. The weather improved, too, as the coast line curved sharply toward Barcelona—now hardly more than sixty miles away to the southwest. A few more minutes and I was in radio contact with the Barcelona tower and was hearing in clear English of the favorable weather there.

The rain had stopped, though beads of oil still peppered the windshield. Still, our 225-horsepower Continental engine was purring contentedly, as if a little thing like an oil leak made no difference. The oil pressure held up, too, though I was a bit less concerned about it than I had been. Now there were plenty of places for a forced landing. So both Tay and I relaxed and began to reflect on our first day's flight, which, in taking us from Paris to Barcelona, had brought us 700 miles closer to Africa!

We were five minutes out when we picked up the airport beacon. The sun had set when we saw it winking at us—white, then green—through the gathering dusk. The tower gave us runway seven zero, and we descended onto the downwind leg to a right-hand pattern, swinging out to sea as we did so, and running through the landing checks: Gas on "Both." Mixture "Full Rich." Propeller to "High RPM." Carburetor heat "On."

We rolled onto the base leg with the throttle closed and let the air speed fall off to a hundred—then flaps down one notch. Onto the final approach. Full flaps, and we were gliding toward the runway at eighty miles an hour.

The runway lights snapped on, though it was still light enough for us to see without them, and in another moment Charlie was on the ground.

We taxied toward the terminal, and I cut the engine alongside a parked Bristol of the Iberian Air Lines. As the propeller came to rest a group of soldiers appeared, marching toward us, but before they arrived I was out of the plane and had reached in through the front opening of the engine cowling. I tried to twist the oil filler cap, but it wouldn't budge. It felt a bit oily, but it was on tight.

The soldiers were coming closer, so there was nothing more I could do about the mystery of the oil on the windshield. Instead, both Tay and I felt it advisable to arm ourselves with our friendliest smiles against the imminent arrival of this most businesslike welcoming committee.

They turned out to be a detail of Francisco Franco's military police, whose ankle-length coats, shiny boots, and large black holsters immediately stirred up memories of Hitler's SS. They halted before us and the officer in charge peppered us with Spanish.

It was meaningless to me, but Tay had at least been exposed to Spanish during her school days.

"What is it all about?" I asked.

"I don't know," she replied. "It's too fast for me."

We thought they might be asking to see our passports, or possibly Charlie's logbook, so, as fast as we could, we handed these documents over. They shook their heads and said much more in Spanish that we did not understand. More than a little bewildered, we were led away to the terminal, and there our guardians ferreted out a civilian who spoke English. It was through him, at last, that we succeeded in answering their many questions about where we came from, where we were going and why, and all sorts of questions about our plane. We answered everything they asked as carefully and completely as we could, but we never did find out just what they wanted. Though we still don't know for certain, we ultimately decided that they merely wished to let us know that they were the police!

Eventually the police, the health, the control and the customs officers all came to the conclusion that we had landed legitimately and were not up to any dirty business. Or at least we assumed that those were their conclusions, for, after impounding our cameras and recorders in the office of the airport police, they permitted us to head for a downtown hotel in an ancient yellow taxicab. The Spanish Civil War took place before World War II began, but that taxi was surely a survivor—and possibly an actual veteran.

We had intended to take off the next morning for Gibraltar, skimping on Spain in order to have a maximum of time in Africa and the lands farther east, but rain and fog decided otherwise and socked us in for three days. Much of our first day in Barcelona was spent at the airfield with Desmond Drea, Pan American's head mechanic there. He is a tall, lanky young Britisher whose genial face was brightly punctuated by a twirling red mustache. Luckily for us, he was generously willing to spend his day off checking our engine for that oil leak.

Dressed in spotless white coveralls and carrying his tools in a black satchel, Des strolled out to call on Charlie more like a doctor than a mechanic. He looked everything over carefully and took a few turns on the clamps around the oil-line fittings.

"They weren't loose enough to leak, though," he remarked, and because he found no other trouble at all, he decided—and later experience confirmed his diagnosis—that the crankcase had probably been a bit too full. Because of that, a little of the surplus oil had been forced out past the filler cap gasket and the rush of air had carried it to the windshield. To this explanation I have nothing to add, except to say that it would have been easier on my nerves if I had known it at the time.

Hoping, as we did from the time we awoke after our first night in Barcelona, that the weather would soon change for the better, we made no real plans to take advantage of our enforced stay. We went to a bullfight, which we did not enjoy. It was far too gory for our taste, and the bulls had too few friends. We did what we could in their support, but rooting for the bulls is disapproved in Spain and we had to give it up.

Tay insisted on visiting the still uncompleted church of La Sagrada Familia, which someone has called "a mystic poem worked in stone," and in the harbor we scrambled over a fascinating replica of Christopher Columbus's *Santa Maria*, wondering as we did so how men had ever dared face the dangers of the unknown sea in such a craft. We rambled up and down the Rambla, a wide avenue in the center of the city, and glimpsed Mount Tibidabo in the distance, but we were constantly on the lookout for good flying weather, and on the fourth morning, on the strength of a not-so-hot weather report, we took off.

Rain, we were told, was falling both in Gibraltar and in Málaga—a city more than five hundred miles ahead. Furthermore, it was working its way up the coast. Our plan, therefore, was to move in as close as conditions would permit to the bad weather. Then we would sit down while it passed over, after which we would push on again. It seemed best to do this, for weather fronts were coming along so rapidly one after another that we might have to wait a long time before being able to make it from Barcelona to Gibraltar in a single hop. When we took off, Cartagena, about halfway down the coast, was the goal we had in mind.

We held Charlie to 500 feet, the better to see the little fishing villages along the coast. One, which was exposed to the sea at the tip of a sliver of land, was complete not only with its *plaza de toros* or bull ring but was also still encompassed by sturdy walls, which may have dated back to the days of the Moorish pirates or even to earlier times. A little over an hour from Barcelona, and before we reached Valencia, we ran off the edge of the map we were following, and, missing the adjoining one, we had to switch over to a general chart of Europe that was prepared on a scale only one fifth as great. That meant, of course, that much less detail had been included, and we had to watch closely in order to keep track of our progress.

As we passed Valencia I called the airport in the hope of get-

ting a line on the weather ahead but got no answer. Probably
the operator had not expected any calls at such an hour, and he
may have climbed down from the tower for a cup of coffee. And
then, about twenty minutes farther along, as we were rounding
the rocky cape known to the Spaniards as Cabo de la Nao—the
"Cape of the Ship," that is—we came upon a great fog bank that
was rolling in from the sea!

The weather report we had been given had forecast nothing
like that, and we promptly took Charlie up to 3000 feet for a
better look.

As far to the south as we could see, the fog hung unbroken
along the coast. The sea was everywhere hidden from sight, but
the land lay clear. For a time we were puzzled, but then we saw
that the fog dissolved as it came into contact with the warmer
shore line. The mountains to starboard descended into a blanket
of white that stretched out over the Mediterranean beyond the
horizon, giving us the impression that we were flying over the
shore line of a soft and silvery sea.

We followed the edge of that sea of fog throughout the slightly
curving, ninety-mile shore line of the Gulf of Alicante, but, at
Cabo de Palos—the tip of the massive coastal spur beyond which
Cartagena lies—we found that the fog bank ended, and almost at
that moment we spotted the long, black-topped runway of an airfield on the coast.

We were still fifteen miles from Cartagena, and the map
we had before us was anything but strong in its details. Still, it
showed this to be the only airfield anywhere near the city which,
twenty centuries ago, had been an outpost of Carthage itself.

Unfortunately, we had no dope whatever about Cartagena's
radio frequencies. Even the Barcelona airport, oddly enough, had
been unable to tell us anything about the place, so we circled
the field for a glimpse of a wind sock. I saw a number of parked
airplanes—tri-motored Junkers, such as the Germans had used
early in World War II as troop carriers. They were clearly a part
of the Spanish Air Force, but that told me very little. Civil avia-

tion was so limited hereabouts that we naturally expected civil and military planes to use the same fields.

We landed on the runway going away from the hangars and other airport buildings, and as we taxied back, a jeep full of soldiers roared out to the runway's end to intercept us.

By now both Tay and I had begun to wonder if, somehow, we had not committed some kind of international *faux pas*. Certainly the approaching soldiers seemed bent on questioning us at once. I cut the engine and, without loosening my seat belt, opened my door. As I did so, the soldiers piled out of their jeep, and I quite consciously put on my very best smile. A snappy young officer who was wearing dark glasses was in command, and I assumed my most genial and confident manner as he approached.

"Hi!" I began, hoping to overcome any suspicions he might have. "This *is* Cartagena, isn't it?"

Stony silence followed. Tay was alert, however, and broke the tension by handing me the map. I showed it to the officer, tracing our route from Barcelona to Cartagena. He followed my explanation intently while he studied the map, and in a moment his solemn manner gave way to a broad grin. Finding that we knew very little Spanish, he began to explain to us in broken English that we had the wrong field. The one we wanted, he said, was a few miles farther south. It was called "Carmelli" but it had no hard runway.

"If," he continued in his labored English, "you—going—that way," and he pointed down the runway on which we had just landed, "you—finding Carmelli—just there." He raised his hand a little and pointed into the distance.

This obviously meant that we were free to take off, and it was a relief to know it. The young officer, whose insignia meant nothing to me but who was too youthful to be much more than a lieutenant, had been most considerate, too.

"Thank you, General!" I replied, with a wave of my hand. "So long!"

And without having stepped from our plane, we fired up the

engine, blasted the tail round, and climbed away. Later we learned that that airfield was one of Spain's most important naval air bases, and that the shoulder pips the young officer wore, as I had guessed, were those of a lieutenant. He must have recognized the U.S. flag that we had painted on Charlie's tail in Paris, and my guess is that he will not soon forget the little American plane that landed by mistake, or the greater "mistake" the American pilot made in calling him a general.

"Wow!" exclaimed Tay as Charlie leveled off. "We were lucky to get out of that so easily."

We soon spotted Carmelli ahead. As the "general" had said it had no hard runway, but there was more to the story than that. Actually, the place was nothing much but a square of grass and dirt, and we went in for a close look, dragging low over it. There was no hangar. In fact, there were no buildings at all except a single tiny structure before which a man lay sleeping.

So far as we could see, there were no other signs of life whatever. No gas truck or pump was to be seen, and though we examined the place most carefully, it was impossible to tell whether or not any rocks or holes lay hidden in the grass. The whole picture was so dismal, in fact, that we decided to fly back some seventy-five miles to Alicante, where the airport was much better. We naturally would have preferred to push on farther to the south, but, lacking a favorable weather report, we dared not make the attempt. The next airfield was two hundred miles away and we didn't have enough fuel to try for it and to return if we failed to make it.

So we turned back, and in less than half an hour were over Alicante. There was the airfield, too, but just as we were all set to drop down, we spotted a row of barracks and platoons of marching soldiers.

"Oho!" we thought. "Another military field. Better not tempt fate twice, or we might land in the *calabozo*."

So on up the coast we flew, regretfully retracing our morning steps all the way back to Valencia. And there, following instructions from the control tower, we landed on the paved runway and taxied toward the hangar where other planes were parked, and where, importantly for us, a gas truck was waiting, too.

Both our gas gauges actually read "Empty," though we knew they weren't quite dry. In fact, they had about seven gallons left —about enough for forty minutes—but that is not enough for comfort, and we called the truck at once.

As our Barcelona weather report had forecast, rain reached Valencia during the night and held us there all the next day. However, the weather did not interrupt the city's preparation for its annual "Festival of Fire." Many side streets were crowded with enormous floats that were in the process of construction, while dancing and fireworks entertained the city's people at night.

With pleasant distractions all about us, we would have enjoyed being weather-bound in Valencia even longer, but despite a mildly adverse weather report, we took off again on our second morning there, hoping to reach Gibraltar, or possibly even Africa, before night. The forecaster warned that we would probably meet a weak cold front on the way, with rain and some turbulence. He was right, too, but Charlie made light of the matter and when we burst through the last shower of rain into welcome sunshine, Tay, looking out her window, saw a brilliant double rainbow that seemed to curve right over us.

We got beyond Cartagena this time, leaving the cold front behind, and found ourselves surrounded by the first spring weather we had encountered. Near Almería, too, with Gibraltar less than 200 miles ahead, we first saw the snowy peaks of the Sierra Nevada, one of which—Cerro Mulhacén—reaches an elevation of 11,-421 feet, thus surpassing even the greatest peaks of the Pyrenees, though it rises hardly twenty miles from Spain's most southern coast.

"Let's fly over them," Tay suggested.

I quickly agreed, and with our propeller control forward to 2450 rpm, throttle to twenty-four inches of manifold pressure, and cowl flaps open at 120 miles an hour, Charlie began to bore upward between clouds that looked like puffs of cotton. At 9000 feet we were above all haze, and the Sierra Nevadas were strung out before us, sparkling vividly against their blue background.

We were flying above a portion of Andalusia that was of particular interest to me, for not far from where we were now, my father, back in the early days of aviation, crashed in an open-cockpit two-seater. He was the one and only passenger, but the plane's French mechanic was riding between his knees, and by great good fortune, he, as well as the mechanic and the pilot, walked away from the wreck. Many times I have heard him allude to his close shave, in what he calls the Andalusian "desert."

Despite Charlie's overload, he almost literally bounded over the peak of Mulhacén, though neither Tay nor I were surprised by that. On a test back home—a test with oxygen—he had taken us to 24,000 feet. No aerial puddle-jumper, Charlie!

Tay opened her window, letting the slip stream hold it against the underside of the wing while she photographed wonderful, timberless snow slopes that made our ski legs quiver. Then I rolled Charlie over, sending him into a long, gentle descent for Gibraltar 130 miles away.

More for amusement than for anything else, I flipped on our VHF radio and gave Gibraltar a call on their frequency of 119.7 megacycles.

"Gibraltar approach, Gibraltar approach," I called. "This is 2343 Charlie. Over."

A clipped British voice replied at once.

"Four Three Charlie. This is Gibraltar. Over."

I had often found it impossible to contact Spanish stations, sometimes when we were as close as ten miles. This kind of thing had happened so often, in fact, that I had begun to suspect that our set had gone sour. It is no wonder that Gibraltar's immediate reply surprised me, or that I fumbled for a few seconds, trying to think of an excuse for having called.

"Gibraltar approach," I replied at last, "Two Three Four Three Charlie is a private American aircraft on a VFR flight plan from

Valencia, Spain, to Gibraltar. We are over the Sierra Nevada at the moment, estimating your station in about five zero minutes. Will we be cleared to land? Over."

Gibraltar replied cheerfully.

"Affirmative. Affirmative. Call again when closer in."

Our flight was different after that. We no longer felt alone over Spain. We were back in touch with the modern, aviation-minded world. Gibraltar, we knew, would make a record of our call, and if, by chance, we failed to show up, a search would be instigated even if no message from us suggested trouble. Radio is a wonderful thing, and our lives were to depend upon it more than once during the months ahead.

Down gently between cottony masses of cumulus, our steady loss of altitude buying an increase in air speed. We were over the coast again at Málaga. Then on a bit, and finally, there it was! The Rock of Gibraltar!

What a thrill to see for the first time this world-renowned and unique landmark—this vast rock that was known to the ancient Greeks as one of the Pillars of Hercules. And it was an even greater thrill to land there, for few private aircraft have ever done so. The tower operator, in fact, later told us on the ground that he had been surprised to learn that we had been given permission by the authorities in London.

While I circled to land, Tay opened her window and aimed the motion picture camera at the ugly Rock, which rears its naked summit 1396 feet above the end of a long and narrow peninsula. Dominating the nine-mile-wide gateway to the Mediterranean with its vasy array of hidden guns, we knew the Rock was honey-combed with miles of tunnels and other defense works. We felt confident, too, that some of those guns were tracking us—just for practice—so Tay stowed the camera before we banked onto the landing approach.

Coming into Gibraltar can be tricky when the wind is not just right. Among our papers was a CAA publication entitled *International Flight Information Manual*, and it warned: "Do not fly

near the Rock—dangerous downdrafts and extreme turbulence,
particularly on leeward side." With this in mind we were alert
as we made our way toward the single runway, which heads
roughly east–west, hard against the north face of the Rock. The
wind, unfortunately, was blowing from the south, which meant
not only that we would have to land "on leeward side," but also
that we would have to contend with downdrafts and a cross wind
as well. I was not at all happy as we approached over the water,
and as a precaution I did not use Charlie's flaps at all and kept
the air speed at a hundred instead of eighty. Charlie bucked a
little over the end of the runway and slipped a bit to port and
into the wind. We floated and floated before finally touching
down, but even then there were thousands of feet of runway before us. I was glad, though, that Charlie was no runway-consum-
ing jet, for if he had been we would never have made it.

A British officer met us on the line.

"I presume," he said, "that you have permission to land here."

We assured him that we had, but he did not ask us to produce
any evidence of that fact. He merely took our word for it with
no fuss or bother whatever, and we quickly got on with the task
of refueling. No one, in fact, paid the slightest attention to our
little ship until a man came dashing up, all out of breath.

He was an American, he told us, and he was in Gibraltar on
business, though he had been swimming when he saw us come
in for our landing. Recognizing Charlie as a private American
plane, he had put on his clothes in a hurry and rushed to the
airfield in order to see just who we were and where we were
going. The British who were all around were matter-of-fact
enough, but there was little that was matter-of-fact about this apparently homesick American.

Charlie took a mere forty gallons of aviation gas from an enormous Shell tanker holding thousands. Then, at the Royal Air
Force meteorological office, we went over the reports. Good
weather was waiting for us over Morocco, so we filed a flight
plan at once for Rabat. By now it was four o'clock in the after-

noon and, suddenly remembering that we had eaten nothing since seven that morning, we headed for the R.A.F. canteen, hoping to correct our oversight. To our disappointment we found nothing edible but Cadbury chocolate bars and Coca-Cola, so that is all we had for our belated lunch before taking off again from close beside the Rock and climbing out above Gibraltar and its harbor in order to span the strait that lies between Europe and Africa.

II. Beyond the Pillars of Hercules

Tay, WHO DISLIKES FLYING OVER water, was all for crossing the Strait of Gibraltar by the shortest way, but that was out. A large prohibited area included the nearest point on the African coast, and everything else seemed to be prohibited, too, except a single narrow corridor that led from Spain to Spanish Morocco about midway along the strait. So that was the way we went, hemmed in on both sides by imaginary lines beyond which we were not supposed to wander lest we bring down all sorts of official wrath upon our heads. But hardly more than fifteen minutes after taking off from Gibraltar, we had left Europe behind and Charlie's shadow, far down below us, was hurrying across the African coast line.

Geologically, I suppose, there is little difference between the land we were flying over now and that which lay some nine or ten miles away in Spain, but this new land seemed much more fascinating and exciting. Here was Africa and the westernmost portion of the Mohammedan world—the land known to the Arabs as Magreb el Aksa—the "Land Farthest West." And, too, here was the first of those "distant" lands we were asking Charlie to carry us to.

Turning westward, we followed the coast line, and before long the white, modern skyscrapers of Tangier passed under our left wing, while on our right many ships, entering the Mediterranean or leaving it, dotted the broadening waters of the strait. Far to the north beyond the strait, the Spanish coast line, softened by haze and distance, drifted northwest toward Cape Trafalgar. Back over our right shoulders, Gibraltar had already faded from view, and as we approached Cape Spartel and turned southwest toward our destination at Rabat, we realized that we were flying over what the ancients had thought to be the very end of the world beyond which no one dared go, except at the risk of falling off the edge.

Continuing along the coast line, we were aware of a lovely beach below and beautiful green fields stretching inland on our left. In a few minutes we passed over the line that divides the Tangier International Zone from Spanish Morocco and, south of Larache, we crossed another unseen line of demarcation and knew that we were over French Morocco.

The coast line still continued unbroken toward the south and west, devoid of landmarks that meant anything to us until we saw Port Lyautey. Then, further on and just at sundown, we spotted Rabat where we made our first African landing at the airport of Rabat-Ville.

There we hitched a ride to town with the Shell representative, and as we passed through an arch in the old city wall, we caught a glimpse of several white-robed Arabs with rifles slung over their shoulders. We wondered if they were a part of French Morocco's discontented populace, but later on we learned that they were guards for the Sultan's palace. And then we found ourselves in the city's principal hotel, which was almost a palace in its own right, with marble floors and towering pillars, high frescoed ceilings and magnificent mosaics everywhere. In the "tourists' bar," which we visited before dinner, we sat on long, low couches while yellow-slippered, white-robed waiters with red fezzes on their heads served us subserviently or hovered silently nearby.

"I feel just like a Sultan's daughter," Tay whispered. "Or at least I would if I were dressed for the part. In a place like this it simply isn't possible to lounge properly in Western clothes."

We had hoped that during our visit to Rabat we would be permitted to film Moulay Mohammed Ben Arafa, the then new Sultan, but we soon discovered that we had arrived at a most unfortunate time. Only the week before one of the Sultan's disgruntled subjects had thrown a hand grenade at him, and many unpleasant pictures of the event had appeared in the newspapers. This press reaction horrified the devout Moslem ruler, who never liked having his picture taken anyway, and for the time being, at least, more photography was out of the question.

Rabat itself offered many points of interest, but our luck was bad in two other ways as well. For one thing, the weather proved a real surprise. It was cold and rainy—the last of the rainy season, we were told. And in addition, the hotel was unable to put us up for more than one night. Before taking off from Paris we had decided not to make advance hotel reservations, for we had no wish to be tied down to a definite schedule. We preferred to take potluck, knowing that we could always fall back upon our sleeping bags. Our idea had not worked out so well here in Rabat, though as it turned out later, this proved to be one of our few close calls, and not a very serious one at that.

Because of all this Tay and I took off for Marrakech early on the morning of March 19. This city, which is 180 miles south of Rabat and about ninety miles inland from the Atlantic, is one of the Sultan's four capitals—only fifteen miles or so from the foothills of the High Atlas and hardly more than thirty miles from the highest peaks in this greatest of Moroccan ranges.

Taking off from Rabat-Ville, we flew over the Sultan's palace, looking down, as we passed, directly into its private courtyards. We even saw the royal laundry hanging up to dry, and with that beginning, we set our course down the coast line toward Fedala, where the American invasion forces landed in 1942, but, as far as we could see, no signs of the war remain. In a few more minutes we flew over Casablanca with its stunning harbor and its white and ultra-modern buildings. Here, turning away from the coast, we headed almost directly south for Marrakech, 150 miles away.

As we made our way inland, the land grew more sandy and more rugged. It was dotted with shepherds' huts and corrals, and tiny villages here and there—an inhospitable and barren land.

Towering cumulus clouds were piled up far ahead of us, and when we looked more closely we made out snow-crowned peaks as well—a surprising sight for Africa, we thought. But soon the sight grew more surprising still, for little by little we began to realize that the peaks we had first seen were merely parts of a whole vast range of mountains blanketed with unbroken snow— the High Atlas, the roof of North Africa. With its westernmost end rising abruptly near the coast, this enormous upthrust extends most of the way across Morocco and forms the central portion of the complicated series of ranges that compose the Atlas Mountains of northwest Africa. Two peaks in this central range reach almost to 14,000 feet, and many others soar to more than 11,000. Rising steeply, as it does, from the thousand-foot plain surrounding Marrakech, this enormous range reaches greater average heights even than the European Alps. No wonder the view was so impressive! And it became even more so when we thought of the tropical flowers and palm trees of the country we had left less than an hour before, and of the arid expanse of the Sahara, whose northernmost sands were hardly more than an hour's flight ahead.

Though our destination was Marrakech, we passed over the city and climbed toward the vastness of that mountain range, up to 10,000 feet where Tay opened her window and photographed the impressive snow-covered slopes.

Back and forth we flew beside the great peaks, taking pictures and looking for the skiing area we hoped to visit. But that was like searching for a needle in a haystack, and we soon gave it up, gliding down to Marrakech airport. There we found another Shell man waiting for us—Monsieur Guy Namini, who not only arranged to refill Charlie's tanks but also drove us to the hotel, telling us about skiing conditions on the way. And he knew what he was talking about, for his wife was Swiss and an avid skier.

Almost in the shadow of the High Atlas though we were, and less than 200 miles from the Sahara Desert itself, we found, on arriving at the Hotel Mamounia, that we had reached a tourist's paradise. Here, deep in Morocco, a region little known to visitors from the West until our own day, we were surprised to find ourselves in a luxuriously elegant hotel with marble halls fit for an art gallery, in which a mammoth dining room with glass doors for walls looked out on beautiful formal gardens. All the rooms had private balconies facing the mountains and looking down on the gardens below, and the whole remarkable arrangement resulted in a hotel just about as beautiful as any we had ever seen. Furthermore, the warm climate, the semi-desert vegetation, and the mountains in the distance all reminded me of Tucson, Arizona, where I had spent a winter in the Air Force. There were even the familiar AT-6s droning overhead, with French student pilots at the controls.

The square of Djemaa el Fna—or the "Concourse of Sinners"—stands at the very heart of Marrakech, in the old section of the city, and is one of the famous landmarks of Morocco. To reach this great market place we walked through wide modern streets lined with shops, and with orange trees, too, that were covered with ripe fruit. Arriving at the famous square, we found it crowded with people and with temporary booths offering an endless variety of articles for sale. The people who were milling about everywhere formed a colorful and varied throng. White-robed, red-fezzed city dwellers mingled with country shepherds. Turbaned farmers, hooded Berbers, and burnoosed Arabs shouldered occasional black giants from the country farther to the south, and here and there we saw a resident Frenchman.

We had barely entered the square when a small Arab in a red fez came up, explaining that he could speak English, and insisting that he should act as our guide. In our efforts to shake

him off, we pretended to pay no attention, but he stuck to us like
a leech, and finally I gave in, hoping that he might be of some
help when it came to taking pictures. This proved to be the case,
too.

As we wandered back and forth through this Concourse of Sinners we marveled at all the things that went on there. Scores of
trades were represented, and the costumes were remarkably di-
versified. Most noticeable were those of the water vendors who,
probably as a kind of trade-mark, wore tall conical hats, from the
wide brims of which dangled brightly colored ball fringes. These
perambulating purveyors of water also wore colorful knee-length
costumes hung with goatskin water bags, metal cups, and tinkling
bells.

Tay and I, of course, were most conspicuous in such a gathering, and we soon found ourselves followed by an insistent little
crowd. Groups of people were at our elbows wherever we turned,
pulling at my sleeve or at Tay's skirt, and whining *"Baksheesh! Baksheesh!"* Nor were their faces particularly friendly,
either, and such curiosity as they showed seemed solely concerned
with what money they might get from us.

As we roamed through the crowded square we came upon a
snake charmer who was already surrounded by a throng. Old
women, and even pathetic little children, were pushing and
bumping against us now, repeating *"Baksheesh!"* constantly, and
plucking at our clothes to attract our attention. We were completely surrounded, and Tay admitted later that for a moment
she felt panic-stricken. But then the crowd around the snake
charmer opened up a little and we found ourselves almost upon
him. He was a wild-eyed fellow, half crazed in appearance, with
disheveled hair hanging to his shoulders, and as he pranced about
he rubbed the snake's head along the sides of his nose and his
chin. He even went so far, a time or two, as to pop the snake's
head into his mouth—all the while giving vent to a weird sort
of chant, with which two fellow Berbers kept time on a couple
of finger-tapped drums and a flute.

"Ah! Something for the camera," I thought, pushing Tay into the scene.

"Closer!" I insisted, as I held my eye to the camera's finder. "Closer!" The snake charmer, up to now, had seemed unaware of Tay, but apparently grasping the meaning of my "Closer! Closer!" he suddenly transferred the snake he held to one hand and grabbed Tay's wrist with the other, waving the twisting snake before her as he did so. This was more even than I had bargained for, and immensely more than Tay was willing to accept. She cried out in fright and did her best to pull away.

I do not know what kind of snake the charmer had in his hand at the moment; it was probably quite harmless, and though the crowd laughed uproariously as Tay tried to free herself, the charmer seemed to think that a cobra would make the show even better. So, he let go his hold on her wrist and turned to pick his cobra from its basket. But we had had enough and took to our heels.

Despite the apparent clutter and lack of order in this busy market place, most activities appeared to be governed by accepted arrangements of some sort. Just beyond the snake charmer, for instance, we came upon an area that was set aside for doctors and pullers of teeth. The members of the latter group, whom I cannot bring myself to call dentists, squatted on the ground with large mounds of teeth heaped before them. So far as I could see, forceps—sometimes rusty—were their only tools of trade, though there were a few bottles of colored liquid, which may have been alcohol. None of these wielders of forceps had a patient just then, and though we waited around for a time on the chance that someone with a toothache might demand their services, no one did. Nor were they willing—lest we make fun of them perhaps—to have their pictures taken, and the nearby group of doctors were just as shy. But I must say that the equipment and supplies the doctors displayed far surpassed in interest the molars and rusty forceps of the pullers of teeth. I remember that there was a moth-eaten leopard's head, the antlers of an antelope, a number of dead and somewhat desiccated crows, and odd bits of bone and fur. And unlike the tooth pullers, some of these doctors had patients, all of whom, we noticed, were veiled women.

One solemn medico was squirting a liquid of some sort through a glass pipe directly at his patient, though with what end in view we could not guess. Another, who had anatomy charts spread out before him, was examining a dirty foot. A third was putting a charm, made up of beads and claws, about the neck of a woman, and all around were groups of curious observers. It was not the ideal way, we thought, to consult one's doctor, but, as Tay pointed out, these women were veiled and covered from head to foot, which, under the circumstances, had its advantages.

The barbers, who were leechers as well, occupied a place "next door" to the doctors, and nearby were the scribes. These "scholars," often with glasses on their noses, labored over their scripts with hand-sharpened quill pens. Most of their clients were women, and it was not hard to guess that letters were being written to wandering husbands.

From the square we made our way into the crowded bazaar area, and if we had not been accompanied by our self-appointed guide we would surely have had great difficulty in finding our way back. This portion of the city is a maze of narrow covered streets through which we must have walked for several miles. Each trade occupied a section of its own—one for blacksmiths, another for cobblers, a third for brassware, a fourth for rugs, and so on. Everywhere clients and merchants were haggling over prices. The streets grew narrower and narrower, and we often had to flatten ourselves against the sides of the passageways or the fronts of stalls to make way for laden burros. Bicycles, pedaled at surprising speeds through the crowded, narrow ways, nearly ran us down, and everywhere we went insistent merchants urged us to buy their wares.

At one point we caught a glimpse, through a half-open door, of a little school that was in session, and we paused. The teacher was an old man, and his pupils were small boys who sat cross-legged on the floor, but as we stepped closer for a clearer view, the schoolmaster started to close the door. We turned away, naturally, for it was obvious that we were none too welcome, and our guide explained that it was because of our cameras. It was an explanation that seemed reasonable to us, so we let him hold the cameras while we returned for another look. But now a couple of boys slammed the door in our faces, and when we turned to go, one of them threw a stone at me. It was small, and even though it struck me in the back, I hardly more than felt it. Still, it was ample evidence of a hostile attitude, and when we remembered that the French had taken over all Arabic schools, we realized that we might have happened on an "outlaw" school that still met in secret.

Up to the time of our visit no open hostility had been directed against any visiting Americans, but as we made our way through the Marrakech bazaar we often felt that the atmosphere was suspicious or unfriendly. Both of us were troubled, now and again, by the many pairs of eyes that followed us with apparent disapproval as we passed through some of the darker, narrower passageways. Tay later admitted that she had sometimes felt hesitant to turn her back on some of those we passed, and we realized how easy it would be for a stranger to disappear without a trace in such a place. We knew little of the prejudices the people held, or of the country's political problems, and in the short space of time at our disposal we could hardly expect to learn much about them. It would be better to leave such matters to the experts. Besides, time was short and our thoughts were turning toward those inviting snow slopes of the Atlas Mountains.

Monsieur Namini, of Shell, who had already told us about the skiing in those great mountains, now offered to take us there himself. And, early on the Sunday morning following our arrival in Marrakech, we piled into his tiny French car for the two-hour drive to the ski area at Oukaimeden—a small settlement high among the Atlas.

For half the distance the road led through irrigated areas and across the foothills, but ultimately we reached a region of cliffs and precipices—of turning, climbing roads that sometimes clung to dizzy mountain walls, and to a region that seemed to us somewhat reminiscent of the Grand Canyon country of Arizona.

Oukaimeden consists of little more than three or four white clapboard chalets, a run-down restaurant, a few small stone houses built directly into the rocky hillside, and a French Foreign Legion post with its barracks buildings. But the ski area itself—several miles beyond this village and higher up the mountain —has only one small chalet, a generous parking lot which we found well filled with cars, and two tows leading up the broad snow slopes.

The room Tay and I were given at the chalet was small and bare, but the lack of luxury didn't bother us in the least. Our only concern was with finding the necessary ski equipment—a tough assignment. All the chalet had to offer were skis and poles, but eventually we located ski boots, and Tay found a pair of ski pants, though I had to settle for my khaki shorts!

"Quelle horreur!" one astonished Frenchwoman remarked when I put in my appearance, but it may not have been quite as bad as that. At any rate, the day was clear and sunny, and despite the vast surrounding snow fields, I did not find my unconventional costume too uncomfortable.

We noticed at once that expert skiers were few and far between, but enthusiasts were numerous. In fact, there were so many French enthusiasts—mostly from Marrakech, but some from as far away as Casablanca—that it was an hour's wait in either of the two lift lines. And in all my winters of New England skiing, and out west too, I'd never seen anything like these lifts. To the cable that ran continually up the mountain and down again, supported by steel towers, a Moroccan would fasten a clamp with a rope attached. Then it was up to the skier to wrap this rope around his poles, thrust his poles between his legs, and sit back against their baskets.

Actually, this system worked very well, although because of

the altitude Tay felt shaky and out of breath when we got to the top. We had reached an altitude of 10,300 feet, which was higher than she had been—except in a plane—for over two years.

The slopes below us were wide, fairly steep, and completely treeless—and buried as they were under a blanket of excellent spring "corn" snow, I found conditions perfect as I started down. Behind us lay an impressive snow-covered mountain wall that reached on up to peaks of twelve and even thirteen thousand feet. And in the opposite direction, far below and beyond the limits of the snow field, stretched endless miles of the vast brown and green plain that surrounds Marrakech.

Though we had been impressed by the size of the crowd while waiting in the lift line, we found, when we had reached the top, that in so great an area our fellow skiers practically disappeared. Most of them were there merely for the day, too, and when we returned to the chalet for dinner that evening, everyone was gone except the proprietor, his family, and another couple. Monsieur Namini returned to Marrakech with the rest, but for the following three days Tay and I skied and photographed and soaked up the brilliant sunshine that flooded the Atlas.

Not until Wednesday afternoon did we set off on our return to Marrakech. A taxi had come up at noon, and we were to leave at three o'clock, but by then a snowstorm had developed and had obliterated all signs of the road. The taxi driver, who obviously had had no experience with snow, lost the road, and though he found it again, we soon bogged down in a snow-filled ditch.

Before leaving the chalet, we had turned in our borrowed ski clothes, and the prospect of walking back to our starting place in our summer clothes didn't appeal to us at all. Luckily, that proved unnecessary, for just as we were steeling ourselves to start, a member of the Foreign Legion, returning from a hike, loomed up in the snow and, seeing our predicament, promised to send help when he had reached his barracks.

He was as good as his word, too, and before long a jeep appeared. We had expected to be helped back to the chalet we had left, but our rescuers decided otherwise and delivered us, instead, at the run-down little restaurant in Oukaimeden some two miles farther down the mountain. And there, to our surprise, we found about a dozen others who were snowbound, too. Even the chalet proprietor and his family were there, having come down on some errand of their own only to find it impossible to get back. And among the rest were the commandant of the local Foreign Legion post and his wife. Snow was still falling, and our situation threatened to become rather difficult, because the little restaurant was much too small to care for such a gathering all night.

It was the commandant who ultimately found a solution to our problem. Disappearing into the snow and the dark outside, he returned with the French Foreign Legion ambulance, apparently the only four-wheel-drive vehicle available. Built a little like a police wagon, it had two long benches that faced each other, and twelve of us crowded in for the trip back up the mountain to the chalet. With much lurching and many sudden stops that flung us about as if we were in a giant cocktail shaker, we finally reached our destination, where, after a belated but most welcome dinner, we turned in with the snow still coming down.

We went to sleep with the expectation of being stuck on the mountainside for days, but we were awakened the following morning by the scraping sounds of a snowplow outside our window. The road had been opened, and though the journey back to Marrakech was far slower than our drive up the mountain had been, we finally entered Hotel Mamounia in a rainstorm with snow still on our shoes. Low, gray clouds hid all signs of the Atlas Mountains, and some of the hotel's more recently arrived tourists would no doubt have been surprised had we told them that we had been snowed in only the night before not very far from the edge of the Sahara Desert and hardly forty miles from Marrakech —snowed in and rescued by an officer of the French Foreign Legion—in an ambulance!

The following day we flew back to Rabat, and there, to our delight, we received permission to land at—and actually photograph—the great airfield of Sidi Slimane, one of the U. S. Strategic Air Command bases in Morocco.

It was about ten o'clock the morning after we had returned to Rabat when we took off in Charlie for Sidi Slimane, a flight of only twenty minutes to the northeast. Flying at 2000 feet, on a "dead-reckoning" course, we could not be sure just when we would spot the base, and I was already talking to the control tower when two Sabre jets zoomed by, and a moment later Tay shouted, "Watch out! There's a B-47 right behind us!" Just then the tower advised us to make a 180-degree turn and let the huge bomber with its six jet engines land first. We gladly did so instantly, and Tay breathed a sigh of relief. We were then told to follow the big plane in. The only trouble was that it made such a wide turn before landing that by the time we were told to come in, we couldn't see the airfield any more.

By now, jet fighters and 500-mile-an-hour bombers were all around us—or so it seemed—and though we were asking Charlie to do his best, his 160 miles per hour, in view of the company we were in, seemed nothing but a crawl.

"Four Three Charlie, you're cleared for an immediate landing," the tower told us. "There's a B-47 circling, waiting for you."

We hurried to the best of our ability and soon touched down on a gigantic runway that looked like half a dozen New Jersey turnpikes laid out side by side. There we found ourselves behind a "Follow Me" jeep but we had to taxi for ten minutes before we came to the parking area! And there, as if to show us just how inconsequential Charlie actually was, they parked us between two Globe-masters, whose towering wings and huge silver bodies made Charlie look a little like an ant between two elephants.

We were met by a group of officers which included Captain Teasdale, head of public relations, and another captain who was officer of the day. There were several lieutenants, too, and a couple of MPs, and after our experience in flying among the bombers and the jets, we were not in the least surprised to hear that Charlie was the very first private plane, large or small, to land at Sidi Slimane.

We were taken for an auto tour of the base, which spread out widely over completely flat land. Except in the vicinity of the small French headquarters, there were no trees or flowers or grass. We passed rows and rows of Dallas huts—small square houses with windows on all four sides. They were drab and gray, but new rectangular houses that were white and homelike were going up nearby.

Despite many aspects of Sidi Slimane that were colorless and bare, it was almost instantly apparent that the men on duty there took great pride in what they had done to make the place more livable. There were a golf driving range, handball and basketball courts, baseball diamonds, and tennis courts, too, though no swimming pools had as yet been built despite the torrid Moroccan summers.

The recreation hall for non-coms seemed to be the most beauti ful building on the base—ultra-modern and mostly glass. And the Post Exchange was remarkably like a big, up-to-the-minute store at home, except that the prices were lower, whether for ice cream, cameras, fountain pens, or diapers.

The permanent base installation included many restricted warehouses, as well as huge stockpiles of trucks, half-tracks, and other conveyances, but much of the base is set aside for bomber wings which come from the United States for training periods that vary from forty to ninety days. These wings bring all their own mechanics with them, and even their own cooks. Thus they are largely self-supporting during the limited time of their stay. The men who are permanently assigned to Sidi Slimane, on the other hand, remain for much longer periods and are permitted to bring their families with them, though those who do so live off the post in nearby towns and cities.

After lunch at the mess hall, Captain Teasdale took us to meet Colonel Frederick R. Ramputi, the base commander. We found him to be a quiet, considerate person who was interested in our filming and writing project and quite ready to help. He briefed us on what we could and could not write about, told us what areas were taboo for photography, and also told us something of the part Sidi Slimane played in the plans of the Strategic Air Command. Then he sent us off to the control tower where we looked down on a whole wing of B-47s—a most impressive sight —with rows and rows of Sabre jets at one side. We watched a flight of returning fighters peel off overhead and come screaming in for their fast, smooth landings, and we saw bombers make "parachute landings" as well, "popping" their drag chutes just after touchdown.

We planned to spend another day at the big air base but were compelled to return to Rabat for the night. So we went down to the flight line, boarded Charlie, and taxied to the runway, stopping behind a B-47 when we reached it, and waiting while five Sabre jets came in over our heads and landed. Then Charlie trembled as the B-47's six mighty engines roared and the big plane lumbered down the runway. Fortunately, we were not directly behind him or Charlie might have melted away in the scorching jet blast.

The bomber rolled on into the distance, gathering speed as it went, but we waited for a surprising length of time before, at last, we saw it leap into the air. Only then did I dare open the throttle, for we were no longer in danger of being flipped on our backs by jet wash. Unlike the bomber, we were in the air in a matter of seconds, though we hugged the ground as we headed for Rabat. We stayed under 500 feet until the field was far behind, for we had no wish to have any more jets breathing down our necks.

We were back at Sidi Slimane again early the following morning, ready for a busy day, and hoping to get permission to take our cameras down to the flight line, but such a privilege is not often granted, and we spent almost all morning going through a maze of red tape. Even when all this was completed, a sergeant was ordered to accompany us so that we might be told what was prohibited and what was not.

First, I took Charlie up so that Tay could get a picture of him landing at the base. Then, in a jeep with the sergeant who was assigned to us, but followed by other jeeps filled with armed men, we went to work. It was a busy and somewhat hectic day, but a fascinating one, and when, at last, we had completed our task, we discovered that we had only thirty minutes left to pack the plane and fly back to Rabat before sundown.

The sun was already only a dull red ball just above the horizon when we took off with a twenty-minute flight ahead of us. Then, to top it all, we lost our way and hit the coast all of twenty miles from Rabat, thus losing another five or six minutes.

We were especially conscious of the French rule that prohibits small planes from flying after dark, and we also knew that Rabat-Ville had no landing lights. Still, we were able to make out the runway as we approached, so we put on our landing lights and came in. A red light was blinking from the tower, but we decided to ignore it, feeling sure that the French were merely letting us know that the sun had set. It was an easy landing, fortunately, and when no police appeared to put us in jail, we parked Charlie in his accustomed place and made our way to town.

Our "shakedown cruise"—which is really what our flight up to now had amounted to—was over. From here on our expedition would be more seriously under way, for now we were about to take off on a 1700-mile flight down the African coast to Dakar, where we would turn inland into the giant interior of Africa. Morocco had merely been a colorful place for trying out our complicated camera gear and stretching our muscles on the ski slopes of the High Atlas.

From here on, Tay and I—and Charlie—would surely find the going different.

III. *Where Ocean Waves*
Meet Desert Dunes

As we prepared to leave Rabat, Dakar was our next important goal, but that distant West African seaport was a long way off. Actually, it was farther to the south southwest than London was in the opposite direction. For the whole distance, it is true, we would follow the African coast line, and so could hardly go astray, but there were difficulties, nevertheless. From Rabat down the Moroccan coast to Agadir, no problems of consequence were likely to arise, but from there on, we would be flying over difficult territory—over the edge of the Sahara Desert where it is washed by the waters of the Atlantic. In this region, for a thousand miles or more, roads do not exist, settlements are rare, and airstrips rarer still. Sandstorms, blowing westward from the desert, often bring visibility to zero for days on end, and make flying more hazardous even than fog.

With problems such as these in mind we naturally made our preparations with great care. Our first hop would be down the coast to the little Moroccan town of Agadir, which, with any luck at all, we should reach in about two hours. There we would refuel and check the weather to the south before beginning what we knew would be our first real test.

As we headed southwest toward Casablanca, Charlie seemed little concerned over his heavy overload, and within twenty min-

utes of our Rabat take-off we found ourselves approaching the
handsome white and ultra-modern city where Churchill and
Roosevelt held one of their important meetings during World War
II. Then, since it was scarcely out of our way, we turned Charlie
toward Nouasseur, which, a dozen miles or so inland from Casablanca, is another important air base of the U. S. Strategic Air
Command.

Casablanca was still visible behind us when we sighted the
base in the distance ahead, but before we could get close enough
for a good look, four F-86 Sabre jets leaped from a runway fully
two miles long, and headed straight at us as they climbed. We
had imagined ourselves more or less alone and all but unobserved
in the bright Moroccan sunlight, but suddenly the sky seemed
full of flashing Sabres as those four swept-wing fighters swarmed
around us like angry hornets. Clearly, we were not wanted in the
vicinity of Nouasseur, and, having no wish to be stung, we rolled
into a steep bank and headed toward the coast as fast as Charlie
could go.

That, apparently, was just what the jets wanted us to do, for
they did not signal us to land, and once we had turned away from
the air base which, like Sidi Slimane, undoubtedly contains great
stockpiles of highly secret equipment, they disappeared. I am sure,
though, the pilots of those Sabres made a note of the number
that was painted on Charlie's wing. They came too close to miss
it.

Now we were over the coast line again and seemed to be alone
in the Moroccan sky once more, but it took us some time to regain our composure. We had been a bit careless, spoiled, no doubt,
by having been permitted to take Charlie to Sidi Slimane. But
the angry jets that had just "scrambled" after us had succeeded
in demonstrating to our complete satisfaction that unauthorized
planes stand little chance of getting near those big SAC air bases.
And this was good to know, for it convinced us that there will be
no aerial Pearl Harbor in Morocco.

For an hour or more we took turns flying. We passed the white

cliffs of Cape Blanco. Mazagan, the port of Marrakech, slipped
by below, the massive remains of its ancient walls still clearly
visible though they were abandoned to the Moors almost two hundred years ago by their Portuguese builders. Lesser towns—
Oualidia, Safi, and Mogador—appeared and disappeared in their
turn. And finally, after two hours in the air, we passed Cape
Guir, which marks the western termination of the High Atlas,
on whose slopes, 120 miles or so to the east, we had been skiing
only the week before. Another ten minutes and we were on the
ground at Agadir.

We had thought merely to fill Charlie's tanks before getting
the latest weather reports and taking off again, but a snag was
waiting for us. The French control officer surprised us by asking
whether we had permission to fly down the coast, explaining that
only such airplanes as were equipped with radio and "desert survival equipment" were permitted to follow that route.

Inspection quickly showed that we met the requirements, but
not having heard of the rule before, we had not applied for a
permit, and Agadir was unable to issue one without permission
from Casablanca.

A message asking for the necessary permit was sent at once, but
we were told that a reply could not be expected before the next
day—a delay that was a bit irritating, though we had to admit
that the ruling was a wise one in view of the desert conditions
ahead. And then our irritation was lessened when we learned at
the weather office that sandstorms were being reported all along
the coast to Dakar.

"*Le vent de sable,*" remarked the French weatherman. "*Pas
bon!*"

We were willing to agree. From our point of view, no sandstorm would ever be good, and plotted on his synoptic chart was
a report from a station about halfway to Dakar showing winds of
fifty miles an hour out of the Sahara, with visibility zero.

No thunderstorms were reported anywhere ahead. There
weren't even any clouds. Only the sandstorm barred our way,

and at ten or twelve thousand feet we might very well have been able to fly above it in clear skies. But that would have been the ultimate in folly, for without being able to see the coast line we would surely have drifted out to sea or wandered off course into the Sahara, and help would not have been available in either direction.

So instead of pausing at Agadir for an hour, we were unable to leave until the third morning when the weatherman finally told us that it looked as if we might get through.

"Il y a beaucoup d'instabilité près de Sidi Ifni," he warned. *"Il y aura des chutes de pluie—visibilité comme ci, comme ça."*

But Sidi Ifni was only about thirty minutes along, and Tay and I were willing to risk the instability and rain showers. We were anxious to be on our way again. In fact, our flight plan called for a 700-mile hop to Villa Cisneros, the capital of the Spanish colony of Río de Oro, and considering the desolate country we would be flying over, we wanted to put that hop behind us.

We took off just before ten o'clock in the morning, and because I knew that range and not speed was what we would need to reach the Spanish town ahead, I chose a slow cruising power that would not burn much fuel. We followed the beach, flying at 2000 feet with a power setting of twenty-one inches of manifold pressure and 2100 rpm, instead of a maximum cruise setting of twenty-four inches and 2450 rpm.

For half an hour there were no signs of habitation whatever, but as we approached the small Spanish colony of Ifni we began to notice the instability of which we had been warned. The clouds ahead were low and alarmingly black. But for all their blackness they were not thunderheads, and as we drew closer they proved to be just nimbus rain clouds.

The trouble was that they blossomed upward far too high for us to top them. We dared not go around them to the east because they were banked up against the high mountain wall of the Anti-Atlas. We might, perhaps, have turned their flank by flying out to sea, but that was not a choice that appealed to us, so only one reasonable alternative remained—to go under them, at least as long as we could see our way.

We were reminded of our flight around the Costa Brava into Spain, though our present situation, we felt, was even more unpleasant. Flying over the water, where there could hardly be any obstruction, we were able to see the rocky coast as it slipped by a little way to port. The lowering clouds had forced us down, first to 1000 feet and then, by degrees, to about 500. Thus we clearly saw the fortress that guards the little Spanish enclave of Ifni and even caught a glimpse of the Sidi Ifni airstrip.

Here was our first precise check point. Tay set up time and distance on the navigational computer, and we marveled at a ground speed of 180 miles per hour. Even though a tail wind had been forecast, this seemed too good to be true, but on the strength of it we reckoned that Charlie could easily reach Villa Cisneros, arriving, if our luck held, with enough reserve for another hour and a half in the air.

The weather grew more threatening just south of Sidi Ifni where the Atlas cliffs fall into the sea. The clouds lowered even more, and we had to slide down and down until we were a mere hundred feet or so above the waves. Tay was all for turning back, and I was about ready to make it unanimous, but just as I began to think we had better retreat, the situation almost miraculously improved. The cloud base started rising and we were soon at 2000 feet again. The storm had saved its worst for the last and suddenly we found ourselves beyond it.

The forts of Foum Assaka and Aroussi, at the southern boundary of Ifni, slid by, and for fifty miles or so we found ourselves above southern Morocco again. But then we passed the Spanish fort of Aereora and knew that we had crossed the northern boundary of the Spanish Sahara.

The time was 11:06—an hour and eight minutes after take-off. But another check of our ground speed showed an alarming de-

crease. It had dropped from 180 miles per hour to 120, indicating
a wind shift from tail to nose.

We climbed above what seemed to be thin scattered clouds,
hoping to pick up better winds, but the clouds closed in solidly,
obscuring the coast and forcing us down to 2000 feet again.

Now we were busy trying to figure out whether or not Villa
Cisneros was really within reach. If we were able to average 125
miles per hour our total flight time would be five and a half hours.
As the engine was turning over now, Charlie's fuel needs were
about nine gallons an hour, though we had to count on ten to
be safe. And that meant burning fifty-five of our usable fifty-
seven gallons (three of our tanks' sixty gallons not being able
to flow to the engine), leaving less than fifteen minutes reserve,
which was plainly not enough.

As a result of this computation we wondered whether to turn
back through all that bad weather to Ifni, or whether it would
be better to land at the emergency strip at Cabo Yubi—Cape Yubi
—about a hundred miles ahead.

We much preferred this second choice, but we had no way of
knowing whether or not Cabo Yubi had any fuel. Still, in a pinch,
ten gallons of ordinary auto gas would do, and we hoped that
we would be able to find that, at least. So we decided on Cabo
Yubi and kept our doubts to ourselves.

Before leaving home, Tay had clipped from our encyclopedia
all the information that could possibly bear upon our journey, and
among the clippings she had mounted in a loose-leaf binder was
one that told something of the portion of the Spanish Sahara that
lay below us now. We were not surprised to learn, when we read
it over, that the region was entirely desert or that its nomadic
population averaged only about one person per square mile. Some
seventy miles offshore—over the horizon to our right—were
Spain's Canary Islands, some of which must be delightful, but
the Spanish Saharan desert bears little resemblance to Tenerife or
Gran Canaria, and we wondered just what we would find when
we reached Cabo Yubi.

The cape itself is prominent enough, for the coast line there changes abruptly. Still, we almost missed the little Spanish outpost, which consisted only of a few adobe houses near where the waves crashed on the beach, together with a windmill and several slender radio towers. So far as we could see from the air, there was nothing else but surf and sand and dunes.

We circled the bleak, unattractive settlement, looking for the airfield, but failed to find it. We circled again and this time Tay saw faint markings that might indicate a runway in the sand, though we could not be sure. But by now we had made out two tri-motored Junkers, parked in the lee of the adobe buildings, as if for protection from the wind.

Those two planes meant an airstrip somewhere, so we kept milling around, hoping to make it out. And then we noticed a soldier standing near the fort and signaling—motioning with his arm as if he were bowling. Over and over he repeated his signal, and finally we realized that he was telling us how we should land.

Without wasting any more precious gas, we wheeled around and came gliding in the way the soldier was motioning. It meant landing in a cross wind from the sea, but—never mind! The wheels touched and we felt the sand grab them, slowing Charlie far too quickly. The plane lurched through one sand drift after another, and I waited tensely with the control column in my lap, fearful lest some bigger drift might nose us over. But to our relief that didn't happen, though I am sure it would have, had it not been for Charlie's tail-heavy overload.

We came to a halt, and I blasted the plane around, but our wheels were deep in the sand and we promptly bogged down. Even full throttle didn't move us, so, shutting off the engine, Tay and I climbed out, and as we stood there beneath Charlie's wing, a truckload of Spanish soldiers in drab blue-gray uniforms came careening down the strip.

We shook hands with their officer when they arrived, and in a few minutes Charlie had been pushed on through the drift. Then, by following in the tracks made by the truck, we taxied to the fort.

Several other officers were waiting there, and we tried our French on them when English proved useless, but to little avail. However, by mentioning Agadir and Villa Cisneros, by showing them a copy of our flight plan, and by somehow getting across the idea of adverse winds, we finally made them understand why we had landed. And they were most considerate, making no requests, fortunately, for written permits.

Tay and I used all the words we knew for gasoline—petrol, *essence, benzine*—and were pleased to see their faces light up. *"Si, si,"* they replied. *"Gasolina."*

In a jiffy several soldiers rolled out a drum. I checked the label and found we were really in luck, for it was aviation gas, even though of a slightly higher octane rating than recommended for our engine, and in a few minutes, by way of their hand pump and our funnel and chamois, our tanks were full. Then, to make it even better, they accepted our Shell *carnet*, which was fortunate, for we had no Spanish pesetas.

The commanding officer, a Spanish Air Force pilot, invited us to the fort for a cup of coffee, but if we were to reach Villa Cisneros by sundown we had to be on our way. We showed him our flying maps and he told us what he could of the route ahead, giving us the frequency of the Villa Cisneros beacon and pointing out the location of a few emergency sand strips—strips our map did not show at all and that we were glad to know about even though, as he marked the location of each one, he solemnly referred to it as *"muy malo"*—"very bad."

The take-off was even more nerve-racking than the landing had been, for we knew, now, just what the situation was. Our heavy load was a real handicap in that soft sand, and to cut our run to the minimum, I lowered the flaps to first notch.

It was necessary to get the plane into the air as soon as possible, and I gave it almost full throttle before releasing the brakes. Charlie plunged through the sand, picking up speed very slowly.

I didn't dare let the tail rise lest we hit a drift and nose over, so I held the wheel back and we staggered off in a three-point attitude. As Charlie broke loose, the tail sank even further before I could bring it up again. With the air speed only about forty miles per hour the stall-warning horn was "beep-beeping" in our ears, which made it rather exciting in view of the cross wind from the ocean.

With Charlie's nose down, we quickly gained speed, lifted the flaps, and after circling the field we rocked our wings in salute to our Spanish friends, and headed south from Cabo Yubi, relieved to have our tanks full with Villa Cisneros still three hours away.

Here and there on the sandy desert below we occasionally saw Bedouin tents—usually in threes—and once we spotted a flock of goats at what must have been a spring—a craterlike area of green in the desert. We kept on under a layer of broken clouds for an hour, but once beyond Cabo Bojador, about 150 miles from Cabo Yubi, we found the clouds more scattered and we rose between them to 6000 feet. The temperature, an uncomfortable eighty-five degrees at the lower level, fell to sixty-five, and, when we were next able to check our ground speed, we found that we had also escaped from the head wind that had delayed us all the way from Ifni.

Tay brought out her loose-leaf "book of knowledge" again and read aloud about the early Portuguese explorers of this coast. In search of a sea route to India, they were among the first Europeans to set eyes upon this barren coast, and during the fifteenth century caravel after caravel crawled over the sea, each voyaging a little farther south than the last. But according to the legends of that day, the "Sea of Darkness" lay beyond Cabo Bojador—a sea filled with unimaginable dangers that neither men nor ships could possibly overcome. And perhaps this legend at least partially explains why the Portuguese took fifteen years to round the cape that vanished beneath our silvery wings even before Tay finished reading to me about it. And the Portuguese searched this "Sea of Darkness" for another twenty years before they got beyond

Cape Verde, the site of present-day Dakar, where, with any luck, we would be in another six hours of actual flying.

Twenty years for the men sent out five hundred years ago by Prince Henry the Navigator, and six hours for Charlie and Tay and me!

Even along this desolate coast of Africa, the world has changed.

Hardly a score of miles to the north of where the Tropic of Cancer crosses the African coast line, the long and slender peninsula of Ed Dajila es Sahria hangs pendantlike out from the coast for twenty miles or so, enclosing a bay so narrow that its fifteenth-century discoverers took it to be a river. Landing there, those early Portuguese came upon a desert Bedouin from whom, by barter or otherwise, they acquired a little gold dust, and the "river" they had discovered was consequently, but much too optimistically, named Rio d'Ouro—the "river of gold." It is true that the Portuguese soon learned that the name was not accurately descriptive. Still, no one ever changed it, though the Spaniards, who took the region over in 1885, translated it from the Portuguese and now this whole Sahara Desert colony, named from the "river" the Portuguese had discovered so long ago, is known as Río de Oro.

Villa Cisneros, our immediate destination, is the capital of the colony, and is situated on the peninsula of Ed Dajila es Sahria. Because of this, we knew it would be easy to find. We could hardly miss it, in fact, and because the colony is fully ten times as great in area as our own state of New Jersey, we expected its capital to be a city of some size.

We found the peninsula readily enough—a slender finger of sand that lay between its riverlike bay and the ocean—but there was no city. In fact, there was not even a town of any apparent consequence. Halfway down the peninsula a string of tiny block-houses stretched across its two mile width from shore to shore, as if to protect its tip from possible Bedouin attack, but there was no town—nothing there at all except a cluster of six white buildings.

"That can't be Villa Cisneros!" objected Tay. "It's too small." We had been measuring off the miles to our destination for so many hours, and worrying so much about getting there, that the size of the place had grown to considerable proportions in our minds, and now below us was a settlement so tiny that we might have missed it entirely had it not been for its unmistakable location. Perched at the tip of its long Sahara Desert sandspit, it was a mere handful of white structures, with a few fishing boats anchored just offshore and a desert airstrip nearby. That is all there is to Villa Cisneros.

The place did not appear especially inviting, but Dakar was still 700 miles away, and we had to land to fill Charlie's tanks. Besides, the sun was sliding down the western sky and we were ready to call it a day. Villa Cisneros appeared to be a place with few extra beds, so Tay and I guessed that we might have to get out our sleeping bags and spend the night in the shelter of one of Charlie's wings.

The airstrip, fortunately, was much more clearly marked than the one at Cabo Yubi. An enormous white arrow was painted on the sand just off its south end, so we needed no hand signals from the ground. We didn't like the idea of landing in the sand again, but the moment our wheels touched we knew there was nothing to worry about. The strip was hard and without sand drifts. We would have rolled indefinitely had I not toed the brakes a bit. No taxiway showed up, but faint tracks led toward the buildings a mile or so away, and we followed them, watching for holes and rocks but finding none.

One building among the rest was surmounted by a radio tower, and assuming it to be the control, we headed toward it. We were right, too, and as we approached, several Negro boys came out and directed us where to park.

Even before the propeller stopped, a huge gas truck pulled up beside us, though its Spanish driver said he had only 100-octane fuel. Charlie's six-cylinder engine would have preferred 80 octane, but the difference was not vital, and in short order we took on an estimated twenty-five gallons.

The Negroes helped us push the plane behind the building where we tied the tail wheel to a ring in the ground and the wings to drums of sand. Then, with Charlie safeguarded against any blow during the night, we entered the control building, and met two cordial Spaniards, one of whom spoke a little English. They just wanted to glance at our log book and the *carnet de passage* and asked when we planned to move on. Red tape created no trouble at all.

"Can we find some food," we asked, a little doubtfully, "and a place to sleep?"

"Why of course," we were told. "The inn is over there."

The most prominent structure of Villa Cisneros was "the fortress"—a blindingly white square building surrounded by a sparkling whitewashed wall. The Spanish colors flew over it, a sentry barred the gate, and the inn stood just beyond, with a wind charger on the roof—an enormous propeller geared to a generator which supplied the inn's electricity. So long as the wind blew, the charger worked well, but that evening, when the wind fell off, so did the lights, and we carried on by candle.

We went straightway to the little dining room. It was empty, as we thought it would be at five in the afternoon, but we hoped for something to eat. At first there was only tea and biscuits, but then, to our surprise, in walked a tall, barefooted dweller of the Sahara—a Berber, as we knew from his blue gown and his turban. His gaunt, sun-parched face wrinkled into a smile as he approached, and to our astonishment he asked, in the best English we had heard since Sidi Slimane, if we were getting enough to eat.

Amazed though we were to find an English-speaking Berber in the Spanish Sahara, we told him we were doing fine.

"But how about some eggs?" I asked.

"Okay," he replied. "I'll tell the cook."

With more food on the way, we began to question him. Where, we asked, had he learned English?

"During the war—at Port Etienne," he told us, "working with the British and Americans."

Port Etienne, we knew, was a couple of hundred miles farther down the coast, and just across the Río de Oro border in French West Africa.

"Where is your home?" Tay asked.

"In the desert," he replied.

"But where?" we asked.

We got out our flying map, and when he had studied it a bit he pointed out an area that was completely blank.

"It takes many days by camel," he explained.

"Is there any settlement?" we asked. "Any village?"

"No," he replied. "No. Just the desert."

The following morning dawned clear and calm, promising a beautiful day and no *vent de sable*. We breakfasted at sunup, filed a flight plan, and checked the weather. Everything seemed fine all the way to Dakar, though whether or not the wind would hurry us along we could not know until we had flown some distance.

We must have taxied two miles over the hard sand before we found the runway and took off, though we might have taken off anywhere, for runway and desert were identical. Climbing slowly, we circled Villa Cisneros, and Tay took a few pictures from her opened window. Then, having reached 1000 feet, we crossed to the mainland, and lined up with the coast line while continuing to climb on to 7000 feet. There I leveled off, setting the throttle and propeller at twenty-one inches and 2100 rpm, and after a time Tay computed the ground speed at 162, indicating that Charlie had found a tail wind of sixteen miles an hour, for our true air speed was only 146. We knew, now, that if that tail wind stayed with us, there would be no question of making Dakar non-stop.

For 220 miles between Villa Cisneros and Port Etienne we did not see a single Bedouin tent. There was nothing anywhere about us but sand and sea and sky, with the sand marching down the coast in giant, wind-formed, crescent-shaped dunes, the tips of which all pointed to the south.

Along this strangely deserted coast, we were flying over the line that separated the great ocean of salt water from another great ocean of sand. So long as the weather remained as it was, there was nothing desperate about what we were doing. We had written on the flight plan we had submitted at Villa Cisneros that our route to Dakar would be over the coast, and the Spaniards had promised to telegraph that information to the international airport at Dakar. There was little likelihood of our being forced down, but even if we were, a landing on the moist beach shouldn't be too tricky, and Charlie would be easy to spot there. But, in order to make doubly sure, our emergency equipment included a signaling mirror, a Very pistol for firing red flares high into the air, and two flashlights. We had two cans of corned-beef hash as well, together with one of pork and beans, two tins of cheese, two of sardines, one of crackers, a little rice, and a small box of dried raisins. We also carried two canteens and six rubber hot-water bottles all filled with water. The hot-water bottles had been General Lindbergh's suggestion, his idea being that they would be least likely to burst in a crack-up. Our food and water, we figured, would last for at least four days—provided we kept to the shade of the wings.

Once before, Tay and I had come this way, but then we had been passengers on a Panair do Brazil Constellation which, at 20,000 feet, had made this coast look much different than it did now. Thinking of the excellent meal the big Constellation had served us somewhere above this stretch of coast, I turned to Tay.

"If we are going to need any emergency rations today," I said, "we may as well start on them now."

My remark didn't make much sense, but both of us were hungry and we were soon dining on crackers and triangular sections of Gruyère cheese, washed down with chlorinated Villa Cisneros water from one of our canteens. Tay was taking a tepid swig when the engine stumbled!

For one horrible second we imagined ourselves being forced to land on the beach 7000 feet below—until I switched the gas selector valve to "Left" and, after a sputter or two, the engine resumed its normal purring. The right tank had run dry, as we had known it must, because we had drawn on it for more than two hours while drawing on the left tank for only one.

I looked at my watch, and calculated that the right tank had given us two hours and thirty-seven minutes, including take-off and climb, both of which require more fuel per minute than an easy cruise. That meant the left tank would do at least as well. It had already gone one hour, so we still had another hour and thirty-seven minutes to go. Barring strong head winds, in other words, we would make Dakar with about twenty-five minutes reserve.

A little farther along, our time over the town of St. Louis, which sits at the mouth of the Senegal River, showed us that we had plenty of gas for the remaining 110 miles. Then, as we flew on down the coast, I called Dakar from fifty miles out and got an encouraging reply.

"Charlie aircraft," the operator replied. "You are clear to start your letdown to 2500 feet."

He talked just as if we were a high-flying 400-mile-an-hour air liner, and we had to chuckle, wondering what he would think when Charlie came buzzing in.

We touched the Dakar runway at 2:21 p.m.—four hours and forty-eight minutes from Villa Cisneros, and when we pulled up to the terminal, there was someone standing on the steps, waving to us.

It was Joe Mankowski, Pan American Airways' Dakar manager whom we had met and liked so much when we had passed this way the year before.

"You came all the way from Villa Cisneros in such a little plane?" he asked in surprise.

But he was not the only one to be surprised that we had been able to fly 700 miles non-stop. We were surprised ourselves, for we had just completed the longest flight Charlie had made so far. And, too, we had reached our first major goal. From Dakar, there on the westernmost tip of Africa, we would turn east—away from the coast and deep into the heart of the world's second largest continent.

IV. Where Camel Meets Canoe

Dakar, the capital of French West Africa, is the most important city on the Atlantic coast of the continent between Casablanca and Cape Town. Though it was founded only in 1857, and had a population of less than 20,000 even when World War I broke out in 1914, it has developed rapidly since then. By far the most important international airport on the western coast of Africa, it has grown to be a thriving city of about 200,000 and, as air travel continues to increase, seems likely to grow larger still.

Because, from Dakar on, we planned to fly into the interior where, for much of the time, we would be well off the beaten track, we were determined to make our preparations with real care. Still, we were willing to luxuriate for a time amid the comforts of Dakar, knowing that for the next 5000 miles or so, luxuries would be nonexistent and even modest comforts would be missing. Our ten days in Dakar, therefore, began as a kind of Easter vacation. We lived in the modern Hotel Croix du Sud where the French cuisine was so appetizing that Tay, thoughtless of Charlie's limitations, gained five pounds. This forced me to issue an ultimatum, for we could not afford to add another ounce to Charlie's overload. Tay had originally been entered on our list of weights at 126 pounds, and anything more than that would never do!

We were in Dakar for Easter Sunday and decided to attend Notre Dame des Etoiles Cathedral—a handsome white marble church built in the style of a Middle Eastern mosque. Dressed in our "Sunday best," we approached the cathedral only to find it so overcrowded that we could barely catch a glimpse of the interior through the door. And of all those who made up that exceptional throng, we, I am sure, were quite the least colorful.

Our fellow worshipers, with few exceptions, were Africans, decked out in the brightest and most ornate clothes that we came upon during our whole journey. Vivid reds and greens and yellows were everywhere, while purples, pinks, blues, and scarlets were intermingled all about us. And, oddly enough, color combinations that would normally have clashed in Western eyes seemed to harmonize here in the strong Dakar sunlight.

Tay observed that the women wore voluminous Mother Hubbard-like gowns called *"bou-bous,"* made of many yards of the boldest, gayest prints imaginable; and, furthermore, that leg-of-mutton sleeves were worn at rakish angles, and that the younger and prettier the girl, the more one shoulder was revealed. Trailing velvet trains of purple or of orange were not uncommon, and the Easter bonnets that most especially caught our attention were intricately wound turbans—their ends poking out or up like rabbit ears. It is customary, we were told, for women in this part of Africa to display their husband's wealth by way of their clothes and heavy silver jewelry, while the men themselves, dapper though they often are in their starched and snow-white Western suits, are notably lacking in color by comparison.

Dakar has a beautiful white sand beach, and swimming in the lukewarm waves of the Atlantic was great fun. However, we discovered one day that fishing was even better when we hitched a ride in a native fishing boat—a twenty-foot dugout canoe. An African paddler sat in the stern, another in the bow, and Tay and I, together with two Africans who had come along to bail, took our places in between.

Once beyond the sheltered lagoon, we met the waves of the ocean, and the need for the bailers became apparent. Because the boat was a dugout, we were in no danger of sinking, but water was forever slopping in over the low sides. However much was bailed out, more always came in again and we were drenched, though that never for a moment interfered with our fishing. Sitting in the water that sloshed back and forth in the bottom of the dugout, we tossed out heavy lines to which three-inch silvery spoons were attached, and almost instantly began pulling in great, struggling fish—king mackerel or flat reddish-brown fish known locally as *capitan,* some weighing twenty pounds or more. A score of fish such as these lay in the water of the dugout within an hour.

We felt we had earned our "Easter vacation," but it came abruptly to an end when we began to prepare for our flight to the east. There were many government officials to call upon for our flight and photographic permits. We had to study maps of the interior so as to plan our stopping points and arrange for living accommodations at various French outposts, where quarters for visitors are rare. Where we were bound, tourist hotels do not exist, but that, we thought, was just as well in view of the steep rates in Dakar.

While I was busy getting permits and looking after Charlie's needs, Tay lightened our load a bit by sending our winter clothes home. She checked our emergency equipment, too, and our medical kit, for we expected to be in the interior of French West Africa and the Belgian Congo for the next two months. But even with that prospect, our medical supplies were few, for a travel-wise doctor in New York had advised against trying to care for any serious illnesses ourselves. Medical help, he had pointed out, was always within a few days by air. So we carried little beside a small first-aid kit, sulfa pills for dysentery, Aralen, which would be a life-saver in the malarial areas ahead, halazone pills for chlorinating water, and some aspirin and milk of magnesia.

Our last few days in Dakar were spent cleaning and carefully checking Charlie, and finally we were ready for a test hop, which, we were convinced, was just a formality, for Charlie, all carefully checked and with a clean oil filter, was in top form.

The test hop would merely take us about the Dakar area, and neither of us expected anything of consequence to happen, but we had not been in the air ten minutes when I reached between the seats to adjust the trim tab, and found it covered with oil. Much concerned, I glanced down and found that my feet and legs were spattered with it, too. Looking under the instrument panel, we could see the golden liquid pouring in through the air vents in the fire wall, and, glancing out the window, we even saw oil dribbling along the struts.

The gauge on the instrument panel still showed the oil pressure to be normal, but it was clear that at the rate oil was being lost it would not long remain that way, so I banked the plane and headed back for the airfield, calling the tower and asking permission for an immediate landing—offering "slight engine trouble" as the explanation.

The oil-pressure gauge was beginning to fall as we touched the runway, but the engine was still running smoothly when we parked in front of the hangars. Climbing out, we found Charlie literally covered with oil. And that was not surprising, either, for we had lost seven quarts out of twelve. Another ten minutes of flying would undoubtedly have ruined the engine.

A Pan American mechanic took a quick look under the hood and discovered that the oil-filter gasket had disintegrated. I should have changed it when cleaning the filter, but I didn't have a spare. Now we found that no gasket the right size was to be had in Dakar. Here at this big field, geared for Constellations and DC-6s, no one had ever seen anything as small as the part Charlie needed, so we had to radio New York for that gasket, which was no bigger than a dime. We thought we would be held up for another week, but seventy-two hours later the tiny parcel arrived, and the following morning, after a frantic hour and a half spent in loading Charlie, checking fuel, oil, and weather reports, and paying our respects to various officials, we were in the air.

Our first major target, as we turned eastward and began our crossing of the 5500-mile-wide continent, was the town of Goundam, a French outpost nearly 1000 miles inland from Dakar, and little known even to those who fly over this portion of the world in Air France planes. Goundam, in recent years, has grown in importance while Timbuktu, its neighbor some fifty or sixty miles further east, has declined. Timbuktu, the famous and ancient city which traces its beginnings to the eleventh century, has long been known as "the port of the Sudan in the Sahara," but the term belongs as well to Goundam. Reached from the south by way of the Niger River, both are on the very edge of the Sahara and so are equally familiar with canoes and camels, but nowadays they are linked much closer to the outside world by a weekly Air France flight from Dakar. With a good connection there, Paris is hardly a day distant to the north while Johannesburg and Cape Town are little more than that in the opposite direction.

Our flight plan now called, roughly, for us to follow the railroad inland from Dakar for some 700 miles to its terminus at Bamako on the Niger River. We would stop for fuel at the Senegal River outpost of Kayes, 400 miles along the way, spend the night at Bamako on the Niger River, and, if our luck held good, would fly on over the Niger for 400 miles or so to Goundam the second day.

This flight promised to be one of the most exciting of our whole trip, and as we buzzed over the beach northeast of Dakar, we were forcibly reminded of the care we must exercise. Only the day before, a young French woman pilot, flying from Villa Cisneros to Dakar in a single-engine plane as we had done, had run out of gas just short of her goal and had cracked up on the beach. Fortunately, she had escaped with only a broken leg but there was little left of her plane, as we could see when we flew over it.

"Inexcusable!" we both said, but not with much conviction, for a little additional head wind, or an error in arithmetic might have caused it, and no one is completely proof against such matters. It is no wonder that we brought our eyes back from that wrecked plane to re-examine our notations of take-off time and distance to be covered.

Turning inland, and planning to pick up the railroad a little to the southeast, we checked various radio frequencies and devoted our attention to flying and to navigation. Finding our way should not be difficult, for only one railroad runs through this region and in the dry expanse below it would not be hard to locate or difficult to follow.

The land we were flying over was almost completely flat, covered with small trees and scraggly bushes. Tiny Senegalese villages were few and far between, even when we found the railroad, but after three and a half hours in the air we spotted Kayes— a small railroad village on the Senegal River—which claimed to be "the hottest place in all French Africa," a contention we had no inclination to question. Flying at 5000 feet we had found the air both cool and smooth, but when we descended toward Kayes and opened a window to take some pictures from 2000 feet, we felt as if we had opened the door of a furnace.

Once we were on the ground, three Frenchmen came hurrying toward us from a little white stucco building—hurrying because the thermometer stood at 120 degrees Fahrenheit, and they wished to gain the shelter of our wings. But they were thoughtful of others, too. Even before beginning the uncomfortable job of filling our tanks, they handed us ice-cold and most welcome bottles of lemonade.

Once the refueling was over, our French friends hurried back to their stucco building, while we, in turn, took off and climbed to the cool comfort of a mile up. And Bamako, when we reached it two hours later, was just as hot as Kayes had been.

Early the following morning, after a breathless night in a one-window hotel room, we took off for Goundam. We had had little sleep, having taken turns under the shower every few hours in a vain effort to beat the heat. So we were glad to reach 5000 feet again after an unsatisfactory French breakfast of lukewarm *café au lait* and stale bread.

We hadn't anticipated any trouble on the flight ahead, for our route was over the Niger River all the way. At first it was easy to follow, for the river was a bright, broad lane paralleled on both sides by carefully planted cotton fields and an extensive system of irrigation ditches, but within an hour the great stream began to wander and to branch. It even began to form lakes and ponds and swamps in such a haphazard, unmapped manner that we could "follow the river" only by guess.

Actually, our map was almost useless, for it merely indicated this area to be swamp, and we soon found that it would be all too easy to follow some riverlike strip of open water that might lead us off our route and into utterly unpopulated regions. And to make matters more distracting still, we began encountering large migrations of storks, great flocks of which occasionally filled the sky around us.

We had been looking forward to seeing these great birds on the roof tops in Goundam, but up here above the Niger River swamps they sometimes seemed to be half as big as Charlie, and they had a most disconcerting habit, when we passed beneath them, of folding their wings in mid-flight and apparently diving straight at the plane. So we divided the bird watching and the river watching between us, meanwhile having an in-flight lunch of cold meat and a loaf of bread. Finally, though, we sighted two large sand mountains ahead and knew that Goundam lay just beyond.

As we flew over the town it looked very large where it sprawls out on the sand beside a river that connects variable and swampy Lake Faguibine with the Niger. Goundam is made up largely of hundreds of mud huts belonging to the native Negroes, though a mosque is prominent among the lesser structures, and a French fort dominates the place from the area's highest elevation. There are also the few small stucco homes for the handful of French residents, and the extensive and ever changing tent encampments of Moors and Tuaregs which are scattered about the outskirts. And even though the city touches the edge of the Sahara, there are green gardens along the river.

Having circled the town to inform the French commandant of our arrival, we headed south and landed several miles away on Goundam's sand runway. The landing strip—for it can hardly be called an airport—boasted no structure at all beyond a white, one-room building toward which we taxied, and there we were greeted by Monsieur Henard, an attractive young Frenchman who explained that he was in charge in the absence of the commandant.

Our plans called for a week in Goundam, and we were concerned for Charlie's safety. There was no telling what damage might be done in seven days by sun and sand and wind, but Monsieur Henard found a solution for our problem. Charlie's nose fitted perfectly in the doorway of the little white building, and though this left his wings and tail at the mercy of the elements, his all-important engine was covered completely. So here we left him, with his engine well protected, and his wings tied securely to gasoline drums. And as additional insurance, Monsieur Henard picked out a nomad shepherd who agreed to act as Charlie's guard both day and night.

With Monsieur Henard at the wheel of a Dodge truck, we then took off on a hair-raising ride to Goundam. Bouncing and careening along the sandy track, now and then at sixty miles an hour, we were given a breathless ride that far surpassed in excitement—and even, perhaps, in danger to our necks—our flight from Bamako. But before long we crossed the rickety bridge over the river, drove through Goundam's sandy streets, which were dotted with white-robed Negroes, turbaned Moors, and veiled Tuaregs, and drew up at Monsieur Henard's home.

The house was dark, and considering the oppressive heat outside, it was comfortably cool. There were no windows, and drawcurtains covered the doorways, but once our eyes had become accustomed to the gloom, we found the interior both colorful and attractive. The chairs and couches were covered with bright native cloth, and the curtains were of similar material. Even the handsome, brightly colored carpets were of local manufacture, and all sorts of local daggers, spears, and shields decorated the walls.

Madame Henard, beautiful and blond, surprised us by appearing both cool and rested, and Katherine, aged ten, seemed equally alien to the heat and sand of Goundam. Her lessons, we learned, came to her each week by air from Paris. And each week the returning plane took her papers back to be corrected and rated—Latin, English, algebra, history, and geography, all studied by way of a correspondence course with two hours' help each day from the local French schoolteacher.

Later we were taken to the "fort" where we were to stay. We found it a kind of *Beau Geste* building, which is actually the commandant's home, though it is windowless and fortresslike, with high thick walls surmounted by a parapet, and with the French tricolor flying from a staff upon the roof.

Here, unquestionably, was a symbol of French supremacy at the edge of the Sahara, but in the absence of the commandant we were told that we had the run of the place. We were given a large, dark bedroom on the main floor, though we were advised, because the nights were almost always pleasant, to sleep on the terrace under the sky. We tried it, too, but the weather was not what it should have been. In fact, throughout most of our stay in Goundam we suffered from constant humid heat that had rolled up here to the edge of the desert before "the equatorial front." It even rained a few drops, and for the entire week we were there we rarely saw the sun. Now and again we nearly collapsed from the heat which, night or day, dropped all too seldom below 115 degrees Fahrenheit.

Luckily we had a large bathroom which was complete with a shower, though this proved to be only a kind of spigot over a sunken area at one end of the room. Still, it served us well, or at least it did until we detected footsteps climbing to the roof each time we chose to bathe. Investigating, we discovered that ten men, who were always followed by a policeman, carried heavy jars of water to the roof in order to fill the reservoir that kept our shower running. The water came from a well some distance away, where the leather buckets that filled the jars had first to be pulled up some 200 feet. The water carriers, we learned, were prisoners, which explained the presence of the policeman, and they no doubt preferred this task to being kept under lock and key. But having learned how the water reached our shower we used it much less extravagantly.

We dined that first evening with the Henards—a superb dinner that would have been recognized as such even in Paris—and during the course of it we learned something of this meeting place of Negroes, Moors, and Tuaregs which, in recent years, has surpassed much older Timbuktu as a center of trade between the desert nomads and the people of the well-watered and more heavily populated regions to the south.

Though the Sahara Desert, throughout most of the distance over which we had flown from southern Morocco to Dakar, extends westward until it actually touches the Atlantic, a different situation exists along this southern edge. Here, between the desert and the hot, moist lands that look out upon the Gulf of Guinea, lies an extensive, well-watered region which forms the western portion of the Sudan, the Bilad-es-Sudan—or the "Country of the Blacks," as it is called in Arabic.

Along the coast of the Gulf of Guinea, and for hundreds of miles inland to the north, much of this portion of the Sudan is jungle and heavy forest—a hot, moist land where fever and dysentery are common—a land of heavy rains and two wet seasons where, at least in certain portions, the rainfall may reach seventy to eighty inches—6 feet or more—a year. Further to the north, however, it grows progressively less moist, passing through a transitional zone of level grasslands partly covered with acacias and mimosas, and ultimately reaching the much drier lands that lie within the great bend of the Niger River. Here, the Niger forms the boundary between the dry, northern limits of the Sudan and the vast arid expanse of the Sahara. And Goundam, lying on this boundary, has more of the Sahara than of the Sudan in its surroundings.

The Negroes of Goundam, and of the country around, have their roots in the Sudan, while the Moors and Tuaregs are peoples of the arid regions to the north, and we learned, in our conversations with Monsieur Henard, that the Moors, like the Arabs of North Africa, are Semitic, while the Tuaregs, like the more northern Berbers, are Hamitic. All of these—and the Negroes of this region, too—are Mohammedan, though their customs differ widely. Among the Tuaregs, for example, it is the men, not the women, who go veiled, and among the Negroes no veils are worn at all.

Formerly, the Tuaregs were the most warlike of all the desert nomads, but now their warlike proclivities are restrained, though they are still nomadic. And despite French efforts to abolish slavery, these Tuaregs still succeed in enslaving Negroes who perform all their menial work.

Monsieur Henard's understanding of these various local peoples was remarkable, and his work involved almost everything from interracial squabbles to petty theft, petty fights, and the endless divorces in which Moslems commonly indulge. He even had to interrupt whatever he was doing each evening in order to wind and set a Negro watchman's alarm clock so that the man, who had never learned to tell the time, could know just when ten o'clock had come—time to turn off the hard-working little generator. And each evening a Goumier—that is, a Moor who was a member of the camel patrol—and a military policeman put in their appearance before Monsieur Henard, saluted smartly, and reported the number of prisoners who were being held, and the number of sick in the Goundam dispensary. Night after night, incidentally, so long as we were there, the numbers remained identically the same—sixty-two prisoners "all accounted for," twenty on the sick list in the dispensary, "and all is well."

On that first evening we were back at the "fortress" before ten, and in bed on the terrace by the time the alarm clock told the watchmen to shut down the generator, but we were still aware of the town all around us, for the braying of the donkeys, the grunts and groans of the camels, and even the tom-toms of some of the local people showed no signs of stopping merely because the few electric lights had been shut off.

Sleeping beneath the stars can be wonderfully pleasant, but with the first light of dawn sleep in Goundam was no longer possible. Flies, in Africa as elsewhere, are always early risers, and by the time earliest dawn had arrived we were forced to get up or to face slow suffocation beneath the sheet. Then, too, reveille blew at six o'clock, whereupon, even though we might pretend to sleep, we were certain to hear bare feet padding about us while the commandant's servants set up our breakfast table within easy reach of our beds.

Wonderful though French meals can be, the *café au lait* we were served each morning—and that was all we got—was far too little to last until twelve-thirty. We did what we could, though without much success, to prepare a little more for ourselves in the commandant's kitchen, but not until several days had passed and Madame Henard learned of our morning starvation period, was the matter corrected. From then on we fared immensely better— starting off the day with ham and eggs, cheese, biscuits, and fruit, as well as with the still invariable *café au lait*.

Each morning we watched as the blue-and-white-robed Goumiers and the well-drilled military police lined up before the fort for morning inspection. They presented arms, the bugler sounded his call with only an occasional off note, and the flag rose to the top of the staff above our heads. Later each day came the review of the fifty-man camel patrol. First we would hear strange sounds which emerged from a vast cloud of dust in the distance. Then, rapidly approaching, we began to make out the fifty galloping camels as they shrieked, groaned, and threw their feet and legs wildly in every direction. Just as disaster seemed all but certain, the mad gallop would slow down to the much less horrifying trot, and finally, after maneuvering in single file, the riders would line up their protesting mounts in formation, each recently ferocious camel now under perfect control, and each robed Goumier impressively equipped with turban and cartridge belt. Their saddles were bright with decorations, their bare feet clutched at the camel's sides, their blue-and-white robes billowed about them, and as they brandished their rifles above their heads they yelled what may have been a kind of Goumier salute.

Having halted, their leader would report, after which the camels complained and groaned again as they were made to kneel. And finally, after much beating and many shouts, the great ungainly animals sank to the sand, the Goumiers leaped off, and we, escaping at last from the heat and the clouds of dust and sand, would retreat to the Henard's clean, cool living room and to the ice water that made it possible to stay alive in all that desert heat.

We became acquainted with Goundam by following Monsieur Henard on his daily tours of inspection—to the school for native children—to the big mosque, which was impressive despite the fact that it was built of mud and straw—through narrow alleyways lined with one story mud houses, most of them built alike.

Each house had a courtyard surrounded by a wall, and there one might find almost anything—horse, donkey, sheep, chickens, ducks, and lots of little children, all of whom were as naked as the day they were born.

The women often hovered over charcoal fires, making delicious-looking stews in black iron pots. A cobbler might be making shoes, or a weaver might be at his loom. Near the river we found the forges of the town and saw sweating Negroes fashioning knives and spears and daggers. Camel saddles were being made nearby.

Cotton cloth in bolts was for sale in a shop a little further on, with Singer Sewing Machines buzzing busily amid the sand and the flies just outside.

In one corner of the market place what appeared to be a pile of not-quite-finished tombstones—grayish-white in color—proved to be slabs of salt recently arrived by caravan from the salt mines of Taoudenni, 400 miles to the north and not far from the very center of the almost trackless western Sahara. Combs, beads and bracelets, mirrors, pots and pans were elsewhere on display. Melons, dried fish, and peanuts were there as well, and we even came upon a butcher shop, though the shapeless hunks of meat, hanging by cords from the only tree in sight, were all but hidden by the unbelievable swarms of flies.

Here and there we passed a tame ostrich that seemed to pay no attention whatever to the people. And down by the river we found women washing pots and scrubbing them effectively with sand. Elsewhere clothes were being washed, along with children, too, and we learned that, in Africa as elsewhere, soap is apt to bring tears and cries of opposition when it gets into youthful eyes.

Later Madame Henard took us "to tea" in the encampment of Moors, and to our astonishment we found that Moorish women perform no housework. They do not even serve the tea when guests arrive, leaving it all, like the Tuaregs, to their black slaves. They merely seem to move from one shady spot to the next, presenting a picture of exaggerated gloom, dressed, as they are, in blue or black, and with their faces smeared—rather unbeautifully in our eyes—with indigo paint. No wonder, it seemed to us, that their men like the laughing, gaily dressed, hard-working Negresses.

Riding down one of the sandy streets to visit among the Negroes on one occasion, we were overtaken by an out-of-breath Goumier. A big Tuareg chieftain had recently reached Goundam, we were told, and, having heard about a camera we had which was supposed to "take a picture in sixty seconds," he wanted us to come and take his picture with it. What he had heard of, as we instantly knew, was our Polaroid Land Camera, which we often used when we wished to give photographs as gifts.

We were more than willing to obey this summons, for the Tuaregs are usually a standoffish lot, and with the Goumier to guide us, we made our way down beside the river where we found a house that differed little from others of its kind. Entering the dark hall, we found it packed with Tuaregs in long white robes, and, having solemnly shaken hands with each of them, we proceeded to the next room, which faced the courtyard. Here, we were told, we were to await the arrival of the chieftain, and, having taken off our shoes, for courtesy requires it among these people, we sat down on a brightly colored blanket that had been spread for us.

Our host entered almost at once, along with others whom we assumed to be his "gentlemen in waiting," or something of the sort. All of them were dressed in white robes and all wore blue veils, other colors being in bad taste among the Tuaregs. The chieftain had handsome leather good luck charms about his neck, a leather purse at his waist, and a long dagger in an exquisitely decorated leather sheath that was strapped to his arm.

He sat down on the blanket beside me, his legs crossed beneath him, while his attendants squatted on the floor. And in a moment a copper tray laden with glasses was brought in, and sickeningly sweet tea was served, each man pulling down his veil to his chin while he drank. Someone was playing odd oriental music on a stringed instrument something like a banjo, but there was little or no conversation until the chieftain, suddenly speaking in French, asked if we would care to see some Tuareg war dances.

This was something I had hoped for but had not expected, so we did not have our recording equipment with us. I explained as well as I could and asked for permission to get it. The chieftain seemed to understand and when I had returned in a quarter of an hour or so, we all moved into the courtyard and the dance began.

Many of the onlookers clapped and sang, but only two men

took part in the dance, "fighting" each other with wicked-looking lances and protecting themselves with leather shields. I filmed the dance, and also caught all the sounds—the sharp clapping of hands, the shouts, and the singing—on our tape recorder. And it was this that delighted and astonished them most when we played back the recording, though the Polaroid pictures we took caused almost equal awe and excitement as the quickly completed prints were passed from hand to hand.

When the pictures had been taken and the recording made, one of the "aides" slipped away and returned, presently, with a beautiful leather pillow, which the chieftain presented to Tay, and as a parting gesture, he slipped his handsome dagger from his arm and handed it to me—a royal gift, indeed—a Tuareg dagger that is really a museum piece.

But that was not all. Clearly Tay and I had been accepted as friends, for as we left we were asked to return the following winter to share the hospitality of their desert encampment. And we, in turn, invited our host to visit us in Princeton—a visit that is likely, if it ever materializes, to astonish the natives of our New Jersey town fully as much as we astonished our Tuareg friends in Goundam.

Our visit to Goundam reached its climax a few days before we left with the arrival on an Air France DC-3 of one of the Negro deputies from French West Africa to the National Assembly in Paris. All in all, there were, at that time, twenty-nine "African" deputies in the Assembly, but of these, I was told, only three were Negroes. It was one of these three who now arrived in Goundam, an important community in this Negro deputy's extensive constituency.

The night before his arrival his local constituents held an impressive celebration in honor of the expected event. Red, white, and blue bunting had been hung all around the city's main square, a powerful gas lantern provided a vivid, glaring light, and crowds surrounded a group of white-robed dignitaries. But even more than the dignitaries, the drummers and dancers were the center of attention.

Wielding heavy, padded drumsticks, the drummers were beating for all they were worth on empty oil drums. These odd instruments resounded most satisfactorily as the performers pounded out their perfect rhythms, and though the dancers, all of whom were men, seemed to have no particular steps, they nevertheless swayed more or less in unison as they walked and pranced in the circle they had formed, waving canes above their heads, or even brightly colored kerchiefs they had snatched from some of the watching girls.

The rhythm and the motions of the dance seldom varied, but we did not tire of watching. There may have been something hypnotic about the scene, as the vividly lighted figures and the vast, moving shadows they cast turned the whole crowded plaza into a huge, black and white panorama of rhythmic sound and motion.

It was the following morning when the Air France plane arrived with the Negro deputy, and a colorful crowd was out in full force to greet him. This was an important event for everyone, and the women, especially, were dressed in costumes that were just as bright, in reds, greens, and yellows, as those we had seen in Dakar. We were on a roof top, well placed to see the parade that accompanied the deputy from the distant airstrip. A galloping group of riders in flowing robes came first, stirring up a great cloud of dust that hung like haze over the crowd. Three flag-covered trucks followed, each jammed with dignitaries, but where was the visiting deputy? It was impossible to tell, though because of the cheers of the crowd, we knew he must be there.

With the movie camera in my hand, I hurried down from the roof in order to follow the rapidly moving procession, and I promptly lost Tay in the process. Noticing this, but being intent on recording some of the developments at close range, I decided to leave her on her own for a time, and hurried on until, by accident more than by design, I found myself in a square toward which the deputy's procession was at that moment advancing.

First came the robed and galloping horsemen, the people cheering as the clouds of dust rolled above our heads. I had my camera working, and in the midst of this, to my surprise, I sighted Tay. Under the guidance and protection of as handsome a little Tuareg twelve-year-old as one could hope to see, she, too, had found her way to this new square. Her little Tuareg friend was carrying her camera case, and somehow the friendly little fellow, who had come to her assistance when I had disappeared, had succeeded in bringing her unerringly back to me.

The dust was blinding, and Tay pulled back, but just then the three flag-draped trucks arrived, and the friendly crowd, with me in their very midst, pushed forward as if each person were intent on being the first to shake the deputy's hand. Exuberant Negroes and Moors were shouting and waving rifles above their heads. A gun went off, Tay told me later, within hardly more than a foot of her ear, temporarily deafening her and making her all the more eager to get away from there. With the help of her little Tuareg protector she managed to do it, too, but as luck would have it, her "escape," which took her away from me again, led her almost directly toward a group of dignitaries who were at the very center of affairs. Tay had no way of knowing who was who, but with admirable presence of mind she nevertheless seized the opportunity to snap a number of pictures.

I, on the other hand, had even better luck. Hemmed in by the crowd until I could hardly move, I finally found myself almost a part of the official group. Then, to my astonishment, I found I was actually being introduced in French to the deputy himself, though, to my regret, I failed to get his name as completely as he failed to get mine.

By now, his group had reached the steps of the house to which they had come, and with such an eager throng crowding all about, a political speech simply had to follow. I could make out hardly a word of it, for it was given in Hausa, a central African language, but both Tay and I, from our two different points of vantage, took note of the deputy's method of delivery.

Standing close beside him was a small bespectacled man who was holding the written version of the speech. The deputy himself, whose voice was powerful and whose gestures were impressive, would intone a sentence with all the vehemence that was in him, after which he would bend down toward the little man and listen carefully while the next sentence was read to him. Then, with head erect once more he would repeat *that* sentence with appropriate gestures, before stopping to hear the next words he was so feelingly to impart.

Tay, still guided by her friendly little Tuareg, finally got away from the densest part of the crowd and ultimately I followed, finding them a little distance off. It was noon by now and we were tired and hot. The speech was still going on, while down the street, as if in competition, a battery of tom-toms was booming. But Tay and I, together with her handsome and helpful little guide, headed back through the narrow streets toward the "fortress," for we had had enough of the reception.

We were grateful to the boy who had stood by Tay so helpfully, and when we parted I gave him several francs—a fortune, I assumed, for the little fellow wore only a short and faded blue robe. He seemed immensely pleased, too, and left us with a smile. But later that afternoon, when we paid a call on an important Tuareg chieftain, whom should we find dressed in white embroidered robes and sitting by the chieftain's side but our little friend of the morning!

He bowed gravely and smiled, and only then we learned, to our amazement, that he was the chieftain's brother—a person of consequence and wealth to whom the few francs I had given him meant nothing—a little Tuareg gentleman by birth, and, as we had observed that morning, a gentleman by instinct, too.

V. Over Greenest Africa

For a week, in company with his shepherd guard, Charlie had waited patiently in the heat of the Goundam airstrip, his wings tied down and his nose inside the one small structure there. The little plane's wings were often scorching to the touch, and I know no way of suggesting how hot it was inside the fuselage, which we kept tightly closed against the dust and the sand-laden breezes. But now our Goundam visit was coming to an end, and Charlie, refueled, aired out, cleaned, and repacked, was ready to take off, with the Belgian Congo next on our list.

Monsieur and Madame Henard, together with Katherine, were at the airstrip to see us off, and with Charlie's engine running as smoothly as ever, we almost literally bounded into the air. Making one circle about the field as we climbed, and waving good-by to our friends below, we set our course to the east. Following the Goundam tributary of the Niger River and then the Niger itself we began our flight along the southern fringe of the blistering Sahara. Up and up we climbed, to 8000 feet where the air that streamed through the cabin ventilators felt wonderfully cool and invigorating after the 115-degree heat of Goundam.

A slight detour to the north took us over Timbuktu, that centuries-old and almost legendary meeting place of camel and

canoe. Time was when this sprawling, mud-walled city was the
most important community of all this vast interior region—a city
that flourished for centuries when great camel caravans plodded
north to Algeria across the thousand-mile-wide Sahara, bearing
gold and slaves from the Sudan to the Arab north. Even yet it is
a city of much consequence, as Tay and I learned when we had
visited it, though only for a single day, the year before, and we
were disappointed not to stop again. But the heat of Goundam
had left us with little desire for more of the same, and with both
our health and our morale in mind we confined ourselves to a
few circles over Timbuktu while Tay took some movies of it, con-
centrating on a crowded gathering of camels that were drinking
at a little pond in the middle of the town. Then, turning Charlie
to the east once more, we flew on above the Niger, following it
for an hour or so to where it makes its great curve to the southeast. In another twenty minutes, we sighted the landing strip
at Gao—first stop on our way to the Belgian Congo, which was
still 1500 miles beyond the horizon.

We landed and immediately refueled, expecting to fly on at
once to Niamey another 250 miles downstream, or about as far as
we had already come, but a report of thunderstorms ahead compelled us to spend the night at Gao's little French hotel, where
we tossed and sweltered before taking off at dawn the next morning.

Niamey, which we reached within two hours, meant more gas
and oil, as well as another look at the weather before turning
eastward into Nigeria. From Niamey we planned to head across
the border of Nigeria for Kano, a town some 500 miles away in
the northern part of that newly independent country. After taking off, we left the Niger River and began our climb on a
course that coincided with a thin, red dirt road. At 7000 feet we
leveled off, and then just as we reached our cruising speed, all
hell suddenly broke loose!

There was a terrifying clatter and a heavy vibration up front,
and my first thought was that a bearing, or something equally

Above—Along a branch of the Niger river at Goundam, French West Africa, where not even a language barrier can keep two housewives from talking things over.   *Below*—Among the Pygmies of the Ituri Forest charcoal paint takes the place of lipstick and rouge. A Pygmy mother decorates her daughter's face with vertical black lines, using a twig for a brush.

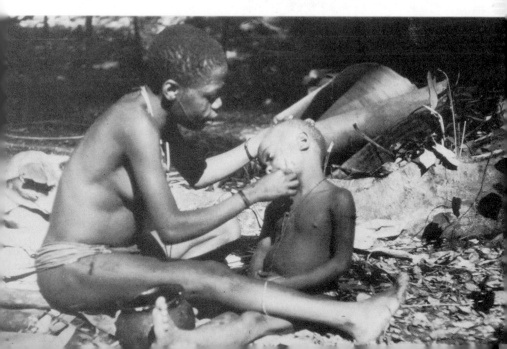

Above — Anne Putnam and Tay talk in Swahili with a Pygmy hunter. Nets, like the one carried over his shoulder, are indispensable to hunting in the dense Ituri Forest. Note the igloo-like configuration of the Pygmies' stick-and-leaf huts in the background.

Above — "Bringing home the bacon." These Pygmy boys are returning to camp from a hunt, and wrapped in their leaf containers are choice bits of antelope killed by their father. Clothing means little to these happy people of the rain forest. *Right* — Contemplation! Saale, a slightly gray-haired Pygmy, thinks things over while sitting in the chair he has quickly made by lashing together four sticks with a piece of vine. Behind him stands an unfinished hut.

Above left—Faizi stands in a rare shaft of sunlight to penetrate the great forest, testing a new bow. The bowstring is a strip of bark, and sometimes Pygmy arrows are dipped in poison. *Above right*—Pygmy hunters scramble up a bee tree in the Ituri Forest to fill their baskets with golden combs of honey. *Below*—Faizi, bravest of Pygmies, steels himself for a flight in Charlie, while Mukabasi, lower left, takes what he probably thought would be his last look at his old friend.

Above — A cow elephant and her baby saunter away from us in Uganda's Park Elizabeth, one of the best spots in all Africa for seeing and filming elephants. *Below* — The legendary Ruwenzori — Ptolemy's Mountains of the Moon, filmed from the Uganda side and from an altitude of about 17,000 feet. Clouds boiling up from the Congo's Semliki Plains will soon hide these equatorial snows that Africans still believe are salt.

Above—Lieutenant Mungo Henderson and his well-armed "Askaris" of Company D, 5th Battalion of the Queen's African Rifles—about to hunt down Mau Mau in Kenya's Aberdare forest. *Below*—At the Athi River Detention Camp, south of Nairobi, loyal Kikuyu work on a captured Mau Mau who sits on the ground, trying to win him back to their ranks. The women and the child may be his relatives.

Above — Eastleigh Airport, Nairobi. R. A. F. Squadron Leader K. R. Bowhill is in the middle and one of his Lincoln bombers stands just behind, after a mission against the Mau Mau on Mount Kenya. *Below* — Soldiers of the Arab Legion take their positions at the frontier town of Qalquilya, where Jordan faces Israel. The "unloaded" Sten gun, just left of center, points directly at Tay, who took the picture, and a moment later it was accidentally fired, missing her by inches.

Above — Mrs. Norman Blake, wife of Pan American Airways' regional director in Beirut, caught us about to take off across the Mediterranean for Cyprus. No room for a box lunch except on Tay's lap. Pinned to the cabin upholstery is the insignia of the R. A. F.'s 214th Squadron.   *Below* — At the Marble Palace, Tehran, Tay chats with His Imperial Majesty, the Shah of Iran, and his lovely, gracious Queen, Soraya.

At Pahlevi, northern Iran, where the world's best caviar is taken, like this, from sturgeon netted in Persian waters of the Caspian Sea.

Tay—almost as frozen as the giant sturgeon under and around her in the fisheries' cold storage at Pahlevi. Russia buys nearly all this frozen sturgeon, but Iran is looking for markets in the West.

important, had let go in the engine. I was sure that we were headed for our first forced landing. Still, the engine kept running. Oil pressure and temperature remained okay. The cylinder head temperature stayed where it belonged. The magnetos were fine. The engine continued to develop the same power as ever. I checked all these and checked them again, for the clatter and vibration were terrifying. We had no idea what was wrong, but our thoughts ran riot, and, recalling our experience with the oil leak over Dakar, we wheeled about in quick order, heading back toward Niamey and calling ahead to let them know that we were having trouble and might have to land on that narrow red road below.

To our relief, we reached the airstrip, and, having landed, we learned that all the clatter and vibration had been caused by the loss of several screws that were supposed to hold the engine cowling in place just behind the prop spinner. The last one must have popped out as we leveled off, leaving the cowling loose enough to flutter in the blast from the propeller.

Other screws nearby also showed signs of shearing under the added strain, and had we been forced to stay in the air much longer we might have lost the whole cowling, which, troublesome though it might have been, need not have been tragic unless, in tearing adrift, it had smashed into our faces through the windshield, or damaged one of Charlie's vitals.

We were naturally relieved to find so simple a reason for all that racket, and luckily our spare-parts kit provided the needed extra screws and washers. Thus we were able to button things up again promptly and resume our journey, though we were not permitted to take off until the French airport officer satisfied himself that our plane was right once more. No doubt he found it difficult to believe that a couple or three missing screws in the cowling had caused all the excitement that had reached him by way of my radio reports, and he had no intention of letting us take off for Kano until convinced that there had been no basic trouble.

Our second take-off was uneventful, and for a hundred miles or so we followed the red dirt road with little trouble. But then the road divided into a number of ill-defined tracks—which were just as poorly defined on our map—and we were forced to continue on a compass heading.

Luckily, both weather and visibility were good and there seemed to be little wind drift. Wisely, too, we had asked the French at Niamey to signal the British at the little Nigerian outpost of Sokoto, asking that their radio beacon be turned on, and after a time we were happy to hear it coming in—"dit-dit-dit, dah-dit-dah, dah dah dah"—S-K-O—and to have the radio compass homing on it. Once over Sokoto we turned a few degrees to the right and headed for Kano, now only 240 miles ahead.

In planning this section of our trip before we had left home we had been much concerned over the possibility of having nothing to follow, but it had not turned out that way. And the Kano beacon, toward which we now were flying, was one of the most powerful in Africa. In fact, it came in on our receiver practically over Sokoto, and for 200 miles we had it to lean on, though we never needed to because Tay's navigation was right on the nose. About seventy miles from Kano we called the airport and had the pleasure of getting a good weather report and of speaking to someone in our own language once more. As we approached the field we called again, and soon landed on an enormous runway which the British jet Comet air liners used before they were grounded.

There to greet us was the Kano health officer, a jolly African in white, who was beside himself with laughter at the thought of spraying the inside of such a tiny airplane as ours. He stuck a DDT bomb through my open window and gave it a little squirt, choking over his giggles as he did so.

"Do you think that will be enough?" he asked, almost doubling over with laughter.

The heat of the Sahara was with us even in Kano, but we had to lay over for several days in order to catch up on our correspondence. We also had to plan the 450-mile jump to Fort Lamy, just south of Lake Chad in French Equatorial Africa, but when we finally took off, the flight proved to be an easy one of only about three hours.

We were anxious to reach the richly rewarding region of the Belgian Congo, but we laid over one day at Fort Lamy, where, to my delight, I was introduced to gliding. For three hours, with a French glider pioneer, I soared round and round to an ultimate height of 8000 feet, amazed and immensely pleased by the hush —the almost utter silence—of motorless flight. But simple though gliding may appear to be, the skill it takes to locate the necessary updrafts almost requires a special sense.

From Fort Lamy our flight plan read direct to Fort Archambault, which lies a little more than 300 miles up the Chari River —southeast, that is—from Fort Lamy. But Lake Chad was to be found in the opposite direction and we headed for it, anxious to see that remote, swamp-surrounded body of water, and hoping to see some elephants on the way. Down the Chari River we flew, very low, looking for the elephants but seeing only crocodiles and occasional hippos basking on the river's sand bars. For miles and miles we buzzed over Lake Chad's vast surrounding swamps, with no place whatever for Charlie to land, and with crocodiles numerous in the vast expanse of reeds. But on we went until we were able to take some movies of the lake itself as well as of its swamps, after which we turned about, passed over Fort Lamy, and made our way on up the Chari to Fort Archambault.

The countryside was greener here than at Fort Lamy, for the rains had already begun. In fact, from here on for a time we had to do most of our flying in the early mornings in order to avoid the thunderstorms that so often developed later in the day.

It was with only a mediocre weather report to guide us that we took off from Fort Archambault and flew almost directly south for a little over 300 miles to Bangui in French Equatorial Africa, across the Ubangui River from the most northwestern portion of the Belgian Congo. We followed a stream early in the flight but soon picked up another narrow, reddish road that was often hard to trace as it made its way through the heavy forest of this tropical and well-watered region.

Halfway to Bangui we ran into a little light rain, but the clouds were high and the visibility excellent. We knew the location of four emergency grass airstrips, too, so we felt safe in keeping on our way. Then the rain stopped and we reached Bangui, where, in the coolness of the rainy season, we had our first sound and comfortable sleep in over a month, though we were now only 300 miles from the equator.

We were in the air again by eight o'clock the next morning, flying over solid jungle. The weather was fine. There was little wind and no apparent drift, so after following the Ubangui River south for forty or fifty miles to the village of Libenge, we turned to the southeast, and, taking a compass heading of 130 degrees, left the river and flew for more than an hour over the unbroken green of the jungle before coming to the mighty Congo and turning east above it to Lisala, there to land on a grass airstrip for enough more gas to assure an uninterrupted flight to Stanleyville.

Here we were on an airstrip near a small Congo River village —a remote spot in Central Africa—and yet, to our astonishment and delight, we came upon another light plane—a Piper Super Cruiser that was being flown by a Belgian couple of about our own age. They had come from Europe by much the same route we had followed and had even had an experience similar to ours at Cabo Yubi. But instead of flying inland from Dakar as we had done, they had kept to the African coast as far as Léopoldville, 200 miles from the mouth of the Congo, and now, as was the case with us, they were on their way to Stanleyville. The husband, whom we did not see, had gone into Lisala on business, leaving his wife to attend to the refueling.

An African helped me "top off" Charlie's tanks, and we took off again, telling the Belgian girl that we would look for her and her husband in Stanleyville, but a little later they ran out of gas somewhere over the jungle and crashed in a village clearing where, fortunately, a group of missionaries cared for the injured pair. The news of their mishap made us shudder—the more so since we had many more hours of jungle flying still to go.

All the way to Stanleyville we followed the broad, muddy Congo River, flying most of the way at 3000 feet, the better to observe life along this enormous and fascinating waterway. Now and then villages of thatched huts were visible at the water's edge, and once we swooped low to buzz a stern wheeler that was slowly churning its way upstream.

By a stroke of luck we reached Stanleyville on the eve of a series of native boat races that had been arranged in commemoration of the fiftieth anniversary of the death of Sir Henry M. Stanley, the great explorer of Africa for whom Stanleyville was named. Now, before leaving home, we had decided to use our motion picture cameras with much discretion, planning in advance everything we wished to shoot. This meant knowing a good deal about our subject matter and working out a story line before beginning to get it down on film, and it kept us from accumulating a lot of miscellaneous material or too many disconnected, unrelated shots. But the races that were about to start were not to be missed, and we covered them both in sound and on film.

With this task in mind, we spent our first full day in Stanleyville beside the river, where, with a few Belgians and any number of Africans, we cheered on the Wagenyas—the people of the river—as they raced in their long war canoes, village against village. They made a striking picture—a dozen great canoes, each with about fifty men, all standing and paddling in perfect unison. Each canoe had been hollowed and shaped from the trunk of a single tree, and each represented a village. When the races began, wreaths of flowers were arranged about the prows of these long dugouts, and standing in every canoe near this floral decoration was a village chieftain dressed in a leopard-skin loincloth with the leopard's tail dangling behind, and wearing a feathered headdress and a necklace of leopard teeth. To keep the paddlers in unison, each dugout carried two drummers and two wooden drums, while the paddlers, standing in apparent insecurity in the narrow, heavily laden craft, wielded their paddles with such rhythm they almost seemed to be dancing.

Having made sound and motion picture records of the races, we found it necessary to work backward, so to speak, in order to create a film story of which our record of the race would be the climax. So, we proceeded to film the Wagenyas in their villages, showing their homes, their children, and their everyday lives. We also filmed their fishing methods, which entail the use of enormous conical baskets that are hung partially submerged from scaffolds erected in the Congo, where the current is utilized as an aid in trapping any fish that may attempt to swim downstream—huge catfish, mostly some more than three feet long.

We centered our story on a young vice-chief named Kalunda, who, along with his necklace of leopard's teeth, wore a St. Christopher medal on his chest. To our surprise, Kalunda knew something about the motion picture business. In fact, he had once actually been on the Hollywood pay roll, having been used, along with others of his village, in the making of *Mogambo,* a picture starring Clark Gable, and in which Kalunda was appropriately cast as an African boatman.

In shooting our story of life in a Congo River village, we were amazed to find how many of the local citizens owned Fords or Chevrolets, how many more owned bicycles, and the surpassing numbers who dressed at least part of the time in western BVDs. We had long since heard, of course, that "darkest Africa" was largely a thing of the past, but we were surprised to learn the direction "enlightenment" had sometimes taken. We were even surprised to find how widely Belgian administrators are scattered throughout the Congo. Hardly a tribe exists without its regular contacts with these administrators, and many tribes, even by our standards, are doing well economically and are steadily increasing their exports of cotton, coffee, palm oil, and other products.

While we were in Stanleyville we were received by, and even

played nine holes of golf with Monsieur André Scholler, the governor of the province, who has had more than twenty years of service in the Congo. Aware, as I was, of the difficulties the British of Kenya continue to have with the Kikuyu Mau Mau, I asked if he anticipated any comparable difficulties in the Belgian Congo. He replied that such a development was not at all likely, for there is little European ownership of land in the Congo and no surplus native population. He pointed out, in fact, that the Africans are forbidden to sell their land without official approval, lest they forfeit their future security for some short term gain, and explained the government's policy of slow, evolutionary changes. The plan is largely aimed at economic and social benefits, leaving major political concessions for the more distant future when the Africans will be better prepared for them.

In all our camera work in the vicinity of Stanleyville, we were effectively assisted by Maurice Le Nain of the Bureau des Affaires Indigènes. He saw to it that the villagers were on hand at the proper times, and, because he speaks the local tongue—Lingala —fluently, he translated for us whenever that was necessary. And when we had finished he computed the value of the villager's time, saying that we owed them fourteen hundred francs—about twenty-eight dollars—which seemed modest to us though it appeared to be satisfactory to our Wagenya friends.

High on the list of the projects that had brought us to this part of Central Africa was our hope of visiting the Pygmies of the Ituri Forest, where we also hoped to find Anne Putnam, an American woman who, we had heard, was living in close contact with these fascinating little people of the jungle. Governor Scholler had told us that the Ituri Forest lay well to the east of Stanleyville, not far from the Ruwenzori Mountains—the fabled "Mountains of the Moon"—which we also hoped to see. He had told us, too, that the best way of reaching both our goals would be to fly to a tiny airstrip at the little settlement of Mambasa. But now, as we began to plan that flight, we were urged to drop in on another group of Africans who, unlike the Pygmies, are developing into prosperous farmers though they still have not abandoned their former rites, including a dance that was said to be unique.

This new idea would involve a detour to the town of Paulis, named after an early Congo pioneer, and it threatened to put too great a strain on Charlie's gasoline capacity until the Shell representative at Stanleyville told us of a few drums of aviation gasoline that had long before been left at Paulis. They were a bit out of date, he said, but the contents should be okay. So, on the strength of that, we plotted on our map all the emergency airstrips east of Stanleyville and then took off, flying once more over the densest kind of jungle with only a red thread of dirt road occasionally showing beneath us.

For 150 miles we followed this elusive track to the east, and then for almost as far north, to Paulis. But to stay with it called for the utmost concentration, for it played hide-and-seek with us under the spreading treetops of the green forest, and two or three times we had to circle back, looking for signs of it beneath the trees. Nor was our map much help, for it showed only the road's general course, not each twist and turn. And the radio compass was no help at all, since there are no beacons in this part of the Congo. But worst of all, the endless jungle, except for the rare and widely scattered airstrips, offered no place to land.

"How could we make a forced landing in that tangle?" Tay and I asked ourselves with a shudder. A question, I at least, had to answer as best I could, because the pilot of a single-engined airplane must be prepared to find himself suddenly at the controls of a glider which, with the weight of a dead engine, is bound to settle fast. I knew that our only hope, if the engine failed, would be to plop into the treetops as though landing normally, just at the stalling speed with the tail low, praying that, after the plane stopped, the forest's heavy canopy would hold it by the wings and fuselage, preventing a crash to the ground more than 100 feet below. Much would depend upon whether the wings would survive the impact. And I was glad we were flying a high-winged airplane, where most of the shock would be absorbed by the landing gear and fuselage.

Even if we came through such a jungle-top landing, what then? The remains of Charlie would settle enough into the forest to be lost to any aerial search. And unless we could shinny down a liana vine and then walk to one of the Congo's few roads, there would be little hope of our survival. That's another reason we were so careful to keep to this dirt road.

Finally, our red thread of a life line intersected a narrow gauge railroad, which we followed for the last fifteen miles to Paulis. Arriving over the town, we quickly spotted its grass airstrip and, as we circled around, we realized that word of our coming must have preceeded us. A crowd was already there, even including a few Belgians, and in a moment Charlie was on the ground—the first plane to come in at Paulis in a long time, and the very first American plane, the Belgian administrator told us, ever to visit that remote settlement. Having greeted us, he gave us a hand as we pushed Charlie into a T hangar that had housed a missionary's Piper until it had crashed long before. What happened to the missionary we never heard, but the remains of the plane lay scattered nearby.

As Charlie's tail wheel rolled onto the hangar's dirt floor, the ground gave way and the wheel dropped into a termite hole. It took six of us to pull it out again and set it back on firmer ground so that the rest of the plane would go in. Then an African soldier was left on guard, with instructions to sleep in the hangar at night, and we were whisked away in a car to the one hotel in town, there to have lunch before going on to the office of the local administrator.

The people of Paulis, it turned out, were in holiday spirit, and hundreds of Mangbetus, who were the tribesmen we had been told about, had left their "cultivations" and come to town to stage one of their remarkable dances. In fact, Tay and I filmed the dance that very afternoon. Men and women wearing feathered headdresses and loinclothes of bark or animal skins danced slowly in a great circle, shuffling in the dust, tossing their red-plumed heads from side to side, and jingling the little bells on their wrists and toes in a cadence that was accentuated by the flop-flop of the women's limp and often elongated breasts. The men waved their spears against a beautiful blue sky that was studded with great pillars of black and white cumulus clouds, and a Mangbetu chief, lolling in an elaborately carved sedan chair, took part in the dance with a minimum of effort as his bearers, still carrying him, shuffled and hopped along with the rest to the tune of wooden horns and wooden drums.

To our ears there was no music, though the rhythm was unmistakable. The horns seemed to give out only two different notes, both of which were harsh and raucous, but the drummers more than made up the difference and could have taught even our "hottest" drummers plenty about "boogie beats."

The next morning we attended to the fueling. Two grades of gas were available in the drums that had been at Paulis so long —100 octane and 73. We decided to use only the 73 because, being an unleaded fuel, it was least likely to have spoiled. On the flight to Paulis we had purposely kept one tank almost full, emptying the other, so now we put the questionable gasoline into the empty tank, and as we did so, someone casually remarked that it was too bad Paulis was losing its supply of cleaning fluid.

"What?" we asked. "Has this been used as cleaning fluid?"

It was the 73 octane, we learned, that had been put to that use, and never, I am sure, has gasoline been more carefully filtered. But once we were in the air and, with the Paulis strip still below us for safety's sake, switched over to that tank of "cleaning fluid," the engine ran as smoothly as if it had actually been designed to operate on the stuff.

So, for two hours we flew on that strangely satisfactory Paulis gasoline, passing over the Ituri River at Nia-Nia and picking up the dirt road that runs east from there to Irumu. Beneath our wings now, hidden under the almost impenetrable cover of the dense Ituri Forest, were bands of Pygmies, hunting, perhaps, with their bows and arrows, and wondering, no doubt, at the sound of Charlie's engine.

Before long our road crossed the Epulu River, and a little way ahead was Mambasa. We made a low pass over the village to let its people know that we would soon be landing at the grass air-strip a couple of miles away, and when we had "dragged" the strip a few times for any anthills or holes and finally landed, Charlie barely stopped rolling before the first sprinting Africans from Mambasa reached the edge of the field.

The Mambasa airstrip was merely a rectangle of grass carved from the forest, with no structure of any kind, and we were wondering how to secure Charlie when Mambasa's Belgian postmaster drove up and called on the African bystanders to produce some stakes for tie-downs. They lopped off branches from nearby trees with razor-sharp bush knives. These we pounded diagonally into the rain-soaked earth with clubs, anchoring Charlie to them with our cargo ropes. Then a native soldier was appointed Charlie's guard—to shoo off any elephants that might try to use a wing tip for a back-scratcher, or any hyena that might fancy chewing up the tires.

We would have preferred more protection for Charlie, but nothing more was to be had, and, trusting that he would not be harmed, we accompanied the postmaster to the surprisingly "metropolitan" village of Mambasa. There, besides a large area of native huts, we found nine Belgian homes, a small hotel—which is really more like a motel—a post office and an administration building, and, having put up at the hotel, we hoped we would have no difficulty in finding our way to the Pygmies.

VI. Tall Trees and Tiny People

IT WAS THE BELGIAN ADMINIStrator at Mambasa who told us that the best way to see the Pygmies was to go to Camp Putnam, and we were lucky enough to hitch a ride through the forest with a young Belgian agricultural expert. It was a two-hour drive to the west by way of the rutted, one-lane dirt road that had served to guide us to Mambasa the day before, and on the way we not only encountered a heavy tropical downpour, but also passed a government elephant-training station where the road crossed the Epulu River. Then, only a little way farther on, we came to a side road and a small roadside sign.

"Camp Putnam. Meals. Lodging," it read, and the side road led off into the forest.

We turned as the sign directed and drove through the rain for a mile or so with the dripping forest pressing closely in upon us on both sides. We passed a tiny village that consisted only of a small cluster of huts and a handful of natives who watched us silently as we passed. We looked about, disappointed at not seeing a Pygmy or two, and not very much farther on, we came to a stop before a large, attractive thatched-roof house—the main structure at Camp Putnam. The rain was still falling as we hurried inside, and there, crowded around a large stone fireplace, were our first Pygmies!

Unexpected happenings are anything but rare so deep in the interior of Africa, but we were utterly unprepared to find a band of Pygmies usurping the hearth in Anne Putnam's living room. We ourselves, of course, had entered very abruptly and informally, and, in a way, were more foreign to the locale than the Pygmies were. Still, we were surprised to come upon them as we had, and we were pleased to see that they were just as small as we had expected them to be. The tallest were no more than chest-high to us, and they wore the barest minimum of clothing—nothing, in fact, but bark loincloths. It is no wonder that they were huddling around the fire, for with the rain falling steadily, there was no real warmth in the air.

We had hardly recovered from our surprise when Anne Putnam appeared—a slender, almost wiry woman in her forties. She welcomed us in a strong deep voice and with an accent that plainly suggested New York City, and it was entirely apparent that she had been busy elsewhere. She wore a pair of faded slacks and a white blouse with the tails hanging out, and her hair, which was drawn carelessly away from her face, was fastened just as carelessly at the back of her neck.

Even from the little she told us before we were taken to our "room," which was an attractive, circular thatched hut at the edge of the Putnam forest clearing, we decided that her story was as interesting as that of the Pygmies, and we promptly went back to sit before the fire and talk with her. Born and reared in the city of New York, her only training for the kind of life she was living now was one summer at a girl's camp in New England and a year among the mountaineers of Kentucky. Wholly interested in becoming an artist, she had studied at the Art Students' League, after which she successfully established herself as a painter in oils and water colors with a studio in Greenwich Village. Africa, to her, was only a name in the distance when she married Patrick Putnam, a Bostonian and a Harvard graduate, but he had already put his roots down in the Belgian Congo. Having been a member of a Harvard anthropological expedition which visited the Congo in 1928, he had come in contact with the Pygmies of the Ituri Forest, and because of the interest these little people and their remote country aroused in him, he had gone to Belgium, and had taken an eight-month *Agence Sanitaire* course—about the equivalent of a nursing program. Then he had returned to the Ituri region and had gone to work as an *Agent Sanitaire* at a place called Pengui.

In 1937, after some eight years of this work, an aching tooth forced him to visit the nearest doctor, who happened to be in Mambasa, but because of the lack of roads—for none had been built in this region as yet—it was necessary to make the journey on foot. It was not an easy one, for it was a three-day hike from Pengui to Mambasa by way of the winding jungle paths. Still, this proved fortunate in a way, for it first acquainted Putnam with the spot on the Epulu River at which he later established the camp we now had reached.

In due course the offending tooth was cared for, but with that accomplished, Patrick Putnam gave up his job at Pengui and arranged with the Belgian Government for the acquisition of fifty-six hectares of land—a little less than one hundred and forty acres—beside the Epulu River. It was on this land, near where the road we had taken from Mambasa was later to be built, that Camp Putnam was established.

Primarily interested in the Pygmies, the new landholder established a dispensary, and ultimately came to be so well acquainted with the tropical diseases prevalent in the vicinity that doctors, missionaries, and others often came to consult him and to learn his methods. But his interests also induced him to study, collect, and tame many of the local animals as well, the rarest and most unusual being that remote and shorter-legged, shorter-necked cousin of the giraffe, the forest-dwelling okapi. And, as if this were not enough, he established his inn for the few travelers who might happen that way, though he apparently reserved the right to refuse to accept any prospective guests he did not like.

In a land where inns of any kind were few and far between, Camp Putnam soon became famous. Its equipment was modest, but its service was good, and most important, it was a place from which the Pygmies could readily be visited. More and more travelers consequently found their way to this remote corner of the Belgian Congo. Scientists sometimes used Camp Putnam as a base from which to study the natural history of the region, and Patrick Putnam, who was an eccentric, much given to such odd ideas as carrying live snakes in his pockets, but whose major interest was the welfare of the Pygmies, came more and more to be accepted by these little people of the forest as their friend.

Anne Putnam, who, from the time of her arrival in Africa, had intended to devote herself to her painting, succeeded in completing a series of twenty pictures she had been commissioned to do, but then found herself more and more occupied with other tasks —mending mosquito nets, feeding baby animals, and even caring for Pygmy children. As the years passed and her husband's health declined she also found it necessary to care for him, in addition to taking over the entire job of running the place—a task that became doubly difficult because of dwindling finances and the increasing cost of living which, by then, was becoming apparent even in the Congo.

Patrick Putnam had died in December 1953, only a few months before we arrived, and the very next day, despite all he and his wife had done to aid the Pygmies, the provincial government delivered a thirty-day eviction notice. Almost any other person, alone in such an area and confronted by so many misfortunes and difficulties, would have given up, but Anne Putnam was stubbornly unwilling to see her husband's constructive accomplishments disappear. She decided to fight the eviction notice, and with the help of the Belgian Embassy in the United States and of the American Consulate in Léopoldville on the lower Congo some 1200 miles away, she finally succeeded in having the order rescinded. Though difficulties still existed and the future was far from clear, Patrick Putnam's widow, surrounded by some two hundred Pygmies and other local natives who looked to her for guidance, was continuing the work her husband had begun almost thirty years ago.

To our surprise, the busy manager of Camp Putnam found time for us in the midst of her many activities. We talked with her, for example, when we went with her to the nearby Negro village which is occupied, for the most part, by those who are employed at Camp Putnam. Explaining to us as she went about her rounds, she stopped in to see some of the older Africans, to visit with a woman who was sick with pneumonia, to listen for requests for more food, and to check up on a problem baby. She spoke to these people in Swahili—a long-established hybrid language from Africa's east coast that has come to be a kind of lingua franca throughout great sections of this part of the continent. She spoke it in her usual boisterous tone, explaining to us that her husband had always insisted that she was the only person in the world who spoke Swahili with a New York City accent.

Though this village lies close beside the road at no great distance from Camp Putnam, none of the Pygmy villages are comparably placed. Scattered here and there through the forest, these clusters of small, round, leaf-covered huts are never much more than temporary camps, though there is a forest clearing near Camp Putnam where the little people stay when they "come to town."

There is a strange and somewhat intricate relationship between the Pygmies and the larger Negroes of the vicinity—a relationship which seems to place the Pygmies under the control of their larger neighbors. A Negro master may have almost any number of Pygmies, though they are neither slaves nor subjects in the ordinary meaning of those words. It is true that the "big chief" may be supplied fresh meat, for example, by the particular Pygmies who are attached to him, but he, in turn, is expected to provide them with salt and other small necessities. Even to

visit a Pygmy village, in fact, it is necessary—or at least advisable
—to obtain the permission of the "big chief." On the other hand,
no one—not even these Negro masters—can make the Pygmies
do what they do not want to do. If conditions do not appeal to
them, they merely slip away into the forest, attaching themselves,
after a time, to some new and more acceptable master, and no
one can do a thing about it. This, in fact, goes far to explain
the relationship which exists between Anne Putnam and her particular Pygmies. In effect, some two-hundred-odd of the little people of this area have accepted her as their "master" or "big chief,"
and this is true even though, in theory at least, they may also
have Negro masters, too.

Mealtime was never dull at Camp Putnam. No one ever knew
how many travelers might arrive at the last moment, and food
shortages were not infrequent. Still, they never proved serious,
for everyone was always willing to have his portions reduced, and
more interesting than the unexpected numbers of visitors who
sometimes arrived were the differing types among them. Congo
government officials, always very formal and proper, frequently
appeared. On one occasion two road workers arrived on a caterpillar road scraper. At another time two young Belgian couples
put in their appearance on motorcycles. They had come all the
way from Belgium, too, and all of them were dressed in the shortest of shorts and wore wide, sturdy kidney belts. Then there frequently were lunch-time tourists who, having stopped to eat,
would take a quick snapshot or two of themselves with such
touristwise Pygmies as happened to be about, so as to add photographic proof to the letters they wrote home of how they had
"been among the Pygmies." And to offset these frequently momentary and always changing visitors was a bearded, vegetarian
Englishman who had dropped in for lunch one day and had
stayed three months.

For our second Sunday at the camp, the Negroes and the
Pygmies planned an afternoon festival—a celebration that led
them to "borrow," though quite without permission and usually

when Anne Putnam's back was turned, a number of native drums and masks that were in the Putnam collection. In fact, their borrowing did not end there, for they took whatever struck them as useful, even including some of the dining-room chairs. Furthermore, with such a celebration in the offing, the usual methods of the camp deteriorated noticeably, and in the end, Anne Putnam found it simpler to dismiss her employees until the preparations had been completed and the celebration held. She even let the "restaurant boys" go and, with Tay's help, passed the food herself, American-fashion.

Two young Belgians who were present were greatly perturbed by this development and seemed to be even more shocked to learn that the borrowers, without having been corrected in any way, had carried off so many of the dining-room chairs that we had to find a stool or two to make up the difference when we all appeared at table. In fact, Anne Putnam's attitude toward her Negroes and her Pygmies differed so greatly from that of most of the white people of the Congo that some among them were convinced that she had "gone native."

Because of these differences of opinion, the atmosphere at lunch was beginning to grow somewhat stiff and a little cool when a band of Pygmies trooped into the garden that lay beside the porchlike dining room. They formed a delegation that had come to invite us to the festival, and they conveyed their invitation by prancing around and chanting in high-pitched voices to the accompaniment of a crude kind of wooden flute. To ears not yet attuned to Pygmy music it was noise rather than melody, though Tay and I, after ten days exposure to such sounds, were able to detect certain melodic passages and even occasional interesting ventures into counterpoint.

We all accepted the invitation, of course, and, making our way to the native village, we spent the afternoon watching the festivities. Anne Putnam supplied the refreshments, which consisted only of beer and cigarettes. The Negroes, fancifully dressed for the occasion and wearing the grotesque masks they had so informally borrowed from the Putnam collection, supplied the dancing. And the Pygmies, having supplied the music and their full share of the laughter, ultimately concluded the affair by gaily swinging from a vine that was looped between two trees.

It was clear from the first that such motion pictures and sound recordings as we could make of Pygmy activities at Camp Putnam would leave much to be desired. The little people are essentially forest dwellers and only by spending some time with them in the forest itself would it be possible to photograph them in their natural surroundings or engaged in their normal activities. And luckily for us, Anne Putnam was willing not only to make the necessary arrangements but also to accompany us into the forest.

We were awakened early on the day we were to leave for the forest camp the Pygmies had selected. Our party consisted of Anne Putnam, Tay and me, and about twenty Pygmy men who were accompanied by an appropriate following of wives and children. Having crossed the road, we turned into a narrow path and were almost instantly swallowed up in the forest.

Giant trees stood all about us, their great trunks tall and straight in the shadowy greenness. High overhead lay a heavy and almost unbroken canopy of leaves through which, here and there, it was sometimes possible to catch a glimpse of the blue sky. All about us, too, almost like a lesser forest within the greater one, were the bushes, vines, and smaller trees, the ferns, mosses, and other jungle growth that covered the soft, moist, springy earth as completely as the vast treetops obscured the sky.

We had progressed no more than a stone's throw from the road before we found ourselves in Africa as Nature made it—an area that was unchanged, so far as our immediate surroundings were concerned, from what it was before the white man came. Henry M. Stanley, who discovered this enormous forest in 1887, spent 160 days in passing through it, "without ever having seen a bit of greensward of the size of a cottage chamber floor." Enormous changes had taken place in Africa since then. Even here, where our forest surroundings were almost identical with those Stanley had known, fundamental changes had taken place. In this very forest, starvation, fever, and the hostility of unknown tribes had confronted Stanley's expedition for months, killing almost half of those who began the journey with him, while we, only sixty-seven years later, were being convoyed by our happy band of Pygmies on a little journey that resembled Stanley's terrible march much less than it did a picnic.

In looking over the journals of some of the early explorers, we had read many terrible things about this forest, but what now impressed us most was that our surroundings were so peaceful, quiet, and beautiful. We were conscious of no dangers, and the only sounds we heard were those of birds and the laughing voices of the Pygmies.

Pygmies, we now learned, have a way of talking to themselves, or perhaps it is to the trees or the spirits that they believe surround them. And they don't just mumble. They give what almost appear to be impassioned speeches complete with gestures, and we heard many of them on our gay, hour-long walk with them through the forest. We were constantly interested in the activities of our forest friends, and Tay, who had been concerned about the possibility of meeting elephants, leopards, or other possibly dangerous jungle dwellers on the way, soon forgot to worry. There we were, in the midst of a vast, wild animal area, and yet we had no guns. The only weapons anywhere about were the bows and arrows of the Pygmies, but no one was concerned—least of all our friendly guides.

The camp site the Pygmies had chosen was a small forest clearing, and we had no sooner reached it than the work of the women began. While the men made pipes out of long banana stems and sat down to smoke, the women started to build the "houses" the new camp would require. They went into the forest and came back with supple saplings from which they made rounded frameworks that were covered with large mongongo leaves. Within an hour the clearing was dotted with a dozen comfortable little ditch-surrounded, rainproof huts. Fires had been kindled from embers that had been brought along, and the newly created "village" was complete even to a few mongrel dogs and an indefinite number of hens and baby chicks, for these semi-nomadic little people of the Ituri Forest carry all their belongings with them when they change camp, and the chickens had been transported in wicker baskets. Oddly enough, however, the Pygmies never eat chickens or even their eggs. They merely look after them for their Negro masters, though how any kind of an accounting is made we do not know.

Having erected huts for themselves, the Pygmies next built two rectangular and much larger huts for Anne Putnam and for us. They were big enough to stand up in, and ours was long enough for two cots and a shelf of sticks. We hung most of our belongings on projecting twigs, shooed an occasional chicken out, and promptly made ourselves very comfortably at home. We washed in a bucket of water from a nearby brook. We even had a shower stall made of mongongo leaves on a frame of saplings. Some earlier visitor had given Anne Putnam a canvas bucket with a shower head on the bottom, and when this was filled with warm water and hung from a tree in our leafy enclosure, it worked almost as effectively as more formal showers did at home.

Though only about a dozen huts had been built in our clearing, we soon learned that another dozen or fifteen were scattered in the woods nearby. Pygmy families that had not been a part of the original "expedition" from Camp Putnam were joining our party a few at a time, for life has definite advantages when white people are about. Anne Putnam, for instance, had brought plenty of palm oil and manioc with her, while Tay and I had laid in a special supply of sugar, salt, and cigarettes which we doled out carefully—the salt to the women for their own distribution; the sugar to the children, a teaspoonful at a time; and the cigarettes, one at a time, to the men and boys.

Among these Bambuti Pygmies the children under five wear nothing at all, and the others wear next to nothing, but they are very modest, nevertheless. Dressed though they are only in limited loincloths, they still seem to have much the same attitude toward nakedness that more completely clad people have. For example, Anne Putnam told of a fight that took place between two Pygmy boys, with all the Bambuti watching and cheering them on. But in the heat of battle, one boy lost his loincloth, whereupon his mother immediately dashed in and carried him off until his loss could be made good and he could once more appear, modestly and properly clad.

The loincloths are made of beaten bark which, properly treated, becomes almost as soft and pliable as woven cloth. Decorated with simple patterns formed with vegetable dyes, these constitute the only "art" the Pygmies have developed, unless one also includes the lines and patterns they commonly draw on their faces. Nor are their handicrafts very well developed. They make strong little bows, the strings of which are strips of bark. Their arrows may be merely sharpened wooden shafts that are dipped in poison, or they may be tipped with metal, but in either case a leaf, and not a feather, is used to guide the shaft.

Their food, so far as we tried it, was excellent—mushrooms cooked in palm oil—antelope meat skewered on sticks and broiled in the fire—manioc pounded into flour, made into balls, and cooked in palm oil—and honey tea. And because their huts are never more than temporary, and their "villages" are forever being moved to new locations in the forest, Pygmy surroundings, as well as the Pygmies themselves, are much cleaner than they have sometimes been credited with being.

The pleasantest part of each day in that forest camp came after supper, when the smoke of the campfires curled upward into the darkness overhead, and the tiny people lay about in happy contentment. Pygmy families are closely knit groups. The fathers as well as the mothers are thoughtful in caring for the children, and at every opportunity any Pygmy group is willing to sing and dance. On our first evening in camp everything was quiet until one of the men produced a small, hollowed-out piece of wood and began to tap on it with a pair of "drumsticks." The rhythm was contagious, and little by little all the others began to sing and clap. No one seemed to take the lead, but a few of the men soon began to dance about the fire, bending toward it, leaping away, and weaving a kind of formless dance pattern about it, and shortly every Pygmy in camp was dancing, singing, or otherwise taking part. Utterly lacking in any formal pattern, the dance nevertheless maintained a character that rarely varied and never really changed. It went on and on, with no end in sight, and finally we went to bed, though there was scant hope of sleep until hours later when the camp finally quieted down.

Photography in the forest was never easy, for little sunlight penetrated to the jungle floor. Even in the clearing in which we were camped more light was necessary, and in order to obtain it the Pygmies obligingly hacked down a few additional trees, but when, on our second day, we went on a hunt with them, we not only failed to come upon any game but also failed to find the light our cameras needed. Thus we returned to camp empty-handed, there to chase elusive sunbeams for photographic purposes or merely to watch the Pygmies.

On one occasion, four of the bravest and most successful hunters—Faizi, Mukabasi, Saale, and Nikiabo—left the camp in search of game, and Tay and I decided to go along. The lithe hunters slipped through the forest without a sound, but Tay and I were quite unable to do as well. The noise we made would no doubt have alerted any antelope long before we could have seen it through the heavy undergrowth, but as it happened this made no difference, for our little hunting companions promptly spotted a bee tree and immediately dropped their bows and arrows and hunting nets in order to build a fire.

As soon as a few sticks were burning they wrapped them in a bundle of waxen mongongo leaves, which they tied with a slender vine. Putting this in a basket, Faizi swung it over his shoulder, and with Nikiabo following after him, he scrambled up the great bee tree, clinging to the heavy vines that had grown about the trunk.

Hand over hand the two hunters climbed, their toes digging into the rough bark while they pulled themselves upward by means of the twisting vines. Bees were buzzing all about them, and ants were there as well, but there was honey to be had, and neither climber paused except to brush away some more than usually troublesome insect now and then.

Finally they reached the opening where the bees had entered the hollow in the tree, and as we moved about on the ground below in order to see what the two in the tree were doing, we saw them hold the leaf-surrounded embers close to the opening in the tree while they puffed and blew through the parcel of smoldering sticks. Angry bees swarmed around them, but they kept on blowing smoke into the beehive, dulling the sensibilities of the bees until, at last, they felt free to cut a larger opening. Then, reaching in, they began to stuff themselves with that welcome forest delicacy.

Now and again, with hands and arms that were covered with the sticky stuff, they dropped down shapeless blocks of dripping honeycomb that were gobbled up by the Pygmies on the ground as soon as they could be extricated from the moss and leaves among which they fell. Wax, larvae, honey, and all were eagerly devoured by mouthfuls, and finally down came Faizi and Nikiabo, stuffed with honey, obviously, to their full capacity. Honey was smeared over their faces, their arms, and in their hair. They had even brought down with them a modest supply of dripping honeycomb in the basket they carried, so that even though we no longer had time to reach the hunting grounds, they would not have to return to their wives and children empty-handed.

By the time we had again reached camp, our four very sticky hunters had licked themselves reasonably clean. They even prepared to answer the angry questioning of the womenfolk. It seemed to us that they looked a little sheepish when their ex-

pected scolding began, but they had a ready reply. With hardly
a word they tossed the sticky basket of honey onto the ground,
and instantly everyone made a dive for it—women, children, old
men, and dogs. In a moment it was gone, and so were the hunters
—more of them this time, gone for more honey.

Now and again adult Pygmies as well as children swung on
great swings made of vines. On one occasion they happily
wrecked several huts while engaged in a wonderful tug of war
with a vine for a rope—a tug of war in which I myself finally
took part to the great delight of these happy children of the
forest.

They sang and danced on other evenings, and late one night,
long after the camp had gone to sleep, we were awakened by a
Pygmy voice that called out loudly, as if making a speech in the
darkness. What the words meant we could not tell, but the next
morning, when Anne Putnam asked what had occurred, she
ultimately learned that one of their ancestors, taking the voice
of an owl, had spoken from the forest. The voice we had heard
had been that of the Pygmy who had answered, and after a time
we were given an approximate translation of what his reply had
been.

"We Bambuti," he had shouted to the forest-dwelling spirit
of his ancestor, "have come in peace to hunt and gather honey.
There are white-man guests among us. We have done no wrong.
Please go away and leave us alone."

It was on a Saturday that we returned to Camp Putnam, leaving
Faizi, Nikiabo, and the rest in the camp in which we had been
their companions. When we had first seen them, they had been
strange little creatures with whom it was hard to imagine that
we had anything in common. But now, as we said good-by, we
knew that they were friends.

By way of a grand climax to our visit among the Pygmies, we
took our good friend Faizi for an airplane ride. We invited others,
too, but Faizi was the only one who seemed willing to accept.

This, incidentally, went hand in hand with his reputation as the very bravest of all Bambuti and the only one in all that section of the forest with an elephant to his credit—an elephant he killed by slipping silently through the forest until he was able from almost beneath the animal to drive a spear into its vitals!

The government agent who was in charge of the nearby elephant-training center—a Greek named Marinos—drove us to the Mambasa airstrip—Anne Putnam and Faizi, as well as Tay and me. Charlie had been sitting in the sun and rain for nearly two weeks, but the native soldier who had guarded the plane had done his work well. No elephants had rubbed against it, and no hyenas had tried their teeth on its tires. I was concerned lest dampness might have fouled the spark plugs or the distributor, but the engine started instantly and checked out perfectly.

We found a little over ten gallons of gas in the tanks, and, having drained it out, we poured it back again, filtering it carefully through a chamois. Then Tay and I took off for Irumu, half an hour away, and filled our tanks, coming back at once.

The flying we planned to do started that afternoon, and never before had I seen so much excitement over an airplane. It must have been similar to the early barnstorming days at home. Not only the Africans but the Belgians, too, were excited, and though many of the Belgians seemed eager to go up—even some who had never been in a plane before—others were more hesitant and did not step forward until later in the afternoon when repeated hops had convinced them that Charlie was reasonably safe.

Because the sun was good for filming, we asked Faizi to climb in first, and he did so without hesitation. At our suggestion, Anne Putnam had given him a somewhat detailed briefing, explaining as forcefully as possible that the control wheel that stood only a few inches in front of him was linked to mine, and that it should be considered as though it were "a charging bull elephant—something to be left utterly alone." On the other hand, the handle to which he was told he might cling was "a tree—a place of safety." And these explanations, having been cast in terms that Faizi really understood, clearly impressed him.

We had wondered if the little fellow might change his mind at the last minute, but he didn't, so I strapped him into Tay's seat, while she climbed in behind with our cameras, keeping the metal fire extinguisher within easy reach lest Faizi, despite his bravery, should succumb to panic amid such strange surroundings.

The door slammed shut. The engine roared, and Faizi grasped the handle that Anne had called "the tree." He looked a little grim, I thought, but I could not watch him as we taxied to the strip and took off. In fact, the first real sign of emotion I detected came when we passed over the Epulu River at the height of a thousand feet and I pointed it out to him.

"*Maee, maee,*" he said. "Water, water." And then, as we returned and banked around the airstrip before landing, he saw some of his Pygmy friends in the crowd below.

"Bambuti," he said excitedly.

When we had landed and rolled to a stop, it seemed to me that Faizi showed some signs of relief, though he did not release his hold on "the tree" to which he had clung throughout the flight. Tay and I jumped out first, and it was only then that we unstrapped Faizi's seat belt and let him out to join his Pygmy friends who, Anne Putnam told us, had so excitedly followed our flight.

"There's a Bambuti up there," they had said almost in unbelief as they had pointed upward. "One of us."

"*Wapi!*" whooped Faizi when he had rejoined his fellows, and that, as nearly as we were able to learn, was more or less the Bambuti equivalent of "Wow!"

His spirit, he told Anne Putnam, had been "tied up" during the flight, as we knew his words had been. But now that he was once more among his fellows, he was wonderfully free with his words again. He jabbered endlessly to those about him, even apparently describing the plane going into a bank—an experience he had evidently not liked. Then, suddenly, he stooped and plucked a blade of grass, holding it before his fellows and pointing alternately, first to the blade of grass and then to them as he graphically explained how small they had looked from so high in the sky above them.

We offered to take him up again but he declined. Still, a second flight would have added little to his first experience in the air and nothing, perhaps, to his reputation. Already his bravery was legendary, for, singlehanded, had he not killed an elephant? And now his unequaled reputation had grown to new and greater proportions, for he was also the Bambuti hunter who had flown!

In Pygmyland, I am sure, that is reputation enough for any man.

VII. *The Mountains of the Moon*

ON THE DAY FOLLOWING OUR return to Mambasa from Camp Putnam, we took off for Irumu again, on our way, this time, to Bukavu—or Costermansville—on Lake Kivu some 300 miles to the south. Pausing at Irumu only for fuel and a hurried lunch, we flew south and west with the snow-covered but cloud-hidden peaks of the Ruwenzori range hardly thirty miles away on our left, but as we approached the outpost of Beni, no more than seventy miles on our way, we saw ahead of us a solid wall of afternoon thunderstorms that stretched as far as we could see to the east and west.

Morning is the time to fly in the Belgian Congo, for convection later builds up the great anvil-topped thunderheads that so often march like cruel giants through the afternoon skies above the almost endless forests. So around we wheeled, beating a retreat to Irumu for the night, and taking off again at a much earlier hour the following day. It was in this way, as we headed south again, that we caught our first glimpses of the magnificent Ruwenzori peaks only a few minutes before we crossed the equator near Kimbulu a few miles northwest of Lake Edward.

Out over the lake we flew, with the land to the west sloping steeply up to elevations that surpass 10,000 feet, and then southward beyond the lake and along the Rutshuru River where

Charlie's roar stampeded herds of buffalo but had no effect on lazy hippos that clogged the river like logs. Groups of elephants here and there flapped their ears in annoyance, and then resumed their peaceful feeding as we passed. On we flew, over the town of Rutshuru with its emergency airstrip, which Tay was so glad to see. On over the gorilla country between the enormous volcanic peaks of Nyiragongo and Karisimbi. Then we dodged a thunderhead and slid downward to lower levels above the eastern shores of Lake Kivu, which, lying at an elevation of almost 5000 feet, is the highest lake in all of Central Africa. But now the weather ahead turned bad, and when we called the Bukavu tower and were given a report of limited visibility there, we reversed our course, and soon landed on the grass strip at Goma on Lake Kivu's northern shore.

There Tay and I waited for nearly an hour, sitting on Charlie's wheels in the shade of the wings, and we were just about to start the walk of several miles to town when, fortunately, a Belgian official drove up and offered us a lift. We accepted and soon were having lunch at the Goma Inn. Then, a bit later, when we had received a more favorable report of the weather in Bukavu, the official drove us back to the strip again and waved us off.

Our purpose in going to Bukavu was to pick up our mail and to send off by air express the film we had exposed since leaving Stanleyville. We also expected to find a case of fresh film from N.B.C., but upon landing, we learned that we would have to wait two days for our new film, which was due to arrive on the next Sabena air liner from Léopoldville.

Unexpected though this layover was, it gave us an opportunity to call on the governor's secretary, and to inquire whether or not we could obtain permission to land at Beni, which lies in the Parc National Albert only about thirty miles from our next goal—Mutwanga in the foothills of the Ruwenzori range. To our delight, we were told that we might do so, but when I made out our flight plan the next morning—which was Sunday—the control officer said that the governor's secretary had been in error—that planes were not permitted to land anywhere in the park. So, rather sadly, we decided to fly to the much less conveniently located town of Rutshuru, where, we were assured, we could readily hire a car for the two-day drive to the foot of the Ruwenzori.

We landed at Rutshuru all right, but quickly discovered that we had reached a dead end. The local administrator wanted to help, but there just was no car or driver available for the two-day drive to Mutwanga.

While the friendly official made more inquiries, we went to the town's tiny inn, wondering what to do next. There we met a couple of Belgian tourists, who told us of an airstrip just across the Uganda border in the newly organized Queen Elizabeth Park, and less than a day by car from our destination. There was no question about the existence of the airstrip, but we were given very little additional information. We understood that lodgings were available in the park, but we did not know whether or not we could get a car there to take us to Mutwanga and back. We did not even know what customs and immigration complications might arise in crossing and recrossing the international border between the Belgian Congo and Uganda. In fact, we knew next to nothing. Even if we were permitted to land in the park, everything beyond that was doubtful.

"How about it, Tay?" I asked. "Should we try it?"

The idea appealed to her, so off we went to talk to the Rutshuru administrator about it. And he not only listened, but also approved our spur-of-the-moment plan, so Charlie promptly whisked us on our way.

The flight was a short one, and we soon found the "airport," though it was only a grass strip in the middle of nowhere. In fact, before landing on it, we had to buzz off a herd of buffalo that was grazing at one end.

Africans came running from a small village nearby after we landed, but there were no signs of any park wardens or cars and—naturally—no telephone. And in an African game sanctuary, one would rather not stand by the road hitching a ride. There are too few cars and too many wild animals.

At this point, however, we could not admit defeat by returning to Rutshuru. Here was a situation, it seemed to us, that required some thought and ingenuity. We knew that Mweya Lodge, only fifteen miles away, had been built in honor of Queen Elizabeth who had come to open the park just a few months before. So we decided to "bomb" the lodge with a note!

"We are two Americans," Tay wrote, "coming from the Congo, and will land at Kasengi, where we'd like to leave our plane for a week while visiting your lodge and Mutwanga. Could you send an auto for us? If so, please wave your arms as a signal. Thank you."

We stuffed the scrap of paper into a cardboard carton, along with a few stones for ballast, and hopped back into the air, feeling like a couple of school kids again, back in the days when we left notes in floating bottles at the seashore.

Flying slowly over the lodge at about 100 feet, Tay released the "missile," which could so easily have disappeared into the dense bushes, or the canal just beyond. But we were lucky (I called it luck, Tay claimed expert marksmanship), for it landed on the center grass circle, right at the foot of the flagpole!

An African promptly retrieved it, and by the time we had completed our fourth circle, a European, wearing a bathrobe, appeared and waved a towel. Obviously, we had interrupted his afternoon siesta.

So back to the Kasengi strip we flew, and an hour later a pleasant young Britisher arrived in a Land Rover. He was our towel waver, and we learned that he was the head game warden, too. He was also in charge of the airfield and was highly amused by our irregular system of communication with the lodge, where most of the guests are British vacationists from east Africa who write for reservations a year or so in advance. But, as game warden, he admonished us for having flown so low during our "bombing run."

"Bad for the animals, you know," he said. "Stampedes them, which is jolly bad for us if we happen to be in their way."

Arriving at Mweya Lodge I sent a telegram to the Belgian administrator at Rutshuru, letting him know that we were down safely, and then we turned our attention to our new surroundings.

The lodge proved to be a group of cabinlike buildings with steep, gabled roofs made of many layers of papyrus stems. Each bungalow had one or two bedrooms, as well as a real bathroom, a living room, and a porch, and whichever way one looked the view was magnificent. From our bungalow the first evening we could see any number of hippos on the shore of the Kazinga Channel, which connects Lake George and Lake Edward, and seven elephants were in a grassy meadow hardly half a mile away. Furthermore, far to the west lay the Ruwenzori range, though its great snow-capped peaks were hidden in clouds.

We spent two days at the park, and one morning took a drive with a German woman in her tiny Volkswagen. Just around the first corner of the rough, dirt road we came face to face with a large herd of buffalo. It was then that we realized we should have hitched a ride with the driver of a massive truck instead! In an instant all forty or fifty of the huge animals galloped toward us, but fortunately the car didn't stall and we scurried away just in time. We saw many more buffalo, and an infinite number of waterbuck, impala, hartebeest, and hippos. We must also have seen a hundred elephants—ponderous but dignified animals that paid little attention to our tiny conveyance. Once, however, we passed between an old bull and his cow and babies, with near-dire consequences. Seeing us between himself and his family, he trumpeted, flapped his ears, and charged. Again we sped away in the nick of time, father elephant thundering down the road behind our puny Volkswagen. We were fast learning that driving through game parks is not always a tame occupation.

On the morning of our third day at the lodge we left for Mutwanga. It had been our idea to hire a car for the drive, but our new German friend was bound for the same destination, so we made the trip in the Volkswagen with her. The Belgian Congo border was only a few miles away, but when we reached it and told the Belgian customs inspector that we had entered Uganda merely to leave our plane there until we could return from Mutwanga to pick it up, he was so confused as to his proper course of action that he let us by without any formalities at all.

From the border a good dirt road led across the Semliki Plains, which were hot, flat, and dotted with distant animals. We reached the Mutwanga Inn without any difficulties, but when we gave our names to the innkeeper, he responded as though we were a couple of ghosts.

"But, but . . . didn't you crash in the forest?" he asked.

Assuring the bewildered innkeeper that we had had no such experience, I hurried off to the local administrator's office and through him scotched the report of our having crashed just before it was picked up by the international press.

We still don't know all the facts surrounding that false report, but apparently it stemmed from a garbled message sent by the administrator in Rutshuru to his superior in Bukavu. In any case, the upshot was a full-scale search for us and our supposedly downed plane. Administrators, missionaries, and Africans spent two days combing the lower reaches of the Ruwenzori, while airplanes were even sent out by Sabena Airlines and the Belgian military to search for us from the air.

Once this most unfortunate incident had been settled, we turned our attention to our surroundings. High in the foothills, at an elevation of about 4000 feet, the inn is beautifully located. Surrounded by bougainvillea, wild poinsettia, and many flowering trees, it looks out across the plains below and up the steep Ruwenzori slopes in the opposite direction. Our room faced the mountainside, and since we were lucky enough to have arrived during a reasonably dry period, we had the good fortune of seeing the snow-capped peaks each morning and each evening when they were clear of clouds.

Not far from our window was a noisy mountain stream, beyond which the slope was heavily covered with tropical vegetation— banana trees, coffee plants, manioc, and elephant grass. Much farther on, and immensely higher, were the six great snow-covered peaks of the Ruwenzori, each approaching or surpassing 16,000 feet.

When we arrived, we were the only visitors at the inn, and for five days about all we did was eat and catch up with our correspondence. The food was equal to any we had ever had— on a par, we felt, with Maxim's in Paris. But that was true to a remarkable extent everywhere in the Belgian Congo. The Belgians like good food and we often found ourselves wonderfully well fed even in remote, equatorial outposts.

Aside from those who ran the inn, our companions, at first, were three dogs, three cats, a couple of ducks, a parrot, and any number of lovebirds. Now and again, however, other guests arrived until there were several Belgian families, two Englishmen, and a loudly talkative doctor and his wife from California.

From the time we arrived I was fascinated—and more than a little tantalized—by the occasional glimpses we got of the great Ruwenzori peaks. I was eager to climb higher up those impressive equatorial slopes, and when a young Belgian arrived on leave from his work as a government veterinarian, he and I promptly organized a two-man expedition, and enlisted the innkeeper's aid in rounding up porters, food, and sleeping bags.

Tay preferred a few more days of rest, and I kissed her good-by on the morning of the sixth day after our arrival, when, with my Belgian companion, our porters, our modest equipment, and supplies for five days, we set out to climb the slippery, muddy trail.

It was in 1906 that the Duke of Abruzzi first climbed the glittering peaks that stood so high above us, and in the years since then several bungalows have been built on the trail that leads upward from the Mutwanga Inn. We had no intention of attempting to climb to the very summit, but we hoped at least to reach the snow line or the terminal moraine of one of the glaciers on Mount Margherita.

For an hour we climbed the slippery trail as it took us upward through the tall, thick elephant grass. Then, having reached the ranger station at the entrance to the Ruwenzori forest, we signed the log, paid an entrance fee of four hundred francs each, picked up an African guide, and went on upward through a strange forest of banana plants, trees with pinkish bark, and enormous tree ferns.

Having left the inn about nine o'clock, we found the going reasonably easy until twelve-thirty when we reached Kalonge. This bungalow, or rest house, overlooked a deep gorge and a steep forested slope, and it reminded me of some of the dak bungalows my father and I had seen several years before on the trail to Lhasa, Tibet, when we were making the initial climb through the forests of Sikkim. It must rain about as much on the Ruwenzori slopes as in Sikkim, but my Belgian companion and I at least did not have to contend with the leeches that so frequently dropped off the Sikkim trees and fastened themselves to the skin of anyone passing beneath. Still, gnats constantly swarmed about our heads and it was all too easy to breathe them in, while all about us other unseen insects sang shrilly in the humid, sticky heat.

We had lunch at the Kalonge bungalow, though our cook, who seemed at first to be competent, soon turned out otherwise. Still, we managed well enough, though after lunch the skies opened and stopped our mountain climbing for the day.

Finding ourselves in a comfortable bungalow, which was equipped with glass windows and had a central room with a fireplace, we settled down to read, and I dug out of my rucksack a treatise that I had brought along with just such a moment in mind. It was a paper Tay had written during her senior year at Smith College when she and one other girl had taken a course in African geography. The paper, interestingly enough, was on the Ruwenzori range—the "Mountains of the Moon"—which my Belgian friend and I were climbing now. I do not know just how proud Tay would be today of its style or content, but as I read it there in the Kalonge bungalow, while the rain drummed endlessly on the roof, it certainly gave me a wonderful briefing for the climb ahead.

"Africa," she had written, with no thought, perhaps, of ever penetrating so far into its interior, "is still a dark, unearthly continent to most people. Its name connotes a land of mystery, of incredibly strange landscapes, animal life, and civilization. Perhaps its greatest mystery of all is that surrounding the Mountains of the Moon. Their very name, their legendary history, their rugged grandeur, and immense altitude, and, above all, their amazing illusiveness present a fascinating subject for exploration.

"The importance of the search for these mountains," she continued, "is accentuated by their strategic location at the head of the Nile watershed, and for centuries historians and geographers have inquired about the source of this river. Homer traced the Nile south of Libya to a land of Pygmies. Aristotle stated that the source of the Nile lay in a silvery mountain south of Ethiopia and in the center of Africa, but it was Ptolemy (A.D. 90–168) who first referred to this source as the Mountains of the Moon."

I learned from my wife's college paper that it was not until late in the nineteenth century that this great mountain range was placed accurately on the map. Up until that time there were only vague notions as to its true location, and along with these were many African superstitions that had to do with mountains that disappeared among the clouds, or were covered with salt, or that shone with a dazzling whiteness.

It was Sir Henry M. Stanley who, on his expedition of 1887–89, first made an accurate report of the existence and location of this great range, and it was he who appropriately named them the Ruwenzori, an African name meaning "The Rainmaker" or "Cloud King." It is after Stanley, too, that the greatest mountain of the range was later named, though, as Tay's account made clear to me, it was not until 1906 that the six great peaks were actually climbed—a task that was accomplished under the leadership of that energetic mountaineer, the Duke of Abruzzi, who made his ascents not from the side on which we were now, but from the Uganda plain. It was not until 1932 that Belgian climbers made the first ascent on the Congo side, and that expedition no doubt blazed the trail my companion and I were following.

We spent that night at the Kalonge bungalow, and though the elevation was only 6500 feet and we were hardly thirty miles north of the equator, we found it most uncomfortably cold. Fully dressed except for my shoes, I tried sleeping under two heavy blankets, with my sleeping bag between me and the bed's wicker surface, but after an hour the cold that crept in from below proved too much, so I turned things upside down and crawled into the sleeping bag.

We were up at six o'clock, and after a breakfast of oatmeal, bananas, toast, and instant coffee, we started out on stage number two. This took us down a steep slope to a running stream which we hopped across from rock to rock, and then up into a forest of bamboo, where the densely massed stems stood twenty feet or more in height and all of three inches thick.

Higher up, the bamboo gave way to gnarled and moss-hung trees that closely resembled cedars, while the ground was carpeted with thick, springy mats of moss that varied in color from green to yellow and even orange. Its water content was surprisingly high. When I squeezed a small bit of it between my fingers it dripped like a crushed and juicy grape, and when we accidentally stepped into it, we sometimes sank almost to our knees.

Now and then as we continued to climb, fast-flying birds took off ahead of us, their wings drumming loudly like those of the American partridge, and our African guide—who spoke in Swahili to my Belgian companion who spoke in French to me—told us that a noise we occasionally heard was that of a monkey, and the tracks we saw were those of antelope.

Periodically, the crests we followed gave us magnificent views of the Semliki Plains far below, but the peaks ahead remained hidden in the clouds. The climb was getting stiffer, too, and we had to advance cautiously in order not to slide backward on the wet and slippery trail.

The second bungalow, for which we were now heading, lay less than a mile straight in from the first, but at an elevation some 4500 feet higher. My legs did not seem to tire, but something did, so I checked my pulse at one hundred and twenty-seven and knew that the altitude was having its effect.

The last hour on the trail was a nightmare, for the way was extremely steep and slippery. Both of us were tired, but finally, as we paused, panting, on the difficult trail, the mist above us opened and the bungalow appeared. Beyond it, too, we caught a glimpse of snow on the higher slopes, and though the clouds closed in again and it soon began to rain, we struggled on until we reached the rest house.

All afternoon it rained, but we were sheltered now. During two successive mornings we had climbed from an elevation of 4000 feet to this rest house which clung to the mountainside at 11,000, and on the following morning we hoped to reach Kiondo —the third bungalow—at 14,300 feet.

We rested all afternoon, but because of the cold we slept none too well that night. However, after an enormous breakfast of oatmeal, bananas, bread and butter, and coffee, we started on again about eight o'clock the next morning.

Our climb of the day before had been difficult, but the one we now began was even more so. The snow line was still far ahead, and we had to climb very steeply upward for an hour or more. The slope was heavily covered by vegetation, and under foot was a confused tangle of roots. Much of the time we had to scramble from root to root, heaving ourselves from one to the next, sometimes straight up for two or three feet—a task that required enormous exertion at the altitude we had reached. Between the roots was black watery ooze, into which our shoes disappeared each time we slipped, while great, dank pits yawned widely here and there, forcing us to make our way around them with the utmost care.

The forest, by now, had become the most unusual I had ever seen. The gnarled trees with their reddish bark and their "umbrellas" of pine needles were much smaller than the ones we had seen the day before. Generally they were little taller than we were, and long streamers of greenish-gray moss hung from their branches. Sometimes, however, these trees gave way to giant lobelias which were covered with thick crinkly bark and supported great bulbous masses of green leaves.

The previous afternoon, while the rain had pounded on the roof of the rest house, I had come upon a paragraph of my wife's paper on the Ruwenzori that seemed particularly appropriate. Tay had quoted a writer named Synge who had referred to these high Ruwenzori slopes as follows:

"'A gray mist made a fitting background for the most monstrous and unearthly landscape I have ever seen. Vague outlines of peaks and precipices towered all around us. Here were plants which seemed more like ghosts of past ages than ordinary trees and herbs. . . . It all seemed unreal, like some imaginary reconstruction of life in a long-past geological age, or even upon some other planet. . . . This strange mountain carried us into a dreamland which was often a fairyland, occasionally a nightmare.'"

At eleven o'clock we wearily reached a level and mossy area known as "the camp of bottles" in honor of a bottle left there by the first expedition to reach the spot, and of other bottles later visitors have added, and half an hour later we staggered into Kiondo, the hut for which we were searching. This had been erected at 14,300 feet, which is only a little over a hundred feet lower than the tallest summit in Colorado, and is about as high as the Pass of Nathu La on the Himalayan frontier between India and Tibet, which my father and I had crossed a few years earlier. But here, unlike the Nathu La, there was absolutely no wind, and the mist hung about us like a wet veil.

All during the afternoon we spent at Kiondo we were enveloped in clouds and rain, and I read still more of Tay's college report. She had written briefly of the six great Ruwenzori peaks, and just at sunset the clouds parted, giving my Belgian companion and me a glorious view of the craggy slopes above us, their snows a rich pink in the sun's last rays.

I had the sensation of being back in the Himalayas of Tibet and found it almost impossible to believe that the equator was just beyond Ruwenzori's southernmost peak.

That night was by far the most uncomfortable we experienced. Fully dressed, and even with a heavy sweater on, I shivered for hours in my sleeping bag, for the bunks had no mattresses to keep out the cold from beneath. Cold, and unable to sleep, I was up early and when I went outdoors at five-thirty I found a quarter of an inch of ice in a drum of water.

Huddled around the fire, we tried to absorb a little heat before cooking our breakfast, and it was seven o'clock before we could bring ourselves to continue the climb to the foot of the glacier. For more than an hour we struggled upward, finally coming to a tiny wooden shelter, but we kept on a little farther until we were a few hundred feet out on the equatorial snows of one of Mount Margherita's glaciers.

We were above the 15,000 foot level, and from that point the way on up to the top looked tempting, but special permission is required before one may set foot on any of the Ruwenzori peaks, and we had not had time to obtain it. So back we went to the little shelter, where we shared some bread and cheese with our shivering, barefooted porter before returning to the Kiondo bungalow at noon.

By now both of us had headaches that had been brought on by the altitude and the exertion. In fact, my companion felt so faint and sick at the stomach that he was unable to take his share of the hot chicken gumbo we had for lunch. Instead, he crawled into his sleeping bag, hoping to revive himself for the descent, and at two o'clock we started down.

Luckily, the clouds were all below us, and we started down in bright sunlight, with the dazzling peaks and snow fields vivid against the sky behind us. From time to time a feathery wisp of cloud boiled up the ridge to shoot over our heads and vanish into the blue.

Ultimately, of course, we entered the mist, and for three struggling hours we let ourselves down from root to root, slipping and sliding on the muddy trail. We spent that night in the Kalonge bungalow again, and started down once more the next morning. I was eager to reach the inn now, and hurrying ahead of my companion and the porters in a long series of skids and falls, I covered in three hours the same ground it had taken us seven to climb.

Our Belgian friend gave us a ride back to Queen Elizabeth Park the next day, and then, two days later, on our way back to the Belgian Congo in Charlie, we took off from the Kasengi strip at eight in the morning, hoping to fly around the Ruwenzori range before the great peaks clouded over. Even as we left the ground they appeared to be obscured from the Uganda side, but when we had climbed to 12,000 feet we could see that the clouds were fortunately all low-lying and that on the Congo side everything was clear. These mountains have seldom been photographed from the air because they are usually hidden from view, but as we circled the peaks at 17,500 feet, the day was perfect and the air was as smooth as silk. The shadowy lower slopes with their black lakes and steep green valleys slipped beneath us, and just ahead the jagged snow-crowned peaks gleamed in the sun against a deep blue sky. We skimmed over steep walls of glacial ice and broad snow fields that seemed all the more uncommon because we were so close to the equator. Then, dipping our wings in salute, we headed south for Bukavu again.

Bukavu has an almost picture-book setting, on lovely hills overlooking Lake Kivu. Tropical trees and flowers are everywhere, but it is rapidly becoming a city, with many cars, much noise, crowds of people, and a hotel that would do justice to Brussels, London, or New York. We much preferred the quiet African countryside, so we hurried through our chores as quickly as possible and early on the morning of June 29, 1954, we took off for the town of Astrida in the land of the famous Watusi tribe, the tallest of all the people of Africa. We hoped to find our way by following a road which, so our map suggested, led directly some seventy miles to the east. From the air, however, we discovered that there were at least five roads, all with confusing branches and forks that got us completely lost and finally forced us to return to Bukavu. The airport authorities were of no help except to say, "You aren't the first pilots to have that trouble." So, taking off again, we kept to a precise compass heading, as we should have in the first place, and consequently hit Astrida on the button.

The grass airstrip was on a hilltop not far from town and because no plane had reached Astrida for several years, a crowd of about two hundred Africans hurried out to welcome us when we landed. Several Belgians were there among them, including a local official. The policeman he assigned to guard Charlie was a Watusi—the first we saw. Clad in a brief pair of shorts, he looked all legs, though he was a mere six feet four inches tall, which is not at all exceptional for a full-grown member of his tribe.

Astrida, with its main street, its four or five stores, and its filling station, had much in common with a good many small Midwestern towns in the United States. The big difference was that ninety per cent or more of the people were black and were dressed in a weird assortment of Western and African costumes. The section of the town given over to the fifteen or twenty stucco homes of the local Belgians, on the other hand, was strangely reminiscent of our own neighborhood in Princeton, New Jersey. Even the green fields and hills in the distance were strikingly similar, but the banana plants, the bamboo, and the tropical flowers brought us back to Africa with a start.

The small hotel, like most others in the Congo, was comfortable and attractive, but we will always remember it for an entirely different reason—an earthquake, which awakened us late one night with loud rumblings and a severe shaking of the whole room. We were both frightened, partly because we had been unaware that this was an earthquake region. The tremor was brief, however, and little damage resulted, except to our nerves.

Early the next morning we rented an ancient Ford sedan from the local garage, and drove twenty miles through hilly, green countryside to Nyanza, the Watusi capital. We looked like a pair of bums in our blue jeans, and no one knew we were coming, so we had grave doubts as to the kind of reception awaiting us. They were soon dispelled, however, when the local administrator, a Monsieur Ackerman, greeted us cordially and immediately took us to meet the Watusi king—the Mwami—at the local restaurant and bar. The Mwami was all of seven feet tall—quite the tallest person I ever saw—and he was dressed in white ducks, with a pale yellow shirt, white sneakers and a handsome gold wrist watch. He was in company with eight other impressive Watusi and about ten of the local Belgians, all celebrating a Belgian Congo holiday—a scene that impressed us as being rare in segregated Africa.

The administrator, who introduced us to the Mwami, explained that we had come to do a film story on the "aristocrats of Africa," and in a friendly social meeting during which everyone wanted to buy everyone else a drink, we planned our "project." To our astonishment, all the basic details were worked out within an hour of the time we arrived, despite the fact that no one in Nyanza had ever heard of us before.

A large number of the spectacular dancers were assembled for our pictures the next day. They were immensely tall, handsome, and striking in their short and brightly colored skirts of red, white, and blue. They carried spears or bows and arrows, and wore anklets of bells and leopard-teeth necklaces, but most spectacular of all were their remarkably handsome headdresses of flowing white plumes.

The sun was hot, and both the dancing and the picture-taking were strenuous. By one o'clock the dancers and we ourselves were worn out and willing to call it a day, so we all retired to the local pub for a last bit of socializing before Tay and I returned to Astrida again, on our way to Nairobi, in Kenya.

VIII. *Stormy Skies over Kenya*

NAIROBI, THE CAPITAL OF THE British colony of Kenya, was our next important goal after leaving the Belgian Congo. It lies only about 500 miles east of where we had been photographing the Watusi in the Belgian mandate of Ruanda-Urundi, but the flight we had to make was a good deal longer than that. Lake Victoria, the second largest freshwater lake in the world, lay in between, and we had no wish to cross so great an expanse of open water on one engine. So, after flying eastward from Astrida to the western shore of Lake Victoria, we turned north to Entebbe, where we stopped for fuel. From there we flew on past Jinja, where the waters of Lake Victoria pour over Ripon Falls to form the Victoria Nile, and then on to the southeast for another 300 miles or so over the green Uganda countryside and the hillier portion of western Kenya to Nairobi.

By far the most important city of British East Africa, Nairobi is an attractive place as well. Although less than ninety miles south of the equator, its mile-high elevation gives it a delightful climate, and though the city dates only from 1899 when it became a railhead camp and supply depot for the construction of the Kenya and Uganda Railroad, it is now a modern city with wide streets, handsome buildings, attractive homes, and fine hotels.

We landed at the Nairobi West Airfield, which is just a few miles from town, and having tucked Charlie into a hangar, we took a taxi to our hotel.

In half a century, or a little more, Nairobi has come to be

known all around the world as the principal outfitting point for those who wish to visit the game fields of East Africa, and in that time its population has passed the hundred thousand mark, though there are only about ten or twelve thousand whites, while more than 60,000 are Africans. The rest are predominantly immigrants from India, and there are also a few Arabs and Somalis.

Nairobi has long been known as the best place in Africa for launching a safari. No other community on earth has so large and expert a group of "white hunters"—professional hunters, that is, who make a business of managing such safaris when they go off "into the blue." Time was when museum expeditions were more or less constantly at work in this part of Africa, and the number of private safaris that have gone out from the city would be likely to strain the imagination.

Even yet, the "safari organizers" of Nairobi do a good business, but some years ago a strangely difficult problem arose, about which the world has since heard so much. Among the local Kikuyu— a formerly peaceful Bantu-speaking agricultural tribe of this region—a widespread and terribly embittered anti-white secret society developed. Known as Mau Mau, this savage and terroristic organization came into existence for a number of reasons, chief of which was that white landowners had taken possession of so much of the area that once was exclusively populated by the Kikuyu themselves. Deprived of land in a region they once controlled, driven on by extremist leaders who ensured their allegiance by the enforcement of blood-curdling oaths to which the Kikuyu give the most frightful meaning, the Mau Mau began a campaign that was frankly aimed at killing or driving away every white person in that whole region.

Not taken very seriously at first by the white settlers of Kenya Colony, Mau Mau terrorism ultimately swept across the whole countryside. Everywhere and at all times, the white people felt compelled to carry weapons for self-defense. Murders of white settlers were frequent, especially on the more detached farms. But even more frequent were Mau Mau attacks against other

Africans who refused to join in the anti-white campaign. A point that has often been overlooked, or deliberately played down, is that while the Mau Mau murdered some fifty "whites," in a period of just over two years, they murdered several thousand loyal "blacks"—mostly their fellow Kikuyus. Only a little more than a year before Tay and I reached Nairobi, seventy-one Africans were killed and about a hundred wounded in a single Mau Mau raid. As a result, hundreds of arrests were made, and in the first of a series of trials, seventeen terrorists were convicted and sentenced to death for their parts in the attack. Jomo Kenyatta, a Communist-trained tribal leader, and several others were found guilty of organizing the Mau Mau and were sentenced to seven-year terms for instigating and aiding the terrorists.

Though the white settlers of Kenya Colony were not at first greatly impressed by the problem, it became clear before long that matters were out of hand. The problem was debated even in the House of Commons in London, where the British Colonial Secretary referred to it as "perverted nationalism and a sort of nostalgia for barbarism" that had developed into an organized uprising that was "more like war."

Had Tay and I reached Nairobi at any other time, our attention would no doubt have been attracted by other matters—by the many East African tribes, for example, and by the fascinating animal life on the Serengeti Plains. As it was, however, the threat of the Mau Mau was of supreme interest, and because there was little understanding of the problem outside of Kenya Colony itself, we felt that any knowledge we could gain of it would be likely to be helpful in explaining the struggle. We had no sooner arrived in Nairobi, therefore, than we went to the U. S. Consulate, and to the British High Commission and the local government, with the idea of getting some firsthand information about this strange war.

It soon began to appear that Tay had best remain in Nairobi, for the Mau Mau business was unpredictable at best, but I was fortunate in meeting Bill Bavis at the U. S. Consulate. Bill, a young U. S. vice-consul, was as interested as I in learning more about the Mau Mau problem, and the upshot of all this was that he went with me a few days later on a visit to a British infantry outfit that was operating against the terrorists.

About thirty miles north of Nairobi on the Nyeri road is the settlement of Thika, and it was there that we found the tents of the first battalion of "Buffs" when, late one afternoon, we were taken to Major Noel Norris, the Buffs' commanding officer. We already knew that there was to be a patrol sent out that night, and that Bill and I were to go with it, but now Major Norris outlined its purpose while the three of us drank warm British beer in the officers' mess.

The patrol had two objectives, we were told. First, it was to search along a stream on colonist Fox's coffee plantation for a Mau Mau gang that at various times had been reported hiding there; and second, the patrol was to arouse Fox's sleeping African laborers and pack them off to a screening center where specialists would try to determine whether any of them were Mau Mau.

Anything, we were told, could happen. A running fight might develop if we stumbled onto the gang. Even if we didn't, Fox's employees might put up a fight or try to run away, and in either case there would be some shooting.

While we were at supper, a message was delivered to the major saying that a gang of fifty Mau Mau had been flushed on a nearby plantation. The local home guard was in hot pursuit through the coffee, but for a time it seemed that this new development might necessitate a change in our plans. It was only after thinking it over carefully that the major decided otherwise. The members of the home guard, he explained, were apt to shoot indiscriminately at anything, and if professional soldiers were sent to join them in that tangle of coffee, more soldiers might be hurt—or even, possibly more Americans, for there were two of us—than Mau Mau. For that reason we were to go ahead according to plan, while the major ordered up a standby patrol to support the home guard if necessary.

A husky young Briton named Jones was in command of our detachment—a brand-new lieutenant fresh from Sandhurst. And the patrol was made up of four British soldiers, none older than twenty, two African trackers, and we two Americans. The four soldiers were armed with rifles and submachine guns. The two trackers carried revolvers only, and Bill Bavis and I, who had pulled on green jungle pants, rubber-soled boots, windbreakers, and floppy campaign hats, were each given a revolver.

Lieutenant Jones loaded his six men aboard a five-ton Army truck, while Bill and I joined him in his "Champ"—a jeeplike vehicle. With the Champ in the lead we drove for several miles along a tarred macadam road, ultimately reaching a side road that led to the Fox plantation. With the lights off, the two vehicles had crawled along the last half mile, and now we stopped. Jones arranged a rendezvous with the drivers, and we started off on foot along the dark plantation road in the hope of accomplishing our mission.

Once well away from the main road, Jones halted us in order to check arms and make sure we were ready for business, and then, in single file, and silently except for the soft scuffle of our boots, we went ahead again.

Off in the distance we heard an auto, but we paid no attention to it until, suddenly, its headlights appeared in the road behind us. We all "hit the ditch" on the double. In fact, I went across it and threw myself into the tall grass beyond, and not a sign of our presence was apparent when the car roared past. The secret of our little mission was still our own while colonist Fox— if that is who it actually was—headed rapidly home from Thika.

We climbed back to the road and marched on again. A half-moon partly hidden by broken clouds gave only the faintest light, and from my position near the end of the column between a native tracker and Lance Corporal Fuller, I tried to make out just what our situation was. There had been only a few snatches of conversation, and what I had overheard had been cast in very low tones. But more than that, it had mostly been in cockney, which was next to impossible for me to follow. Still, even Lieutenant Jones, whose English was of the best, was himself hard to understand as he occasionally made some low remark or gave some order from the head of the column.

Thika, we knew, had long been a hotbed of Mau-Mauism. There had been many acts of butchery in the country round about, and such patrols as ours were necessary, though they rarely came upon the enemy. In fact, that was a characteristic of this whole emergency. The Mau Mau were almost literally everywhere but were almost always invisible. Many Kikuyu who worked in the coffee, or who walked the roads or appeared in the villages, were undoubtedly sworn members of the secret terrorist society. Ninety per cent of them, it was said, had actually taken gruesome Mau Mau oaths and were consequently subject to Mau Mau discipline, but unless they were caught while actually engaged in Mau Mau activities, no one could know for certain.

Among the Kikuyu the oath-taking ceremony has always been of exceptional importance. For one thing, they believe that an oath, once taken, has the power to kill. Many important phases of Kikuyu life are marked by oaths of one sort or another. Even the transfer of land becomes final in their minds only when a certain oath has been sworn to by the parties concerned, and it is in this that one important explanation for the Mau Mau trouble lies. The Kikuyu says—and no doubt believes—that he merely *loaned* his land to the white settlers—that no oath was ever taken and consequently that no transfer of ownership was ever involved. The settler on the other hand purchased the land in good faith. From what I was told, however, there seemed to be many other complications. Jomo Kenyatta and his disciples, for example, had corrupted the Mau Mau oath and had turned it into a hideous, debasing, loathsome pledge that is almost beyond belief.

These were some of my thoughts during the half hour it took to reach the stream beside which we were to hunt the terrorists.

Having reached it in the dark, we divided into two groups, each with a tracker, and began the search, silently cursing the mosquitoes. We found no Mau Mau, but after pushing through dense brush for several hundred yards, we came upon a matted place in the grass where something—a lion, one of the trackers said—had been lying only a little while before. We could hear animals drinking not very far away, too, but we found no sign of any Mau Mau, so we left the stream and made our way toward a dark cluster of round huts with peaked thatch roofs.

Lance Corporal Fuller whispered to me from behind to be careful about entering any of these African dwellings. Two of his buddies, he said, had been picked off on just such a mission as this by a Mau Mau gunner who was hidden in the peak of his hut.

"Look up into the peak," he whispered, "before you go in."

We crept forward silently, or so we thought, but as we approached, a dog began to bark, and we heard the sounds of cattle and horses as they moved nervously in nearby corrals. And while I was marveling at the ability of the animals to detect us, my companions suddenly dashed forward, each toward some predetermined target.

I had been told to stick with Fuller, but he almost vanished before I hurried after him. He made directly for one of the huts where, as I came up, he was pounding on the door with the butt of his rifle.

"Open up!" he shouted in Swahili, and though the corporal was not more than twenty, and was a small man besides, his huge voice and the noise he made must have given those inside the idea that a veritable giant had arrived.

At first not a sound came from within, but then a baby began to cry, and we heard a woman's voice. People were awake, certainly, but the door did not open. Fuller threw himself against it, but it still held, and then we heard the sound of a shrill whistle as someone inside blew it again and again. We had no way of knowing what the whistle meant. It might be a call to the Mau

Mau. On the other hand, it was quite possible that these were loyal people who were whistling for the home guard.

Fuller was still pounding and shouting orders in Swahili, and the baby was still screaming inside. No one had appeared, but presently the door opened. A man came out clutching a bow and arrows to his chest, and obviously ready to surrender. Another man followed, and then a woman who was carrying the screaming baby.

There were eight huts in all, and by now all their inhabitants were coming out. The soldiers hurriedly rounded them up and went through the huts, finding little of significance except bows and arrows. One of the arrows, a tracker said, was tipped with poison, and in one hut someone came upon a two-foot section of three-quarter-inch pipe. So far as I could see, it was only a piece of pipe, but there was more to it than that, for homemade Mau Mau guns were made of pipe like this, and the owner of this piece of metal would surely be asked some pointed questions.

By now colonist Fox had put in his appearance. He was in slippers and bathrobe, his hair was mussed, and he seemed almost as bewildered as his frightened laborers when Lieutenant Jones explained the reason for the raid. He insisted that his people were all loyal. He himself had given them the bows and arrows for their own protection, and he had given them the whistle, too, so that they might call for help in case of a Mau Mau attack. But when the piece of pipe was brought to his attention he could not explain it and merely nodded when Jones said that the men were to be taken away for screening.

"Better send a truck for them in the morning," suggested Jones.

"Let 'em walk back!" grumbled the planter.

The lieutenant fired a Very signal into the sky, and when, in reply to it, our two vehicles arrived, the captives were taken aboard the truck for delivery, half an hour later, to a flood-lit, wire-enclosed compound near Thika. Once screened, they would be released if found to be loyal, though they would be sent to a detention camp if they were not.

As we drove back to Nairobi through the darkness, I found myself wondering about the difficult and complicated problem that confronted the British. Such patrols as the one I had accompanied were a necessity, of course, but no one knew better than the British that the Mau Mau could hardly be overcome by such means alone. Other plans were necessary, and a good many were under way. Loyal and would-be-loyal Kikuyu were being helped to defend themselves, thus cutting down the terrorist society's principal source of new members. Village educational programs were also being used to counter Mau Mau ideas, and Kenya Colony as a whole appeared to be moving toward a multi-racial government based on something like proportional representation. Furthermore, the newly organized United Country Party was hopeful of encouraging the integration of Europeans, Asiatics, and Africans.

Though all these and other reforms and measures were getting under way, the brutal terrorism of the Mau Mau still forced the British to continue their tough military policy. Terrorists who were caught were being shown no mercy. The trouble was that they were so hard to catch. Hidden away, as they were, in the hundreds of square miles of the Aberdare forest, and on the heavily forested slopes of Mount Kenya, they were able to organize bands of greater or lesser numbers, to collect and replenish their supplies, and to maintain or even increase their strength by forcibly administering their terroristic oaths to new recruits. They were also able to raid loyalist Kikuyu settlements, and though the members of the white community had long since been alerted to the danger, attacks on outlying farms and on lone autos on the country roads were a constant possibility.

The Buffs with whom I had been at Thika had explained that if I wanted to get closer to the heart of the fighting, I should go on a patrol in the great forests of the Aberdare range, and I was able to arrange to do so.

This time I was accompanied by a tall public relations officer of the British Army—Major Westerman—and was taken to the town of Nyeri, about seventy miles north of Nairobi. There, having met the officers of the 5th Kenya Battalion of the Queen's African Rifles at dinner, the major and I were driven, the next morning, out through the Kikuyu countryside to where the men of the 5th Battalion's Company D had pitched their tents within a barbed-wire enclosure on a grassy hilltop about a thousand yards from the edge of the Aberdare forest.

The men of the Queen's African Rifles are well-trained African troops—"Askaris" is the East African term—with British officers; and Company D—"Dog Company"—of the 5th Battalion was to send out a patrol that morning which Major Westerman and I were to accompany.

It was ten o'clock when we arrived, and the patrol was getting ready—twenty-five well-trained young African soldiers and two Europeans. One of these—the patrol leader—was redheaded, nineteen-year-old Lieutenant Mungo Henderson. The other was the company's equally youthful dog handler, Private Jones, who had charge of Jake, a well-trained but somewhat scarred Doberman pinscher.

This was the group that Major Westerman and I were to accompany, and after Lieutenant Henderson had inspected his men, we headed, single file, for the Aberdare forest at the edge of which Jones harnessed Jake, letting him run ahead of the column on a fifteen-foot rope.

Only the day before, the dog had located three Mau Mau on this very trail, pointing as a bird dog might have done, and giving the patrol fair notice when it passed near the three while they were carrying a butchered sheep. Two of the men had escaped in the bush, but the third had been caught, and now that Jake was back on this trail again, he picked up another scent almost at once.

Off he went at the end of his long rope, with the rest of us trotting after him along a faint forest track, dodging branches, leaping obstructions, and trying to watch our footing. The scent petered out after a time, and an African tracker took over, but without success. We came upon elephant tracks—big saucerlike depressions—and tracks of other animals, too, but the Mau Mau for whom we were looking had left no signs.

The firepower of the patrol was astonishing, as the Mau Mau understood. There were three or four Bren guns—heavy automatic rifles—and a number of Pachet submachine guns. There were several grenade-throwing rifles, as well as the usual clip-loading ones. There were hand grenades, knives, and bayonets. My armament, this time, consisted only of my Bell & Howell motion picture camera, which I tried to hold overhead each time I lost my footing. I was surprised to learn, during one of our pauses, that it weighed only about as much as a Pachet submachine gun— nine pounds.

From time to time Lieutenant Henderson talked about the Aberdare Mau Mau.

"There are thousands of them in this forest," he said, "but it's like looking for a needle in a haystack—a haystack covering 300 square miles. Best way to bag them is in night ambushes."

Private Jones told me of a time when a patrol he was with was attacked by a large gang. He was in the lead with Jake, so he dropped down to be out of the way of the Askaris' fire. But, instead of fighting, the patrol "panicked" and took to their heels, leaving Jones and the dog alone. When he realized what had happened, it was too late for him to run, so he opened up with his rifle.

"They could easily have wiped us out—Jake and me," he said, "but instead, they ran off too."

He went on to point out that the Mau Mau usually ran at the first sign of return fire. They like to snipe from cover, or to ambush a car at night on a lonely road. They also delight in hacking up defenseless Kikuyu and, occasionally, an unprotected European or two, but rarely, he insisted, were they willing to launch an attack against an armed group. Still, some of their attacks had been hideous. On one occasion, for example, hundreds of doped or maddened Mau Mau unsuccessfully stormed the barbed-wire barricade of a home-guard fort, and before the onslaught was over, many had actually impaled themselves on the sharpened wooden spikes that lined the moat.

Our patrol covered eight grueling miles—eight miles of dodging branches and pushing through the undergrowth, of scrambling up and down, of fording streams, of slipping, sliding, and occasionally falling in the red mud. Major Westerman, who was almost old enough for retirement, had stepped directly from an office desk to this, and before that march was over he was near exhaustion.

According to the lieutenant, the Mau Mau were not well armed. In fact, the only precision weapons they had were a few they had captured. So far as anyone knew, they had only three Bren guns, and their supply of ammunition was naturally both limited and irregular. They were poor marksmen, too, and ingenious though most of their firearms were, they were very ineffective. Made of pieces of pipe such as we had found at colonist Fox's farm, their "rifles" had crude wooden stocks and firing pins made of door bolts. These bolts slid in slots in the wooden stocks, and their tips were filed to a point. To fire one of these weapons, the bolt was pulled back, slingshot-fashion, against a strip of rubber tube. When the bolt was released, its sharpened end struck the cap in the cartridge and the gun went off. Almost any caliber of ammunition could be used, though the cartridge had to be kept from sliding through the pipe by collaring it with a hollowed-out East African penny. Fired in this way, of course, the bullets had little muzzle velocity, and in the utter lack of rifling the guns had very little range and no accuracy at all.

I later visited the Athi River Detention Camp south of Nairobi where nearly two thousand captive Mau Mau were being held, and where the camp was divided into compounds according to the degree of individual prisoner co-operation, as well as according to age and former position of Mau Mau leadership. The camp was run by eleven British officers and one hundred and fifty

African soldiers. Its purpose was to redirect and rehabilitate the Mau Mau, not merely to detain them, and though results left much to be desired, progress was being made. There were four hundred and seventy detainees who were definitely co-operative, and two hundred and thirty of these had confessed to having taken the Mau Mau oath. These received the most favorable treatment, but the great majority, who were constantly given the hardest jobs—road work and the like—were still stubbornly "non-co-operative."

Early one morning Major Westerman and I went to a briefing of three R.A.F. bomber crews of Squadron Leader K. R. Bowhill's 214th Squadron in Hangar Number 2 at Nairobi's Eastleigh Airport. Then, loaded down with parachute, helmet, goggles, and camera equipment, I managed to crowd my way into the bombardier's compartment of the squadron leader's big four-engined Lincoln.

Sharing the nose with the navigator-bombardier, I watched with some excitement as we flashed down the runway almost to its end before the pilot hauled back on the wheel and lifted the big brute of a plane over the trees.

We climbed to 10,000 feet in the brilliant equatorial sunshine and saw snow-capped Mount Kenya ahead. Our target area was somewhere in that direction, and a little Piper Tri-Pacer was already out there, flying around at treetop level, searching out a gang of terrorists for our flight of bombers to blast.

There! A little way up Mount Kenya's western slope a white column of smoke suddenly appeared above the trees. The Piper—"Eagle Yellow"—had heaved a marker out his side window, and we were already beginning to line up on the smoke. I watched the bombardier as he readied his release controls, flicking his switches and arming the bombs that hung in their racks a little way behind us.

"Bomb bay open!" he called, and, after a moment, "Bombs away!"

Looking through the tiny door into the bomb bay I saw eight brown "eggs" fall free—not all together "in salvo," but slightly staggered.

I could not see them hit the forest, nor was it possible to hear their delayed bursts twenty-five seconds later, but in a few moments we were back over the target, with our guns blazing on a strafing run.

Scarcely a quarter of an hour later we were on the ground again at Eastleigh Airport, and, once back in the operations room, I remarked that the best way to film the bombers in action, which had been my purpose all along, would be from another plane.

"I wish I could take my Cessna on one of your strikes," I added.

"Why not?" the R.A.F. replied, and almost at once it was agreed that Tay and I should fly out with them the very next morning.

We were off from Nairobi West, where we kept Charlie, at the first light of dawn. We headed north over Nairobi, but a little beyond Thika it began to rain, and the clouds hung so low that we were forced back.

Sure that with such foul weather the whole business would be canceled, I radioed Eastleigh Airport for permission to land there rather than return to Nairobi West, but when we entered "Ops" a few minutes later, we were told the strike was still on—that the sun was shining on the target area part way up Mount Kenya. Already several flights of AT-6 Harvards were taking off on dive-bombing assignments, and the Lincolns, too, were beginning to taxi. Having come back to Eastleigh we would now be late, of course, and would surely miss most of the show. Still, I thought, if we got a move on we could see some of it, and the R.A.F. agreed.

Tay would have objected if she had had a chance, but she was given no opportunity and away we flew, just ahead of the last Lincoln, making our way up and up through the gray stratus with that huge Lincoln, which we couldn't see, somewhere behind us and coming fast.

Charlie didn't shake off the overcast until we had passed 12,000 feet, but then a glorious view lay beyond our propeller. We were flying over a dazzling sea of white cloud, with the sky a clear deep blue. And in the distance stood the snow-clad 17,000-foot summit of Mount Kenya, with its dark green lower slopes rising out of the clouds. And there, off on our left, was the big Lincoln that was now pulling rapidly ahead of us.

We reached the target area not far behind that last bomber and we saw Eagle Yellow—the little spotter plane—milling around just above the trees. We heard one of the Lincolns calling, but Eagle Yellow's radio was out of commission and he could not hear.

"Eagle Yellow," the Lincoln called again. "This is Avenger One. If you're reading, drop your marker now. I'm ready to run in."

Eagle Yellow still made no answer, and no marker was dropped, so Avenger One announced that he was going to run in anyway. I tried to figure which of the three Lincolns was Avenger One, but I could not tell, and without a smoke marker I had no idea where the target was. Because of that, when one of the Lincolns let its bombs go, Tay and I were in the wrong place and failed to get a picture of what happened, though we saw the orange flashes in the forest and the cauliflowers of smoke and earth debris.

Now it was the second Lincoln's turn, but again we were out of place. We saw the bombs falling in the distance and I headed for the spot where they entered the forest, counting the twenty-five seconds until they would go off, and hoping to put Tay in a good filming position. We were about 2000 feet above the treetops, and Tay was ready, with the window open when——

"Whump!"

"Good Lord," I thought. "The window's blown off."

But it hadn't. I banked and, looking down, saw that we had been directly over the bombs when they had exploded. The "whump" was their concussion, and I am glad we were no lower.

Now it was up to Avenger Three, and this time we were lower

than the bomber. I tried to arrive near his release point at the correct moment so that Tay might film both the falling bombs and their bursts, but my timing was off again. I nearly flew Charlie under Avenger Three's open bomb bay.

"Cessna!" he called. "Ah! Ah——!"

But we pulled clear and he didn't finish what he planned to say. His bombs fell instead, and we missed getting a picture of them, too.

Back at Eastleigh Airport, Tay and I were saying good-by to Squadron Leader Bowhill before taking Charlie "home" to Nairobi West. We had failed to get the pictures we wanted, still we had had an experience we would not soon forget. We were commenting on that fact when the squadron leader snipped his unit's insignia from the shoulder of his flying suit and handed it to us as a memento of our mission with his Lincoln crews.

The crest of the 214th Squadron is a diving nightjar with the motto *Ulter in Umbris*—"Avenger in the Shades"—and we accepted the insignia gratefully when Squadron Leader Bowhill handed it to us. In fact, Tay later sewed it to Charlie's cabin upholstery so that we might have it with us as we continued on our way.

Flying with those Lincolns would have been a perfect finale to our adventures in East Africa, but, before taking off for Ethiopia, we still had a flight to make to Zanzibar, the island of cloves and Arab dhows, which sits twenty miles off Africa's east coast some 400 miles southeast of Nairobi.

The flight was an easy one, and we spent a weekend on that lovely island as guests of Acting British Resident Alford and his wife. However, we had come at the wrong time of year for both the cloves and the Arab dhows, so, promising ourselves to return someday at the right season, we flew back to Nairobi, swinging a little out of our way in order to fly over Tanganyika and Africa's highest mountain—Kilimanjaro—which rises in solitary splendor from the African plains to the ice-capped height of 19,565 feet.

We took Charlie around and around the mountain until, even without oxygen masks, which surprised us, we were above the summit and still conscious! We flew directly over the great mountain's perfectly symmetrical extinct crater, and as we looked down into its yawning green crevasses, our altimeter showed 21,000 feet.

That was the high point of our flight across Africa, and it was from there that we went into a steep descent for Nairobi 125 miles away, there to prepare for our flight from the land of the Mau Mau to Ethiopia, the land of the King of Kings—the Emperor Haile Selassie.

IX. Wings over Ethiopia
and the Nile

$\mathbf{L}$AY AND I LEFT NAIROBI ON FRI-
day, July 23, bound for Addis Ababa, the capital of Ethiopia. We
knew the flight would not be an easy one, for Ethiopia was in the
midst of its rainy season, and much of the country is high, mountainous, and exceedingly rugged. We consequently made any
number of checks on the weather, pestering the Eastleigh Airport
weather office, and cornering every Ethiopian Airlines pilot we
could find.

With these sources of information at our disposal we did not
seriously consider flying the direct route to Addis Ababa. It measures more than 700 miles, and much of it is over country that is
not only mountainous but is also without roads. Furthermore, even
if such a flight were otherwise free of incident, it would bring us
to Addis Ababa in the afternoon—a bad time for thunderstorms.
Then, too, we were advised against this route because of "wild
tribesmen" who occupy much of the area.

We also decided against the long and roundabout route through
low, flat, and oppressively hot Italian Somaliland, and ultimately
charted our course along a kind of middle route. Even this left
something to be desired, for it would take us over many miles of
arid country, much of which is without roads, and all of which—
especially along the border between Ethiopia and Italian Somali-

land—had little to offer either Charlie or ourselves in the event
we lost our way or were forced down. Still, there was a landing
strip at Mandera about 500 miles from Nairobi where we could
refuel before continuing to Hargeisa, in British Somaliland, where
we planned to spend the night, going on to Addis Ababa the
following morning.

We took off about nine o'clock and, as the clouds were low
again, we hopped along over Thika, the Tana River, and the
Lorian Swamp until we reached the desert area of northeastern
Kenya. There, under a clear blue sky, we picked up an isolated
dirt road, following it northeastward toward the desert outpost of
Wajir.

This whole northern frontier region is usually prohibited to
single-engine aircraft, for it is a desolate land with few landmarks.
In order to come this way we had had to obtain special permission,
which was granted when the authorities learned of our flights in
the Sahara Desert and the Belgian Congo, and when we promised
to keep this road in sight.

We saw no town or any other sign of life until we found Wajir,
a small white fort surrounded by a village of mud huts. We circled
three times, for that was the prearranged signal we had been told
to give, and then continued on our way to Mandera, but that was
much more easily said than done. The trouble was that there were
four roads leading from Wajir, though our map showed only one.
I chose one of them (the decision was a contested one, for the
co-pilot had picked another), and we followed it until we noticed
it was running too much to the north. With the co-pilot assuming
"I told you so" airs, we angled over toward her choice, which we
soon decided was probably right. But, twenty minutes later we
came to a totally unexpected fork, and once again couldn't agree
on which of the two routes to follow. I took the lesser road,
which was more in agreement with the compass course, and almost gave up again when it narrowed into little more than a foot-
path. We were about to admit defeat, and were longing to land
for a peek at a signpost, if such a thing existed, when suddenly

the track broadened into a well-traveled road leading across that utterly arid land in the direction we wanted to go. We followed it carefully, and finally relaxed when a narrow ribbon of green showed up in the distance ahead. This was the Dawa River, and it wasn't long before we spotted Mandera, a tiny British outpost where Kenya touches Ethiopia and Italian Somaliland.

This remote frontier station had the type of grass airstrip that we had encountered so frequently before, and the moment we landed hundreds of Africans came running from all directions, completely surrounding us as soon as our roll had stopped. There was no question about the warmth of our reception, but we had never before seen any such Africans. They were tall, handsome Somalis of the Eastern Hamitic family of tribes, with long stringy hair that was wiped with grease, and all of them—men and women alike—wore ample lengths of orange-brown cloth that were draped about them from shoulder to knee.

Having no words in common, all either they or we could do was to stare curiously and smile until two British soldiers—the local administrators and only Europeans at the field—came running up. They had had no word of our coming, they told us, and were surprised by our arrival. This, in turn, was something of a shock to us. It would not have mattered especially on a flight from New York to Washington, but there in that desert country it could have spelled disaster. For if we had been forced down, no one would have known about it, and no attempt would have been made to help us. The two Britishers were much concerned over the breakdown of their communications system, and we were even more so, though it confirmed the wisdom of keeping to roads in such desolate lands.

I promptly refueled Charlie with five-gallon tins of gas that were brought up, while several hundred fascinated Somalis watched. The two Englishmen then asked us to join them in "a spot of tea," but we had to refuse, for Hargeisa, which had to be reached before dark, still lay some 400 miles ahead across a land with no roads, no radio, no nothing. We would have to make the flight by compass all the way, and there were no emergency airfields within reach. If we lost our way, or bad weather developed, we might have to return to Mandera, so we told our two British friends that if they heard our engine after dark to please line up a few jeep and truck headlights along the airstrip.

We had hardly taken off before we began to see that the land we were flying over was more than a little rugged. There were no roads and no villages. It was merely a land of nomadic tribesmen, though we saw none of them. Even the hills and rivers were unidentifiable—especially the latter because for more than half the year this country has no rivers at all, but now, in the rainy season, almost every gulch, wadi, or depression held a stream or a pond. So we kept to a compass heading with the utmost care and, something over two hours after taking off from Mandera, we spotted a distinct dirt road twenty miles or so from Hargeisa.

It was with real relief that we turned to follow it, the more so since by now we counted four different thunderstorms that had appeared from nowhere. I called the Hargeisa tower and was told that hard rain was falling on the north end of their field but that the south end was still clear. The situation struck me as highly dubious, while Tay was already looking for places to land on the road beneath us, but the tower reported no strong wind and no gusts, so I kept on despite the ominous clouds ahead. The field, when we found it, proved to be almost 10,000 feet long, and the far end, as reported, had indeed slipped under the edge of a thunderstorm, but the end nearest us was still clear, so we came straight in, landed, and taxied down to the parking area. It was there that the rain caught us. We had made it, though only by the skin of our teeth.

We tied the plane to some blocks of cement and hitched a ride to town with the British airport official. Tay and I knew Hargeisa was the capital of British Somaliland, but we had no idea what to expect in the way of overnight accommodations. In a community of anywhere from thirty-five to fifty thousand Somalis, there were only about a hundred Europeans, and no hotel. But there was a local club where travelers could stay—an attractive, low, white building—and after a long, tiring day we looked forward to a good night's sleep there. When we greeted the "innkeeper," however, he threw up his hands in despair and said he had absolutely no room left.

"Sleeping-bag time," I thought, but I noticed Tay glance toward the living-room couches. The manager noticed this, too, and came up with an even better idea, although he was rather apologetic about it: he would set up two cots in the small library.

We had a substantial supper and turned in immediately, though it was only nine o'clock. Sleep came at once, too, surrounded as we were by shelves and shelves of books, and even with a violent thunderstorm going on outside.

Next morning Tay and I were in the air again by eight o'clock, with few signs left of the thunderstorm except some puffs of cumulus that still hung over the highest hills. Addis Ababa was little more than two hours away to the west, and our route ran along the edge of a high plateau, past Dire Dawa, Ethiopia's second largest city, and across the spectacular great Rift Valley where its sheer and rocky sides drop abruptly down to the flat and grassy valley floor that is dotted, here and there, with small extinct volcanic craters—some of them transformed into beautiful clear lakes. Beyond the Rift Valley the land lay high again, and mounted even higher as we approached Addis Ababa, which is at an elevation of 8000 feet, with mountains rising three or four thousand feet more both to the west and the south.

We followed a road and a railroad on the approach to the capital and finally saw Addis Ababa just ahead of us—a large city sprawling extensively over green mountain slopes.

Landing at the big up-to-date airfield, no one seemed to know where we should park, and Charlie finally ended up among three brightly painted DC-3s of the Ethiopian Airlines—a subsidiary of TWA—and we went into the terminal to tackle the customs. To our great concern, the officials blew their tops when we told them we could not produce a flight permit. We tried to explain that the local American Embassy had it, but to no avail, and just as we had premonitions of being led off to jail, two Embassy men—Mr. Cassidy and Mr. Anderson—arrived and cleared up the situation.

Once our papers were stamped and Charlie had been tied down, Mr. Anderson drove us to his home for lunch, and on the way we noticed that Addis Ababa was a city of surprising contrasts. Magnificent, thoroughly modern government buildings here and there look out on rows of cluttered shops and shanties. New and many-storied office buildings stand beside unkempt hovels. Palatial homes sometimes have huts for next-door neighbors.

Many streets are modern and well paved, but donkeys and carts make up most of the traffic. Here and there we came upon well-planned city squares with statues, fountains, and bright flower beds, past which flocks of sheep made their way to market, or hay-laden donkeys ambled. Near some of the city's modern department stores we saw a large outdoor market, crowded with people, cluttered with cattle, sheep, and goats, and filled with such sounds and odors as only an Ethiopian could identify. Pedestrians, donkeys, and dogs were everywhere, and frequently we passed robed and barefoot horsemen riding on padded saddles, but with their big toes thrust through circular little metal stirrups not more than two or three inches in diameter. Automobiles and bicycles, too, passed us with much honking of horns and ringing of bells.

Though we had reached Addis late in July, the day was cold. The Ethiopians were bundled up in heavy robes or Army coats, and the Europeans all wore woolen clothes. Tay and I, freshly arrived from milder Nairobi and lightly dressed, were thoroughly uncomfortable, but we quickly warmed up at Mr. Anderson's, with our first American food in over five months.

We learned before lunch was over that we had arrived at a most opportune time, for in honor of the birthday of His Imperial Majesty, Haile Selassie I, Emperor of Ethiopia, King of Kings, Elect of God, and Conquering Lion of Judah, a ball was scheduled for that evening despite the fact that the Emperor himself had not yet returned from his trip to the United States, and Dr. Joseph Simonson, the American Ambassador, wanted us to go with him.

We were glad to accept, of course, though neither of us had any evening clothes. But our hosts immediately produced an extra tuxedo that fit me remarkably well. Tay, whose evening dresses had been left behind in Paris when we were cutting down on Charlie's load, was forced to fall back on a white and gold cotton halter dress which, with a woolen stole and some jewelry, may not have set a new style for the diplomatic corps of Addis Ababa, but which served remarkably well under the circumstances.

Once lunch was over, Mr. Anderson took us to our hotel, and this we found to be another Ethiopian anachronism. It had formerly been a summer palace, and so was strikingly impressive with its handsome, high-ceilinged rooms, its ornate chandeliers, beautiful paneling, and highly polished wooden floors. Closets and bathrooms had been added, apparently, when the palace was turned into a hotel, and modern hotel furniture had been added as well, but, having once been a summer palace, with high ceilings, many windows, and no heating, it was like an icebox and we spent much of our time there wrapped up in blankets.

Ambassador Simonson, with Mrs. Simonson and their daughter, came for us at eight-fifteen that evening while I, as luck would have it, was finding it quite impossible to tie my tie. Tay, however, was ready—halter dress and all—and though neither of us had met the Ambassador before, she at once told him of my problem, and he—a most human Lutheran minister who had left his church in St. Paul, Minnesota, to accept the post in Addis Ababa—chuckled while he tied my tie for me in the hotel lobby before taking us off to the ball.

The ball was held in a lavishly decorated armory and the entire diplomatic corps, as well as many important Ethiopian officials, were present. There was a great hubbub when Dr. Simonson and his party entered, and it was immediately apparent that he was accepted as the dean of the diplomatic corps. We were shown to one of two vacant tables on a raised area at one end of a large room, and Dr. Simonson had just begun to greet some of the other diplomats and Ethiopian officials when everyone jumped up, bowing from the waist.

It was a member of the royal family—a brother of the Emperor —who had arrived, and he took his place at the table beside ours, though he remained there only a moment before getting to his feet and leading the way to the banqueting hall. Following after him, we found that the walls of this other room were covered with greens and flowers, and that there were many pictures of the Emperor and his family. Long tables which ran the length of two walls were covered with an astonishing array of food, but little of it looked familiar to us.

Uncertain of what many of the dishes were, we conservatively sampled most of them. There were many different kinds of bread, and just as many meat pastries. There were saucelike dishes, along with chicken and fish in unusually disguised forms. And, most obvious among the rest, though we avoided them, were great platters of raw meat—dripping red beef, which the Ethiopians especially relish.

Sitting on chairs placed against the walls, and balancing our plates as best we could, we nibbled at the spicy food. We still wondered what much of it was and were relieved to find that we had cake and fruit for dessert. Once the feast was over, we returned to the main room and sat around our little tables watching the dancing.

The whole affair was formal, and we found it difficult to converse effectively with anyone. On that account we were glad to tag along when the Simonsons left early.

On Sunday, our second day in Addis Ababa, the Ambassador sent his car to take us around the city. The driver was a young Ethiopian who had been a member of the Ethiopian brigade in Korea. He had learned his English from American soldiers there, and now he proudly pointed out all the admirable aspects of Addis while overlooking or explaining away both the poverty and the undesirable details. He drove us past the handsome new palace, which is in a section of the city that was then under construction. We stopped at the zoo, where the only animals were lions, for the lion is the national symbol of Ethiopia. We visited the city's oldest church, a simple circular stone building with the Star of David on the roof instead of the Cross. Ethiopia has been a Christian country since Christianity was first introduced in the fourth century, and the Ethiopian Orthodox Church was once a part of the Egyptian Coptic Church.

We had a pleasant informal supper with the Simonsons that evening, but an audience with the crown prince the next morning proved to be the highlight of our visit to Ethiopia.

Formality and reverence for the royal family are strong at the Ethiopian court, and when an Embassy car came to take us to the palace, we paid the strictest attention to the briefing we were given. If, we were told, we were received in the throne room, I was to bow and Tay was to curtsy three times—once at the door, once in the middle of the room, and once very deeply when we shook hands. If we were received in a smaller room, we could omit the second of these.

That seemed clear enough, but once our Embassy friend delivered us at the palace doorway and deserted us there, we began to worry lest we had misunderstood. A formally dressed Ethiopian official greeted us just inside the door and led us upstairs to a cozy little living room where a man in a plain business suit was seated on a couch.

"The crown prince's secretary," we thought, and somewhat casually shook hands.

It was only then that we discovered that we had been taken directly to His Royal Highness, but he obviously did not hold our blunder against us. In fact, he was most friendly and informal, though he spoke in Amharic in spite of the fact that he knows English well.

The interview was a pleasant one and the prince was especially interested in our travels—particularly in the trip I had made into Tibet in 1949 with my father. In fact, he seemed to recognize the similarities between his country and that of the Tibetans, both of which, as I had an opportunity to point out, are high, mountainous, isolated, and deeply religious.

At the end of the interview we were permitted to take a few still pictures, but once that had been done, we tried to atone for the informality of our entrance by making the deepest bow and the very best curtsy of which we were capable. Then we backed politely out the doorway and made our way down the steps and out to the waiting car.

Tay and I planned to leave Addis Ababa early the next morning, but when we awoke the clouds were hanging close to the ground and it was pouring rain. We went to the airfield anyway and hung around while three American pilots employed by the Ethiopian Airlines took stock of the situation.

About ten o'clock the clouds began to break up, and the three took off, one of them radioing back a little later that he had been able to reach the Rift Valley VFR—flying, that is, with the ground visible all the way.

That was good enough for us, so we took off, too, bound for Asmara, the capital of Eritrea. Our destination was about 500 miles directly north of Addis Ababa and within thirty miles or so of the Red Sea, but here again the direct route was not feasible. Our course, at first, led to the east, toward the great Rift Valley.

Despite Addis Ababa's elevation, Charlie took off readily enough, but we soon began to feel that if the pilot who had reported had actually flown VFR, he must almost have wheeled his DC-3 along the road. That, at least, was about what we seemed to be doing, and the clouds appeared determined to force us lower still. Within minutes we found ourselves no more than 200 feet above the road, and there was no way of knowing just where some hill might be. But then the ground began to drop away and in another ten minutes, or even less, we were over the Rift Valley with its smooth floor a thousand feet below us.

We were relieved, of course, but we still could not turn north, for the valley was choked with thunderstorms and we added fully fifty miles to our flight before finding a way around them on the valley's eastern side. That meant—if we were to get through to Asmara—that our total distance for the day would be just under 700 miles, or five hours of flying. We would have to watch our ground speed and fuel consumption very carefully indeed.

Fortunately the weather cleared and the sun came out, hot and glaring, as we began to make our way northward over the deadly Danakil Desert, first crossed by a white man as recently as 1928. The land beneath us changed until it was monotonously flat and uninteresting, and we soon tired of just sitting. Except for our emergency rations, we had been unable to bring any food with us, so we took turns flying and reading, until some time later, near the border of Eritrea, we were startled to see three towering thunderheads blocking our path in the distance.

On the route we were flying there were no airstrips between Addis Ababa and Asmara, and because of our earlier detour, we had already passed the "point of no return." We could still head for the port of Djibouti, in French Somaliland, which now was about as far to the southeast as Asmara was to the northwest. But, as I remembered from having been told about it by an airline pilot earlier that morning, a nearer alternate airfield was at Assab, a little Eritrean port on the Red Sea, about a hundred miles to the east of our position—if we could find it.

I figured, now, that we had about an hour's supply of fuel left, and Assab was little more than half an hour away, so I did my best to set an accurate compass course for it. I also slowed down our cruising speed a bit more to increase the ratio of miles to gallons and began to use our radio on all frequencies, even including the emergency one (this had a terrible psychological effect on Tay) though I was unable to get any answers.

Already we were overdue at Asmara. Soon they would be looking for us, but they would hardly think to look where we were now. Our map showed far too few details of this Danakil Desert, and I noted, to my concern, that the land below us was growing rougher. There were no roads to follow, and there were no towns. On the other hand, if the course I had chosen was right, we should be picking up a road before long—one that had been built by the Italians leading across the desert to Assab.

We were keeping a careful watch on the arid and boulder-strewn valleys we were flying over when, in the midst of a landscape that would not have been much out of place on the moon, we saw the road—a black, winding strip of tarred macadam. We followed it eagerly, and soon came to Assab, or what we felt certain was Assab, for it was a town on the shore line, and the map showed no other anywhere about. But where was the airfield?

We circled for ten minutes, but still we found no airstrip. Perhaps we would have to land on the black-top road after all, but we could look a little longer, so back we went above the road, and finally, almost twenty miles north of the town, we spotted an airport, though it seemed to have been abandoned.

Circling around the place, we saw three hangars—all without roofs—and the other buildings were in comparable condition too. We saw no men—no trucks—no cars. No lived-in house was anywhere about. Still, the gravel strip seemed to be in good shape, so we landed, wondering how far we might have to walk for help.

We taxied toward the biggest hangar, which had once been a fine building, and still bore battered signs in Italian reading "Waiting Room" and "Airport Commander." It occurred to us that this must have been an Italian air base during the war and, from its appearance, one that had been well bombed.

As we stopped the engine and sat staring at the waiting-room door, three Arabs walked out. We were so surprised to find human beings in such surroundings that we both jumped. But when they smiled and "salaamed" we knew they were friendly, and were probably the airport attendants, although we had no way of talking to them.

We followed them into the old waiting room, where they took turns shouting over a battery-driven telephone that must have dated back to World War I. I even took my turn and tried shouting over it in English, and to my immense surprise and relief I got a reply from someone who spoke English with a definite Oxford flavor. He told us, too, that he would come and get us, and within half an hour he did—a handsome young Ethiopian who spoke fluent English, and who brought with him a disreputable-looking Italian who just mumbled in his own tongue.

It was five-thirty and we had had no food since six that morning, so our first thoughts were of a possible hotel. Yes, there was one—but it had no roof! There was a Shell Oil representative, however, and we decided to turn to him for help.

The town, when we reached it half an hour later, proved to be terribly hot and totally run-down, though efforts were being made to restore it. It was twelve years now since the Italians had surrendered Assab to the British, and at least a third of the buildings were still in a bombed-out state.

The Shell representative in Assab was Peter Turpin, an attractive young Englishman, a bachelor, and the only non-Italian European in town. He helped us send a message to Asmara, reporting our arrival in Assab, and insisted that we go home with him, not only for dinner but also to spend the night. We accepted with real gratitude, though first he took us to an outdoor café where, over foaming glasses of beer, we met the town doctor and three of Turpin's Italian friends. Then, while we were having an excellent dinner on the screened veranda of our host's home, the night watchman reported for duty. Instead of a dog at the end of a leash, he had a scrawny rooster! Obviously, the watchman was planning on a sound night's sleep, with a reliable alarm clock to awaken him the next morning. We went to bed laughing and quickly fell asleep despite the intense heat.

Mr. Turpin drove us back to the field early the following morning, and after Charlie had been refueled by turbaned Arabs, we took off, hoping, because we were in the air by eight o'clock, to fill our tanks again at Asmara and then go on to Wadi Halfa on the frontier between Egypt and the Sudan.

Our course, now, was north along the Red Sea coast for 300 miles, to a point due east of Asmara where we turned inland for fifty miles to where the town is perched at the edge of an 8000-foot plateau. Over the Red Sea lowlands, the weather had been clear and hot, but it was cool in Asmara, and we barely slipped onto the lofty plateau under low-hanging clouds. Even before we left Charlie and went in to get the latest weather reports, we had to put on our sweaters and jackets again. The Asmara tower officials, we learned, had been worried about us the day before and had sent out messages trying to locate us. In fact, they were readying search planes when our wire came through from Assab.

By the time we had been passed by the customs and had gone over the latest weather reports it was almost noon, and the idea of trying to reach Wadi Halfa before dark began to grow less appealing. For one thing, the distance was more than 700 miles, and for another, our route would take us across the Nubian Desert. Besides, Asmara was wonderfully cool and comfortable after the heat of Assab, and we could not resist the temptation to have one cool night's sleep before tackling the torrid heat of the Sudan and Upper Egypt. Anyway, we had heard about the U. S. Army Post Exchange in Asmara and the thought of the first chocolate milk shake in six months could not be dismissed.

We had been surprised to learn of the presence of American troops in this remote Eritrean town, where they operate a radio relay station. Apparently the location is one of the best in the world for such a thing. When the Pentagon can't get through to Hamburg, for instance, or to Okinawa or Tokyo, they send their message by way of Asmara.

The town is attractively Italian in appearance. The countryside is green, the climate is delightful, and though it was raining hard when we checked in at Asmara's ultra-modern hotel, we did not let that keep us from walking several miles to the Army base and the Post Exchange. There, to our surprise, we learned that the commanding officer knew of our arrival. Apparently the American Consul had passed the word on, so we not only got our chocolate milk shakes—each of us had two—but got them in the company of the C.O. himself!

When we took off the following morning we found that getting out of Asmara was as hair-raising as leaving Addis Ababa had been. We had to skim along beneath low clouds, following a road and a valley, with mountains rising here and there into the over-cast. Fortunately the ground kept falling away while the valley widened, and before long the greenery disappeared and the mountains became great arid piles of stone.

At the border between Eritrea and the Sudan the Ethiopian escarpment dropped steeply to a level plain where two dome-shaped mountains rose abruptly and Gibraltar-like. At their feet was the town of Kassala, and we landed there for gas and to clear the Sudan customs.

From Kassala our course was over the Atbara River to its junction with the Nile. Then we stayed with the Nile until, about a hundred miles downstream from the Fifth Cataract, it made its great turn to the southwest, leaving us to follow the thin straight line of the railroad that runs almost without a curve for more than 200 miles across the Nubian Desert to Wadi Halfa and the Egyptian border.

This was no desert such as we had seen near Goundam, with thorn trees and occasional mimosas to interrupt the arid expanse. Instead, we flew for mile after mile over sand dunes and sandy levels where nothing but an occasional rocky hill broke an otherwise featureless desert. There was no detail that we could follow except the straight and narrow line of the railroad, for though a road of sorts parallels it all the way, it was as colorless as the surrounding sand and was always difficult to see. Not a town exists along all that lonely desert railroad—only service stations spaced at intervals of twenty miles where water is stored for the trains, and gasoline for the few cars that pass that way.

Wadi Halfa is on the east bank of the Nile only four or five miles from the Egyptian border, and though its airport is large, the town is not. We landed without trouble, and when we caught a lift into town we found that it stretched out along its sand streets so close beside the Nile as to give the impression that both the town and its fringe of palm trees were shrinking from the quivering heat of the nearby desert. The hotel was good enough and its gardens were beautiful, especially by contrast with the arid surroundings of the town. But the Nile—muddy brown and featureless—was far from beautiful despite the welcome presence of so great a stream in so vast a desert.

We were up at five o'clock the next morning and off on one of our longest flights—five hours and twenty-four minutes. For the first half hour we flew just above the river, taking pictures of the lateen-rigged sailboats. At Abu-Simbel, as we made our way downstream only a few hundred feet above the smooth brown water, we passed a cliff and saw four huge Egyptian figures carved there in the rocks—three in remarkably unworn condition, considering that they have kept their silent watch over that portion of the Nile since before the days of Greece or Rome.

We climbed higher as the air grew hot and "bumpy," and ultimately passed Luxor. It was there that we dropped down once more, circling again and again about the ruins of ancient Thebes, and marveling at the size and state of preservation of the enormous temples.

From Luxor to Cairo is an overnight journey by train, but within two and a half hours of the time we left the ruins of Thebes, we sighted the pyramids of Gizeh, with Cairo five or six miles away across the Nile. In another few minutes we landed at the Heliopolis Airport where we parked Charlie among multi-engined international air liners.

We were back, once more, at one of the crossroads of civilization. The African portion of our flight was over, and the Middle East now beckoned.

X.   East to Aqaba and North
to Jerusalem and the Bosporus

C<small>AIRO, WHICH TAY AND I HAD</small> visited before, held few attractions for us now. On our previous visit we had paid our respects to the everlasting pyramids, as well as to the Sphinx and the city's famous bazaar, but now we had arrived at the end of July, when the heat approaches the unbearable, and the city's flies and smells are at their worst.

Under the circumstances, Cairo typified what we especially wished to avoid. Certainly it was a far cry from the beauty and laughter of the Ituri Forest, and we would have gladly passed it by and gone directly to Jerusalem had that been possible. However, we dared not do so without first checking in with the Egyptian Civil Aviation office in order to learn how we might fly to the Holy City without running the risk of being shot down by the Arabs on the one hand or the Jews on the other.

Would it be possible, we asked, for us to skirt the Mediterranean coast of Israel, keeping just outside the three-mile limit until we could turn inland by way of some corridor across Israeli territory to the Arab portion of Jerusalem?

The answer was "No!" We would have to swing south and east, crossing the Suez Canal, the Sinai Peninsula, and the Gulf of Aqaba. Then, having reached Jordanian territory by flying over

Arab lands all the way, we could go north to the Dead Sea, and could approach Jerusalem from the east.

"I wish we could spend the rest of the year in Africa," said Tay, and I agreed with her, though Cairo in midsummer was not the part of Africa we had in mind. We were glad to get away from its heat and flies and odors on the morning of August 2, and we dipped our wings to the whole fast-awakening continent as we swooped over the Sphinx and roared between two of the pyramids so low that we saw a camel-mounted tourist as he clung to the saddle of his excited and long-legged mount—so low, too, that when I banked Charlie, Tay shot one of our best flying scenes by filming the pinnacle of Cheops' Pyramid with the lens pointing nearly straight up.

We flew east from Cairo as far as the Suez Canal, above which, to our surprise, the Egyptians had given us permission to fly. We reached the canal just north of Great Bitter Lake, where, turning south, we respectfully maintained an altitude of 5000 feet, for we recalled having been told by a pilot who had once flown low where we now were, that he had plainly seen the muzzles of anti-air-craft guns as they had tracked him—an experience we had no desire to duplicate in view of the trigger-happy potentialities of the Middle East these days.

On to the south we flew for thirty miles or so over the canal. Then, from the port of Suez, we followed the eastern shore of the Gulf of Suez for another ten minutes to put ourselves indisputably south of a prohibited area which lay north of the line from Suez to the little Jordanian port of Aqaba. And finally we turned east to cross the barren waste of the Sinai Peninsula, where Moses and the Children of Israel wandered for so long on their journey to the Promised Land.

Not the slightest patch of green or the faintest sign of habitation appeared beneath our wings. The arid landscape was as devoid of life as the Nubian Desert had been, while off to starboard, through the hot haze of noon, several peaks loomed against the horizon. One of these was marked Jebel Musa on our map—

the Mount of Moses, which, so some believe, is Mount Sinai where Moses was given the tablets of stone. We knew, too, that the renowned monastery of St. Catherine stood somewhere in this desert waste, near that biblical summit.

Although Jerusalem was all of 200 miles to the north, I got a message through by using our long-range, high-frequency set, and reported our route and ETA—estimated time of arrival. This could be important in case of a forced landing, and both of us felt better when we knew that the Jerusalem control tower had a line on us.

Early that morning Tay had arranged with our Cairo hotel for a box lunch of sandwiches and fruit, and we were munching on one of our rare meals aloft when the Gulf of Aqaba appeared some twenty miles ahead. Far off on our left lay the southern tip of the Negev, the southernmost portion of Israel. To avoid this we had taken the route we were following, but when, at last, the greenish-blue waters of the Gulf of Aqaba were beneath us we knew that we could turn northward.

In a few minutes we spanned the narrow gulf to its eastern shore, and we set our course for the town of Aqaba at the head of the gulf. Aqaba, besides being Jordan's only outlet to the sea, is also the very near neighbor of the Israeli airfield of Elath.

The course that we had earlier drawn on our maps showed a distance of nearly 200 miles to the city of Amman, Jordan's capital, and, in our customary way, we followed the road that leads northward from Aqaba, keeping it always within Charlie's gliding range. This was our usual policy whenever a road approximated the course we were flying, and one might wonder if we would not have been better off traveling by car. Sometimes, I must admit, we might have been, but it wouldn't have been half the fun. Traveling by car would have been more time consuming, too, as well as far more tiring, and many a place we visited could not have been reached at all.

At the town of Ma'an, sixty-five miles northeast of Aqaba, we picked up the Hejaz Railway and followed it for a time, but then we headed almost due west from both the road and the railway until the narrow valley of Wadi Musa came in sight. It was here, according to tradition, that Moses smote the rock and produced the Spring of Moses—the 'Ain Musa—which, even today, still waters this parched valley. And here, too, lies Petra, "a rose-red city, half as old as time," though most of its wonders, largely hidden among the cliffs, were lost to us as we flew over. It was not until we came back weeks later and made our way on horseback through the deep, narrow, and vertical-walled gorge known as the Siq that we were able to see and marvel at "Pharaoh's Treasury," and the other ruins of this strange city of the rocks, which flourished more than two thousand years ago and provided a desert port of call for the caravans of Biblical times when they were bound for Syria, perhaps from the Queen of Sheba's land of myrrh and frankincense.

Flying north from Petra, we followed the eastern edge of one of the world's strangest valleys—the Rift which we had seen as it crosses Kenya and Ethiopia, and whose northern end was now leading us toward the great depression wherein the Dead Sea lies. Charlie slid down and down through the air until the altimeter, unwinding far past the zero mark, recorded an elevation of minus 1000 feet! And even then, as we flew on above the milky-blue waters of the Dead Sea, its surface was almost 300 feet below our wings. Here we were, flying 300 feet above the lowest point on the face of the earth, and 1000 lower than the surface of the Mediterranean, whose waves were beating on the shores of Palestine only fifty miles away.

On our right the mountains of Moab rose 4000 feet against the eastern sky, and in the distance ahead, shimmering in the sunlit haze, we could see the River Jordan with the date groves of Jericho showing up as dark splotches against the white and barren valley floor beyond.

With the northern end of the Dead Sea still below us we climbed to 3500 feet, for the Jerusalem airfield, now only twenty miles away, lay at 2500 feet, and we radioed the control tower for landing instructions.

Back came the reply with a thick Arabic accent.

"Roger, Four Three Charlie, landing to the west. Call me when you are three miles out."

We approached over the wilderness of Judea, an expanse of rocky eroded hills without a tree and even, so it seemed, without a blade of grass.

"There it is!" Tay called out suddenly as she caught the white gleam of the Holy City beyond the Mount of Olives. "But don't get too close," she cautioned. "The Israeli frontier runs right through the city."

I rolled Charlie to a more northerly heading, toward the airfield which is five miles or so north of Jerusalem, and as I set up landing approach I could see why the tower had asked us to call from three miles out. Traffic had been stopped, as if at a rail crossing, on the asphalt road to Ramallah, which ran across what appeared to be a recent extension of the runway. What had happened was that when Palestine had been split up, Jordan had lost access to the original Jerusalem Airport, and so had created this one in a hurry. By the map, the border between Jordan and Israel was barely one minute farther west and, as Charlie glided down, the voice of an air liner came in clearly on our loud-speaker as it called "LOD tower" at the nearby Israeli airfield.

Waiting at the terminal to vouch for us before the Jordanian authorities, was Anna Grace Lind, who, with her mother, Mrs. Bertha Spafford Vester, and her brother, runs Jerusalem's illustrious American Colony. With her was Father Eugene, a genial Franciscan friar who, with others of his order, is a caretaker of Jerusalem's Christian Holy Sights.

The Jordanians are still sharply critical of America's support of the Israelis, and they do not warm up to Americans readily. Still, Tay and I appeared under ideal auspices when we were met by Anna Grace and Father Eugene. One was the daughter of Jerusalem's respected and beloved modern Florence Nightingale —a person who, ever since the days of the Turkish Sultan, has lived and worked for the multi-racial inhabitants of the city that is sacred to three great religions—while the other was a friendly and highly respected member of one of Jerusalem's most important Christian orders.

We rode into the city in Father Eugene's little British Ford and were grimly reminded on the way that all is not well in this divided land. Slowing his car down, Father Eugene carefully zigzagged through several staggered rows of heavy, white, conical blocks of concrete.

"Tank barriers," the Franciscan remarked with unmistakable distaste. And as we entered the city's outskirts we drove in the shadow of a high, thick wall of stone on which turbaned Arabs were still working. This was a protective wall which, running through the very heart of Jerusalem on the Jordan side of no man's land, dramatically cut the Holy City in two with the idea of stopping sniper's bullets from the Israeli sector.

"The too often promised land!" remarked Father Eugene as he turned his car into the American Colony driveway.

The American Colony was founded as a charitable institution in 1881 by Anna Grace Lind's grandparents, who gave up a secure and comfortable life in the States in order to care for Jerusalem's needy, regardless of race or creed. Today it runs a baby nursing home, an infant welfare center, and a general clinic, and it hopes to find funds enough for the creation of a desperately needed hospital. The Colony also operates a hostel as a partial means of support for its charitable work, and it was here that Tay and I put up while we remained in Jerusalem. The hostel and the American Colony Headquarters both stand directly against the defense wall, whose daily progress we noted with keen interest, the more so because distant gunfire in the night grew so common that we ultimately came to sleep through it undisturbed.

Within Jerusalem, no man's land varies in width from a very few yards to several hundred. It is at its widest in front of the American Colony, where it is also distinguished by its desolation and its deserted, partly demolished stone houses. No one has safe access to this forsaken zone except stray dogs and cats, and even they are safe only in the daytime. We were told, in fact, that any person entering this desolate area even to pick daisies would draw rifle fire from both sides.

On one occasion, anxious to get some movies of this tragic area, I poked the lens of my camera across the sandbagged wall in the heart of Jerusalem and nervously filmed the Cathedral of Notre Dame, whose gaping shell holes, I was told, had been made into gun positions. The Arab soldiers who were with me urged me to make my stay on the wall both short and snappy, for I would be plainly visible from the other side, they said, and there was no way of telling what might happen. And then, to emphasize their point, they told me that the spot I had chosen was about where one correspondent had already been shot.

I insisted on making the movie but wasted no time about it. In fact, the scene I shot would surely win a prize for brevity.

The best view of no man's land is from the roof of the Frère's School near the Jaffa Gate through which General Allenby made his triumphal entry into Jerusalem after defeating the Turks in World War I. Tay was with me when we were taken there by an American captain of the United Nations Truce Team, and though we were even more exposed than I had been before, we were now under the protection of the U.N. Thus we were not hurried as we looked down into Israel across a zone of emptiness and ruin beyond which we could see people in the streets a hundred yards away.

Just below us stood a sinister three-story building, with the glass broken from its windows and layers of sandbags piled upon their sills. This, we were told, was "the green house," which greatly concerned the United Nations.

The reason? Under the terms of the armistice, we were told, it was to be occupied only by civilians, but it had nevertheless been heavily fortified by the Israelis. We stood there for a moment looking at the discouraging scene, but the captain then suggested that we remain no longer. The roof top was exposed and there could be no doubt that we were under observation.

The only people who cross from one side of Jerusalem to the other are United Nations' observers and tourists, and the latter are permitted to go only one way—from Jordan to Israel—in the divided City of Peace.

Tay and I were in the Holy Land the whole of the month of August except for the first week after our arrival when we flew 150 miles farther north to Beirut, Lebanon. In this Mediterranean city we busied ourselves for a time writing up our diaries, catching up on our correspondence, swimming, and taking life easy. With that behind us, however, we returned to Jerusalem where, while we drank "lemon squash" one afternoon, we were fascinated by the stories of an English-speaking Jordanian captain of the Arab Legion.

We had had tentative plans that would have taken us on before so very long, but the more our friend, the captain, told us of the force with which he served, the more we were convinced that we should stay in Jordan longer in order to film some of the things he told us. And, so enthusiastic were we over this new idea, that we postponed our departure and flew to Amman, the Jordanian capital, the very next morning. Then, for the next ten days, we commuted back and forth almost every day, for the hotel at Amman could not compare with the American Colony hostel in Jerusalem, and Jerusalem, being closer to the sea, was much cooler at night.

Each morning we would leave the Jerusalem Airport between seven o'clock and eight, returning just before it closed at six—a twenty-minute flight each way across the Jordan Valley. The customs men and the police came to know us so well that they paid little attention to our comings and goings.

"Oh," said one of them as he beckoned us through. "We consider you Jordan citizens now."

Our photographic plan was to follow a young Bedouin from the tent he called his home through his Arab Legion training to his military assignment, and then back to his tent again, though as a local hero now. With this in mind, we spent the first three days at the Arab Legion training center outside Amman, picking out our "star" and taking pictures of various phases of legion training.

Problems arose, naturally, but those that confronted me were much less troublesome than some that confronted Tay.

"Needless to say," she wrote in describing her situation, "certain problems have arisen because I am a woman in the middle of a Moslem Army camp. For one thing, I have found it necessary to wear the one dress I have with me that has sleeves and a high neck. For another, I try to be as inconspicuous as possible, though I certainly feel that all eyes are on me.

"That was especially true one morning when, as I was standing by the roadside waiting for Lowell, a company of recruits came marching by.

" 'How well trained they are,' I thought. 'Marching perfectly—looking straight ahead.'

"But just as they reached me the sergeant barked an 'eyes right' command in Arabic, and instantly I had the whole company staring directly at me as they marched past."

Most of the time we were out around the base, taking pictures, but we often had to visit Jordanians in their offices, and that invariably meant first having a glass—not a cup—of tea. And it was always served so steaming hot that Tay insisted—privately, of course—that if this was to continue we would have to develop asbestos fingers.

Most people, I believe, imagine that the Arab Legion, whose British leader, General Glubb—Glubb Pasha—was so unceremoniously dismissed long after our departure, is made up exclusively of Bedouins. On that account, we explained that we preferred to have a "tent dweller"—a Bedouin—for our hero, though the men of the legion now come largely from the towns and cities. And, having completed our photographic work at the training center, we picked up the star we had selected and, with another cadet as interpreter, flew north over the rolling desert hills to Mafraq, the home of our leading character. The countryside appeared completely barren, but we were assured that in the spring the whole area was green, that flowers were numerous, and many hills were covered with wheat—hills where now, as we flew over, we saw the black tents of the Bedouins, and even saw their herds of goats and camels.

Mafraq was an air base, and once we had parked Charlie, we were whisked away in an Army Land Rover to the home of our star. To our surprise—for we had thought him to be a Bedouin—he lived in an adobe house in a nearby village where, in order to be polite, we went in and met his family.

We were still hopeful of salvaging as much as we could of the story we had in mind, and, having learned that this particular family had no Bedouin friends, we decided to head out into the desert and make ourselves known at the first black tent we came to. And, as luck would have it, we soon came upon a group of four.

No one came out to greet us, perhaps because they thought the legion had come to recruit more men, but when one of our soldiers entered a tent and explained our problem, the Bedouins agreed to "adopt" our star for an hour of picture-taking. They could not have been more considerate, and they co-operated with the greatest gusto, obviously enjoying every moment they spent before the camera.

The tent we chose to be our soldier's "home" was divided into sections—one in which the women did their cooking, and the other where the men were sitting on beautifully woven rugs while they smoked and talked. This, perhaps, was the "living room" while the "kitchen" section was used for everything else, even including three sheep.

"While the men had coffee in the 'living room,'" Tay wrote when she came to set down her account of the visit, "I joined three women in the 'kitchen.' Of course, we couldn't talk to each other, but I made a fuss over their cute, plump children and we admired each other's clothing. I noticed a baby in a tiny canvas crib in a corner, and there were assorted sizes of children peering at me from other dark recesses. There were piles of blankets, too, and cooking utensils, and a big tub of water—probably their entire supply—stood by the door. At the moment I entered a scrawny chicken was drinking from it.

"The women wore plain black dresses, with bright and beautiful embroidery down the front. I wore blue jeans, but I had on a bright red silk blouse over which they ohed and ahed. Then one of them pointed shyly to my very brown arms.

" '*Shamps*,' she said, which was a word I knew. It means 'sun' in Arabic.

"To these bronzed women, who must always live out of doors, any woman not a Bedouin has enviable lily-white skin, but after four months in Africa mine was nearly as dark as theirs. Maybe they thought I was a Bedouin, too, but from a far-off land.

"I had been told that it would be extremely difficult to take pictures of any of these women—that they would not allow it. But when I brought out the camera they could hardly wait to be photographed—perhaps because I was a woman and a friend—and they insisted that I take pictures of each of the children, too."

While Tay was making headway among the women and children, I was winding up my task with our star and the various male members of his "momentary family." Much to my surprise, these Bedouins had fallen in with all our ideas, and with the camera record completed, we thanked our hosts and returned to Mafraq, flying back to Amman that same afternoon.

To simulate the graduation ceremonies of our recruit-star, the Amman training camp arranged a dress parade for us, and we also filmed cavalry drill and artillery practice. And finally, with our movie sequence largely completed, we drove to Qalquilya, a frontier town in northern Jordan, where, for the purpose of the film, our star, his training completed, was to be assigned to a border patrol.

Qalquilya was chosen because it is typical of many border towns which, in the partition of the country between Jordan and

Israel, lost the agricultural land they were formerly dependent upon. Much fighting had taken place here and Qalquilya now occupies a wedge of Jordanian territory that extends far into Israel.

Prior to the establishment of Israel, the people of this vicinity had been successful farmers for centuries, but now that they had lost their fertile land, they had been compelled to turn to the semi-desert hills to the east where, with extensive irrigation, they have made remarkable progress in creating new agricultural land for themselves.

Among the scenes we took in the vicinity of Qalquilya, the most important were of a border patrol simulating some defense maneuvers. Armed and wearing their tin helmets, they ran through a network of communicating trenches, as if to take up their positions in "the front line." And there, with the idea of getting some pictures from in front of them, Tay and I, cameras in hand, went out beyond them, having asked the lieutenant in charge to make certain that the guns, which were now pointed at us, were all unloaded. Most of the men were armed with rifles, but I concentrated on one who had a Sten gun, while Tay, at work with a still camera not far away, was photographing two riflemen who were within her range. Wanting a little action, I asked the Sten gun operator to work the bolt of his weapon, and when he did so, the gun we all thought was unloaded, went off with a sharp report.

The lieutenant, as surprised as we, instantly seized the weapon and emptied it of cartridges, but then I realized that the bullet had cut a shallow little trench in the soil and had buried itself in the ground within a yard of Tay. It had happened so quickly that no one had any feeling of fright, but we were so close to the Israeli border that we began to wonder if that accidental shot might not attract some "return fire." As it happened, nothing of the kind occurred, but it might have, and we all got out of there immediately.

"I've had enough of front lines," said Tay a little later, "to last me a lifetime."

The very next day was our last in Jordan and, in an effort to see something that we had so far missed, we flew to a frontier post in the desert wilderness of southern Jordan about fifteen miles from the Saudi Arabian frontier. The post was Wadi Ram—pronounced Rum—in a region where many border raids formerly took place but which had now grown more quiet. So that we might appear under proper auspices, two Arab Legion friends—Lieutenant Mahmoud and Lieutenant Gazi—went with us. Tay and I, dressed in our oldest clothes and well supplied with sandwiches and water, picked the lieutenants up at Amman and, with them sitting a little uncomfortably on the floor behind our seats where our baggage was usually lashed down, we took off toward Ma'an and Aqaba.

Once past Ma'an, all signs of civilization fell astern except the black line of the tarred road that wound on toward Aqaba. This we followed until, at last, we could make out the Gulf of Aqaba in the distance ahead. Then we turned to the east, and with even the road now out of sight behind us, we began searching for the tiny little fort which was represented by a mere dot on our map and which no doubt would be hard to find in that vast expanse of yellow sand and pink eroded cliffs.

Pink and utterly arid hills and mountains rose here and there, and one, looming higher than the rest, appeared to be Jebel Ram, the mountain that had given its name to the fort of Wadi Ram. And there, after we had carefully searched the sandy valley floor, we found what we were looking for—a tiny speck between two mountain walls.

The canyon in which it lay was hardly broad enough to turn around in, but because both its north and south ends were open we flew right through it with the rocky walls high on either side of us. We had been told that there was a sand airstrip some three miles southeast of the fort, but a mountain rose about there so we searched farther.

While we were circling and searching, Tay got some striking motion pictures of the pink canyon walls that flashed by our wing tips, and finally, after half an hour of this aerial hunting, half a dozen camel riders, hurrying from the fort, directed us to the landing strip which, even when we made it out, appeared to be nothing but a patch of sand that had been cleared of shrubs. It was hardly longer than a football field, was not marked in any way, and worst of all, it was close against the canyon wall.

If I had been in my right mind, I never would have tried to land there. The risks were far too great. As it was, I unwittingly came in downwind, and Charlie shot off the cleared area into the thinly scattered brush, but he missed the larger stones and ultimately stopped safely, though with a whole bush dangling from the horizontal stabilizer.

The six camel-riding Arab legionnaires who had pointed out the airstrip had wisely kept their distance as we came in, but now they came galloping toward us through the sand. Tay said later that the scene reminded her of a Hollywood *Beau Geste* movie— the galloping camels with their red trappings and dangling tassels, the long khaki robes and flowing white sleeves of the riders, the black leather cartridge belts, and the red-and-white checked kaffas, or headdresses—and all this against yellow sand, pink cliffs, and a deep blue sky.

Having welcomed us, these policemen of the desert invited us to a large Bedouin tent just inside the fort compound, Tay riding a camel all the way across the valley. She was a bit frightened when the animal threw her violently backward and forward as it rose to its feet and when, after reaching the fort, it folded them up again with many groans and snarls and dropped to the ground. Actually, I think she would have preferred the difficult walk. And then, for an hour, we sat on leather cushions in the cool half light of the spacious black tent while we were given the traditional Arab welcome. Coffee was poured from a copper samovar—was poured three times as tradition requires—and was followed by hot glasses of tea. Only after this did we venture into the desert sun

Above — The veiled Tuareg chieftain at Goundam, French West Africa, who for his picture "in sixty seconds" gave us the stunning dagger strapped to his arm. Hanging from his neck are leather good luck charms. *Below* — Two Moorish Goumiers, desert police, ride into Goundam from a patrol in the Sahara. Note the numerals branded on the neck of the nearest camel.

Above — A Wagenya chieftain, wearing a necklace of leopard teeth, directs the landing of his village's slender dugout after the boat races at Stanleyville. To the right of the chieftain's feathered headdress a Wagenya woman does her wash in the Congo River. *Below* — The bespectacled chief of the Mangbetus, lolling in his ornate sedan chair during the dance at Paulis in the Belgian Congo.

Above — The Watusi, the "aristocrats of Africa" and the tallest people on the Dark Continent, dance gracefully with spears and bows at Nyanza in the Belgian mandate of Ruanda-Urundi. *Below* — Kilimanjaro! A rare view of Africa's icy pinnacle. At 21,000 feet Charlie swept us right over the great mountain's dead crater and jagged glacier, which is visible just beyond.

Opposite — The legionnaires at Wadi Ram, who patrol the Saudi Arabian border of Jordan, are striking figures with their red-and-white kaffas, flowing white sleeves, cartridge belts and daggers. And their mounts are the best-trained camels we've ever seen. *Below* — A contrast in transportation at Wadi Ram where we've made a barely safe landing in the pink sands of southeastern Jordan and Tay is glad for a lift on an Arab Legion camel.

pposite — A friendly and color-lly dressed nomad woman of fghanistan uses all fours to weave cargo net for a camel. Her jewelry cludes a silver ornament fastened the side of her nose. *Below* — t home with another nomad oman who is preparing to bake a *ippattie,* a thin leaf of bread, over fire of twigs and sun-dried dung thered during the day's migra-on.

Above — Safy, aged leader of our band of Afghan nomads, visits our tent while a girl and a boy peek in amazement at the two *feringi*. Safy is clutching his yellow prayer beads.

Opposite — Hunza Valley! The treacherous trail out. Tay wears the red hat and jacket, and right behind her is her sister, Frances. The fields across the valley are in Nagar state.

Above — Naibullah Beg, a friendly twelve-year-old student at Baltit's Agha Khan school, shows me his text-book. In the upper left background a plume of snow blows from the summit of Raka-poshi, which, at 25,550 feet, is one of the world's highest unclimbed mountains. *Op-posite* — Dancing in Hunza seems to be for men only, like this Hunzukut with sword and ancient leather shield who wears a broad woolen cap and a gown of silk. Part of the orchestra can be seen at the lower left.

Above — Sailing with the "Sons of Sindbad" on an Arabian Nights' adventure across the Persian Gulf on a wooden dhow. Sitting on my left is the captain. The mate is at the wheel behind the compass box.
Below — Looking down from Cotton's Beaver upon the fantastic sand mountains of the great Saudi Arabian desert — the Empty Quarter. Some of those peaks of solid pink sand rise 1000 feet above the desert.

again, visiting the foot of Jebel Ram where the ruins of an ancient Roman temple lay scattered about. Among the rocks across the way we could see the seven stone pillars that some say gave Lawrence of Arabia the title for his famous book, and this reminded me that my father had visited Lawrence in this very valley when, during World War I, the dashing young English leader of the Arabs was making his destructive raids on the Hejaz Railway.

We ate our picnic lunch in the shadow of the fortress wall and were royally entertained by a band of legionnaires returning from a patrol along the Saudi border. Their camels brought them trotting across the sand as they sang their lusty songs.

It was not until the sun slid down behind the peak of Jebel Ram that we took off, clearing the end of the airstrip with space to spare and rocking our wings in salute to our friends as they galloped their camels back to the fort. A little over an hour later, having dropped off the two friendly lieutenants at Amman, we landed at Jerusalem. The next day we flew to Beirut, but there, worse luck, we both came down with miserable colds. However, we managed to catch up on our correspondence and made our plans to fly on to Turkey.

September 12 was the day we took off for Ankara, going by way of the island of Cyprus. It was on this flight that we made the longest open water crossing—about a hundred miles—of our whole trip, and to keep our minds off the waves below we polished off two box lunches (courtesy of Pan American Airways). We stopped at Nicosia (which was peaceful then) just long enough to refuel, and when we took off again we set our course for the Turkish coast across fifty-three more miles of open water, before climbing over the Taurus Mountains and landing at Ankara late in the afternoon after a 350-mile flight.

Here, while Tay went sight-seeing and nursed her cold, I spent almost a week trying to get permission to climb Mount Ararat, which soars to an ice-crowned altitude of 16,946 feet practically on the border between Turkey and the U.S.S.R. Such a climb, of course, would not have been intended to prove anything. There is little thought these days that Noah's Ark ever really came to rest on Ararat, though there is at least a certain poetical fitness to the notion, for the mountain rises more or less midway between the Black Sea and the Caspian, as well as about midway between the Mediterranean and the Persian Gulf. But permission to climb it was not forthcoming, which is not strange. After all, its summit overlooks Russian territory from a part of Turkey that has been "off limits" ever since the close of World War II.

It was on September 18 that we landed in Istanbul, where Tay was really "grounded," this time with an ear infection.

"It all began," she wrote later, "after our flight from Beirut. Autumn had come to the capital of Turkey and it caught us with our summer clothes. We both still had colds from Beirut, and we sniffled our way about Ankara, visiting Ataturk's tomb, wandering through the old section, and paying our respects to various government officials.

"Then, having flown to Istanbul at 8000 feet in order to clear the rugged mountainous area between, we found the deep blue of the Sea of Marmara below us and, with the mosques and modern skyscrapers of Istanbul not far away, we spiraled down over the airfield, losing those 8000 feet in no time at all, our colds completely forgotten.

"It was a sad mistake, as I realized as soon as we had hangared Charlie and found a ride into town. My ear began to ache and by evening I was in agony, pacing the floor of our hotel room."

By morning Tay's ear was even worse, and she also had a high fever. We located a doctor through the Pan American representative in Istanbul, but when he came we found that he spoke no English, while Tay, befuddled with her earache and her fever, was unable to describe her symptoms adequately in French. The doctor frowned and shook his head, though he obviously knew what he was about. He would have to puncture the eardrum, he said, and before Tay could open her mouth to say, "*Mais non,*" it was done.

Tay spent most of the next two weeks in bed, surrounded by

medicine bottles bearing directions in Turkish. We were fortunate to be in a large and modern city rather than in some one of the remote towns or villages we had visited, but even in Istanbul there were problems.

We were staying at the luxurious Park Hotel—the best in the city, for the new Hilton Hotel had not yet been completed. Tay had a breath-taking view of the Bosporus even from her bed, with ships and blue water in the foreground and green hills beyond. All day long, too, she could hear the deep-toned signals of passing ships, the cries of vendors in the streets below, and the muezzin's periodic calls to prayer from a minaret not far from our window. But after four days, to our astonishment, the hotel asked us to leave.

We objected, naturally, but to no avail. Firmly and icily the hotel manager repeated what he had said. We were being asked to leave, bag and baggage, ear or no ear. Our room was needed for a convention group and, for all the management of the Park Hotel seemed to care, we could go and sit on a park bench.

Istanbul was then a "one-hotel city," as it continued to be until the Hilton opened, and such pensions and rooming houses as existed were jammed with tourists. And Tay was seriously ill. In desperation, I went to Charlie Waggoner, our generous friend who is the Pan American Airways' station manager. I explained our situation, and the answer came at once. Charlie and his wife, Ollie, promptly took us in and they treated Tay like a daughter. Furthermore, as if to dispel any sense of homesickness, the nurse who came from the American Hospital to give Tay her penicillin shots was Molly Bliss, a girl with whom Tay had grown up at home in Connecticut.

Meanwhile, I had received word that Cinerama, in which both my father and I were interested, was to be shown at the international fair at Damascus, and with Tay much improved and in the best possible hands, I decided to visit Damascus myself. My purpose in going was to see what kind of reception the visitors, who came from all over the Middle East, were giving Cinerama, and I also hoped to do a film story on the fair. I planned on going alone, but at the last minute Bill Kayser, Pan American's thirty-year-old chief mechanic at Istanbul, decided to come along, and off we went in Charlie on a round-trip flight that started quietly enough, but that ended under conditions that I have no desire ever to see repeated.

XI. From the Golden Horn
to the Land of the Peacock Throne

Iᴛ ɪꜱ 700 ᴍɪʟᴇꜱ ꜰʀᴏᴍ ɪꜱᴛᴀɴʙᴜʟ
to Damascus, and the flight down was a breeze. Bill Kayser, my
companion, whose regular task was to keep Pan American's
enormous DC-6s flying, was taking a kind of busman's holiday,
and he, as well as I, enjoyed the flight. We made it by crossing
the Anatolian Plateau and the Taurus Mountains to Adana, flying
south from there over the Cedars of Lebanon and the Lebanese
Alps. We passed above the ancient ruins of Baalbek and, a few
miles farther on, landed at Damascus, the oldest living city in
the world.

The Damascus International Fair was on, and America's exhibit
featured an Arabic version of *This Is Cinerama,* whose impression upon the Arabs I was anxious to observe for myself after
having heard that its popularity had caused riots—people fighting
by the thousands to get into the open-air theater. One evening in
Damascus was enough to convince me that these reports were
more than true. Even the Syrian Army had been called out to
maintain order at the theater gates. Cinerama had completely
stolen the show at that great fair. So, with little else to occupy us,
our stay in Damascus was short, and the second day after our
arrival, Bill and I took off on the return to Istanbul. However,

we got a late start because of troubles at the Russian industrial exhibit where I tried to rig up lights for indoor movies—not that the Russkies minded, the difficulty had to do with too many volts.

When, at last, we managed to get off, I decided to land at Beirut forty miles away in order to send a case of exposed film to New York by air express, that sort of thing being very difficult in Turkey. The result was that when Bill and I finally made our start for Istanbul, it was nearly three o'clock in the afternoon. Furthermore, in my shirt pocket I now had a weather report that told us of a cold front over Turkey—a front that was expected to weaken with nightfall, though we could not know as yet whether it would break up enough to permit us to make Istanbul. We understood that we might have to land somewhat short of there.

At 3:06 we were over Tripoli, and having passed Tartus and Latakia on our way to a point near Adana, I tuned our long-range transmitter to Istanbul Control's 5551.5 kilocycles and called across the intervening 500 miles.

The pleasant voice of a woman came through my earphones, speaking English that was flavored with an exotic Turkish accent. I reported our position and estimated time of arrival, and requested her latest weather report. She told me that Istanbul's wind was from 270 degrees at five knots—visibility eight miles, broken clouds at 4000 feet, overcast at 8000. She also gave Ankara's weather—wind 300 degrees at seven knots, visibility twenty-five miles with scattered clouds. Both these reports, I noted, showed improvement over the one we had been given at Beirut.

We passed just west of the 11,000 foot ridge of Bulgar Dagh, not far from the narrow rock-walled pass of the Cilician Gates, and then headed out over the Anatolian Plain. We were above the village of Karapinar near the great salt lake of Tuz Golu at five-twelve, but to make this course good I had to hold a ten-degree drift correction, crabbing into a southwesterly wind. I figured our ground speed to be 142 miles per hour and estimated that if it held we would reach Istanbul at seven fifty-five after a total flight of five hours and nine minutes. This, I thought, would leave us nearly an hour's fuel reserve at the low power settings I had chosen—2200 rpm and twenty inches of manifold pressure.

Sunset came at six o'clock as we flew over a solid overcast with tops at 8000 feet—the work of that cold front. The overcast was made up entirely of stratus clouds, with no boiling cumulus, and its leading edge was so clear cut that from our 10,000 feet it looked like the front of an enormous sheet of ice.

Ankara was only twenty minutes away on our right by now, and I thought of going in there while there was still a bit of light. Not to do so would be gambling, all or nothing, for once night had fallen there would be no alternate to Istanbul. Not even the airfield at Ankara, the Turkish capital, was lighted for night landings. Still, Istanbul's weather seemed to be improving, and the cold front looked harmless.

"What do you say, Bill?" I asked my companion. "Shall we go for it?"

"Suits me," he replied. "I'd like to get home tonight."

"O.K.," I agreed. "Let's go on."

Far ahead, against the pink afterglow of sunset, the sky was crystal clear and there were no signs of higher clouds to come. This, too, was reassuring, though when I tried to call Istanbul for another weather report our tiny transmitter was overwhelmed by the more powerful voices of air liners and military planes that were talking with Istanbul, Athens, Rome, Beirut, and even Cairo. My voice was completely lost among all these.

By the time I realized that Istanbul could not hear me, the pink had faded from the western sky and we had been swallowed by the night. The blanket of clouds beneath us hid any ground lights and there was no moon. Oddly enough, I have no recollection of any stars either, though the heavens must have been full of them—an indication, no doubt, of how busy I was watching the plane's instruments and simultaneously studying the map under the little spotlight on the left doorpost. Every time I looked up, the gyros showed Charlie in a turn, and I would have to get him back on course and level again before returning to the map. How I missed my co-pilot navigator! If she had been there she could have taken over the map work, but Bill couldn't. He was a mechanic, not a navigator, and though he had learned to hold Charlie on course during daylight, I could not expect him to fly the plane on instruments.

While I had been fiddling with the radio, the engine had spluttered as the right tank ran dry, and I had switched over to the left, letting the radio go while I checked and rechecked our consumption. The right tank had carried us for two hours and forty-five minutes. At that rate, Charlie would be all done five hours and thirty minutes from the time of our Beirut take-off, not "almost six" as I had supposed.

"How much reserve will that leave us?" I wondered.

I figured it out quickly. The answer was twenty-one minutes— twenty-one minutes, that is, if our ground speed held. But a twenty-one-minute reserve is not much after a flight of more than five hours, and it is dangerously little protection against losing one's way.

I wondered exactly where we were. Eskisehir's beacon—the one crucial fix now—had gone to bed. There was dead silence on the radio where that station should have been, though I had been counting heavily on it. It was one of Turkey's major jet bases, and all my information indicated that it was supposed to operate day and night.

The fact is, though I could not know it then, that if Eskisehir had come through, the radio compass would have shown that we were already drifting off course. Without our knowledge, the wind had swung around from southwest to northeast—perhaps to almost due east, the change having undoubtedly occurred about the time we climbed above the overcast, while I had continued to hold our earlier heading. So, instead of drifting just ten degrees off our course, we were drifting ten degrees plus the effect of the new wind.

We were still too far away to rely on the radio signals from Istanbul, but I tuned in the range station there and heard a solid N signal through the headphones. I watched the needle of our direction finder—our A.D.F.—trying to search out the direction from which the signals were coming, but it swung back and forth through a range of sixty degrees, refusing to make up its mind. Still, its average reading indicated that Istanbul was due north at that moment, not northwest as we were heading.

"No!" I thought to myself, still holding to the course we were flying, "the A.D.F. is crazy. We're still too far out to put any faith in it."

The world seemed terribly small up where we were. We had no sweeping panorama of plains or mountains now from which to pick out check points on the map. We had nothing but the ghostly glow of needles and dials on the instrument panel. To Bill, who sat silently beside me not understanding just what was going on, it may have been as though we were droning along through timeless space, but to me it was a little like being closeted with a ticking bomb, and I was already searching for an escape key as we groped through the dark on what was becoming an almost desperate race with time.

Instinctively, I began to follow the needle of the radio compass, which was still tuned to Istanbul, but then I began a silent conversation with myself.

"If you start wandering," I thought, "you'll never make it. Hold your heading until your estimated time of arrival is up. You just can't be this far off course."

"But what if we are?" my other self asked. "We haven't got much gas."

Ten more minutes and there was no change in radio signals, so I changed our heading desperately, thirty degrees to the right. I was intent on striking the southeast leg of the radio range so that I might follow it in, but even as I was doing all this I still had no realization that we were due south—later we were actually southwest—of Istanbul.

Unable to raise the control tower on the long-range set, I tried them on VHF—very high frequency—and they replied. The weather was worsening, they said. Beneath the overcast, lower clouds were forming.

We were still not any closer to the steady hum of the beam, so I shifted our heading once more—another thirty degrees—to due north. I was frightened now. If the radio compass was wrong and the range signals unreliable, we would soon be flying over the Black Sea with our tanks about to run dry. On the other hand, if the radio was right and I persisted in holding to my dead-reckoned heading, we would wander out over the Aegean— an equally watery grave.

I called the tower again and asked if they would use their direction finder to steer us in, which would give a double check on my A.D.F.

"Four Three Charlie," came the reply. "Sorry. We don't have a direction finder here."

At that I actually broke out in a cold sweat. In fact, I nearly panicked. I could feel it beginning to well up in me. But then I took myself in hand.

"Look!" I said to myself. "If you give up, you've had it. There *must* be a solution. Believe your instruments!"

Although I couldn't see it in the dark I thought of the poem Tay had pasted to the instrument panel in front of her seat:

> *Peace be in thy home*
> *And in thy heart,*
> *Or if thou roam*
> *Earth's highways wide,*
> *The Lord be at thy side*
> *To bless and guide.*

I repeated it to myself and found that it meant as much to me as the blind flying instruments. Then I followed the needle of the radio compass, banking the plane to a heading of twenty-five degrees—then to thirty.

From northwest I had now swung the plane to northeast! "Incredible!" I thought. "But what else to believe?"

In the midst of calling the tower again, the radio failed.

"Check your transmitter," the tower ordered. "You're modulating, but there's no R.T." Which meant that the tower heard only the carrier wave of the transmitter and not my voice.

The trouble was the microphone, but I didn't think of it until several other frequencies also failed. Then, remembering a similar experience in Africa, I rapped the microphone on my knee a few times, and that brought it back to life.

There was not a light beneath us, and the tower reported a solid overcast above Istanbul, so we, at 10,000 feet, could pass directly over the city without ever seeing it. We dared not try slipping beneath the clouds for, not knowing where we were, we might strike a mountain. So the radio compass, though I still questioned its accuracy, was all I had to count on.

Our estimated time of arrival came and went. Our gas dwindled, and the suspense increased as the gas gauge sank farther and farther into the red.

"Why didn't you land at Ankara," I asked myself, "while it was still light?"

The answer was obvious.

"Because I was a damn fool," I thought.

In fifteen hundred hours of military and civilian flying I had had my share of nervous moments, but none of them had ever equaled this. Of course, I should by now have learned about not flying a single-engine plane at night over terrain where no radio aids existed, where there were no lighted airports, and when there was not light enough to land safely in a road or a pasture. And, above all, I should have learned not to fly without ample fuel plus reserve to permit reaching some alternate field in case of necessity.

Even if it were still possible for us to arrive over Istanbul with gas left, what would I do if the airfield, which is directly on the Sea of Marmara, happened to be socked in with fog?

By now the on-course signal of the Istanbul range had grown louder, though I still assumed that we were approaching the southeast leg, not the southwest. But suddenly both Bill and I spotted a faint dome of light in the overcast immediately ahead— the reflected lights of a great city! With only five-minutes gas remaining, we were over the lighted area and the radio compass needle swung 180 degrees.

Our destination was below!

I heard a plane identified as "Clipper Five" call the tower for permission to start its landing descent from 11,000 feet, and I grabbed my microphone. We were over the city at 10,000 feet, I reported, requesting immediate clearance to let down as we were "a bit low on gas."

"Cessna 43 Charlie, Roger," came the reply. "Roger. You are cleared number one."

I pulled back the throttle, and with the rpm's cut to the limit to save gas, I began an instrument letdown through the overcast. I circled to stay within gliding range of the field in case the engine quit, and reported each thousand feet on the way down.

Charlie broke out of the overcast at 2000 feet, with the runway lights to port. We quickly entered the traffic pattern and for the first time in an hour I spoke to Bill.

"Whew!" I exploded. "You can tell your missus you sure had an experience tonight."

I rolled Charlie onto the final approach to the lighted runway, slowed to 100 miles per hour. Then, with flaps down, I slowed to eighty and, from force of habit, I set up a slight power approach, using the engine a bit. I was just congratulating myself on our good fortune when——

Cough—splutter—silence.

We were out of gas, and the engine had quit!

Bill was surprisingly calm.

"Can you make it, Lowell?" he asked.

Flaps down—air speed slow—altitude about 500 feet.

"Bill," I replied, "I don't think so."

Without consciously thinking of what I was doing, I flipped the gas tank selector to the "Both" position. The other tank had run out long before, but perhaps our maneuvers in the overcast might have slopped a few drops of unused gasoline into the stand pipe.

We held our breath as the plane inexorably sank—too rapidly to make the end of the runway.

It was at that very moment that the engine caught and surged momentarily. For perhaps as much as two seconds it pulled strongly. It coughed again and hesitated, but then it pulled once more, for perhaps another two seconds. Then it quit—for good.

It had given us a final three or four seconds of power, but that had been enough. We barely cleared the lights at the head of the runway. The wheels touched and we bounced before settling down.

Charlie had done all he could for one night, and so had Bill and I.

With the propeller standing straight up and down, the plane had just enough momentum to roll off the runway onto a taxiway where Bill and I climbed out.

"Lowell," said Bill, "I could kiss you."

Perhaps he really felt that way but he would almost have been justified, it seemed to me, if he had murdered me on the spot!

Clipper Five—a huge, brightly lighted DC-6—swept in behind us, with what seemed great dignity, and I had to radio the tower that we were out of gas and needed a tow to the hangar. The tower threw a spotlight on us and sent out the gas truck. We took on only a couple of gallons before taxiing to the terminal, and there I apologized to Pan American's freckle-faced Captain Watt, of Clipper Five.

"Well," he smiled, when I explained the situation I had been in. "You've got a good story to tell 'em now."

Bill's wife and their two children were waiting anxiously at the airport, and I'm sure he was never happier to see them. And an hour or so later Tay greeted me in Istanbul. She seemed to know that something desperate had taken place. She told me that when she heard I was coming through, she had looked out the window at the reflection of the city's lights on the overcast and had said a prayer. It is easy to say that Bill and I had reached the Istanbul field "on instruments," but even then I knew that there had been something more.

The next day I got out the maps and reconstructed what must have been our course. To have reached Istanbul on the heading we were on during the final minutes of that flight, we must have flown from the southwest for all of eighty miles, passing in that time over a prohibited area where Turkey has established its jet defenses for the straits. Furthermore, we must have flown over the whole of the Sea of Marmara, and on just about our last drops of gasoline. Not only had we been blown off course, but also the shifting wind had miraculously pushed us along faster and faster. Had there been a head wind, we would never have made it.

But there is another explanation, too.

I was flying without my partner—without Tay whose caution balances my brashness. We had become a team, and when we were separated the result was far from pleasant.

Tay was better by the time I got back from Damascus, and within a week she had the doctor's O.K. to fly again. By that time, too, we had replaced our summer clothes with some winter woolens sent from home and had made our plans to fly on east to Tehran. We tried to express our thanks as we said good-by to the Waggoners. Then we took off for Iran in Charlie, keeping just ahead of the first winter weather and flying over some of the ruggedest terrain so far.

A cold front awaited us between Istanbul and Ankara, but we made our way through it with only a bit of turbulence, and then we had good weather on to Kirsehir. A little farther on, in the neighborhood of Kayseri, the air was filled with dust and sand, after which, for an hour or so, we passed over some of the wildest and most rugged country we had yet seen. It boasted no roads and

few settlements, but we sped across it with a strong tail wind
that boosted our ground speed to as much as 190 miles per hour.

Over Malatya I called on various high-frequency channels to
report our position and got a reply on 116.1 megacycles in Turkish. The operator could not understand English but he knew that
an American plane had called, which would help if we turned
up missing. The Turks would know that we had gotten as far as
Malatya, at least.

Over a beautiful blue lake a few miles south of Elazig we
changed our course toward the Turkish F-84 jet base at
Diyarbekir and when we saw the two-mile-long runway I called
the tower.

"Aircraft 2—3—4—3," a Turk replied in painfully slow English.
"Run-A-Way—three—four."

"O.K.," I replied, but then I thought to use a bit of Turkish I
knew.

"*Tammam. Choc tesakeraderim,*" I added. "All right. Thanks
very much."

"*Besadir,*" came the reply with a smile in his voice. "You are
welcome."

A jeep met us at the taxiway and directed Charlie to a position
close beside a Thunderjet in one of several rows of fighters. The
Turkish air base had been warned of our coming so there were
no delays. With Charlie tied down, we were taken to the officers'
mess for lemonade, and then to the "Tourist Hotel" in nearby
Diyarbekir—an inn that wasn't there when I came this way in
1947 with Max Thornburg, who was surveying the Turkish
economy for the Twentieth Century Fund.

Back at the base next morning we filed a Turkish flight plan
with the aid of an English-speaking Thunderjet pilot who dis-
couraged us from flying to 17,000-foot Mount Ararat by telling
us of heavy clouds in that sensitive corner of Turkey, beside the
U.S.S.R. border. So we agreed to fly directly to the frontier "gateway" that Ankara had instructed us to use, crossing into Iran at
a point on the border due west of Lake Urmia's northern tip.

Once away from Diyarbekir, however, we altered our course a little for Bitlis Gorge, which Max Thornburg and I, with our Turkish companions, had arduously negotiated in a jeep seven years earlier. It was not easy, in that rugged country, to locate this famous landmark, and luck, more than anything else, steered us to the town of Bitlis and then to the narrow gorge itself, through which we flew with the high rock walls on either side of us. I even saw the ruins of Alexander's Castle, where I had picked up a piece of white stone which my father used in building his "History of Civilization fireplace," though I now found that the castle looked remarkably insignificant from the air.

We flew on over the deep blue waters of Lake Van and then over the city of Van which was once the very heart and center of Armenia. Near there, too, we circled the ruins of a once great castle where, seven years before, I had found cannon balls scattered about the plain below.

By the time we reached the frontier, we had climbed Charlie to 10,000 feet, and with a forty-knot wind blowing from behind and across the many ridges, the air was bumpy. Tay was at the controls, for her stomach always behaves better when she does the flying in rough air, and now, even with seat belts fastened, we both bumped our heads against the cabin ceiling. I think we actually crossed into Iran about ten miles south of the prescribed spot, but no border guards fired at us, so far as we know, and Lake Urmia soon appeared ahead.

I tried Tehran Control on 5604.5 kilocycles and though the distance was all of 400 miles the answer came back at once. They read us, they said, at about strength three, out of a possible five, and I reported that we would refuel at Tabriz and expected to reach Tehran two hours thereafter.

We got a purely military reception at Tabriz, though it was cordial enough. They knew we would be landing for fuel some day that month, and we did get it eventually, though the field is used only occasionally, and it was necessary to telephone the representative of the National Iranian Oil Company for the six tins of 91-octane gas we needed—there being no 80 octane. We had to wait an hour, but we had tea with several friendly officers to help pass the time.

We paid for the gas with American "greenbacks," for Ambassador Loy Henderson had told us of Iran's need for dollar exchange. Incidentally, that was the cheapest aviation fuel we ever encountered—twenty cents a gallon, while at home 91 octane sells for about forty cents.

Up again to 10,000 feet, with a gentle tail wind, and we flew eastward over Zenjan and Kazvin. Off on our left rose Iran's Elburz Mountains, which, continuing to the east, reach an altitude of almost 19,000 feet in Mount Demavend—the Everest of the Middle East—whose snow-capped summit can be seen from Tehran.

We were again in contact with Tehran Radio, who, it seemed, wanted our position almost every other minute. We learned later that Steve Campbell, the American Embassy press officer, had phoned for news of our progress and by way of the radio he saved himself a long wait at the airport. As usual, we were behind our estimated time of arrival.

The sun had barely set when we came in for a landing at Mehrabad International Airport, and they flicked on the runway lights for us, though it really was not necessary.

As Charlie glided toward the end of the runway, I remembered how several years before I had arrived at this same field alone and in humdrum fashion on a KLM air liner. I had been a little forlorn then because I had had to leave my girl friend on the other side of the globe, but now she was my "missus," and we were coming in our own "air liner." No wonder I felt pleased.

Steve Campbell was waiting for us. He had served as a navigator-gunner in an 8th Air Force B-17 during World War II and had arrived in Tehran not long before from Paris. He gave us a grand reception and, because he had already greased the wheels of customs and immigration, we were handled like home-coming royalty.

Steve had an Embassy station wagon, and after we tied Charlie down before the Iranian Airways' hangar, he drove us to a new hotel—the Persepolis. It was not the best, he said, but all he could find for us, and we found it occupied exclusively by new "Point Four" Americans who were still apartment hunting. We also found it all we needed—clean, quiet, well run, and with fairly good food—all unexpected commodities throughout most of the East.

I had often told Tay of Tehran, for it is an incredibly colorful place, and now she was able to see it for herself. Not many years ago a wall still surrounded the city, and even the Lalezar—the city's Park Avenue—remained narrow and unpaved. The Ala-Dowleh, too—the "Road of Diamonds"—hardly lived up to its name in those days as it made its way past the Maidan Tupkaneh to the wonderful palace of Gulistan—the "Place of Flowers." But Tehran has changed tremendously in the years since then. Even when I had first seen it, the wall was gone, the principal streets were paved, and this Eastern city of over a million Iranians had already been immensely altered by influences that had reached it from the West.

However, the city's water supply still remained as I had seen it first. The oversize gutters of the streets still flowed with rushing water in which dead leaves, sodden paper, old rags, and scattered bits of garbage drifted with the current. Horse-drawn water carts carried water for those who cared to pay for it, but many of the people of the city dipped their water from the always flowing gutters. Camels, dogs, donkeys, and fat-tailed sheep drank there as well, and little children dabbled in the gutters or waded in them with as little thought as the animals had for the ways in which they contaminated the water. But this ancient water system was scheduled to be replaced soon by an up-to-date one, befitting the modern city Tehran had become.

The city's taxicabs, too, were just as I remembered them— rattletrap, madly driven little vehicles with dented white fenders. And the city's many shops were as fascinating as ever. Tay went wild over their silver and brassware, their inlaid boxes and turquoise jewelry, their delicately painted ivory, camel bone, and mother of pearl. There was silver filigree work so intricate and so delicate in design as to defy description, and Persian rugs of unbelievable beauty were displayed everywhere. Fortunately, Charlie's lack of space placed a severe limitation on the co-pilot's shopping spree, and she finally had to settle for a pair of earrings, which she could sneak aboard in her pocket.

Most of our time in the Iranian capital, unfortunately, was spent in getting travel permits, press cards, and photographic licenses. The American Embassy, and even Ambassador Loy Henderson personally, helped us constantly, and we almost beat a path between our hotel and the Embassy building, which was the last word in modern architecture—red brick and glass. It was functional, of course, but seemed wholly lacking in beauty or style. "Henderson's High School," the Embassy staff called it.

Once our permits were all in order, Tay and I were honored by having a photographic interview with His Imperial Majesty, the Shah and his Queen. Remembering the formalities of the Ethiopian court, we asked the Embassy to tell us what to wear and how to act.

"Don't worry about etiquette or apparel here," we were told. "The young couple prefer informality both of dress and manner."

The Marble Palace is surely one of the world's most beautiful, though it is small, as palaces go, with simple lines. It is a lovely pastel green and we walked toward it through large formal gardens and along a driveway lined by tall pine trees. Red roses circled a fountain at the palace entrance and as we entered we caught a glimpse of snow-clad Mount Demavend far off to the northeast. But though it was in this palace that we saw the Shah and his Queen, they do not live there. Palaces are not built with comfort in mind, and they prefer an ultra-modern home that stands across the street.

Upon entering we were greeted by several morning-coated, white-gloved gentlemen who led the way up a circular marble stairway to an ornate, high-ceilinged room on the second floor. The Shah, we were told, would be a few minutes late, but Queen Soraya would receive us in the meantime. With that, we were ushered in and found the Queen sitting on a couch. Tay curtsied and I bowed, whereupon we walked over and shook the Queen's hand, leaning somewhat awkwardly across a circular table as we did so.

We had seen many pictures of Her Majesty, but now we realized that none of them had done her justice. Her manner was friendly and, surprisingly, she wore a simple pink cotton dress, plain white shoes, and no ornaments or jewelry at all except a diamond wedding ring.

For half an hour the three of us chatted quietly. She likes sports, and we talked of skiing and swimming, and of her coming trip with the Shah to the United States, but our conversation was beginning to wear thin when in sauntered His Imperial Majesty, Shah Mohammed Riza Pahlevi—the Darius of today— wearing a tweed sport coat and gray slacks.

I had met the Shah on my first visit to Iran, and I noted that he looked both older and grayer now, which was not surprising after the dark years he and his nation had just passed through. But His Majesty is an aviation enthusiast, and we were soon discussing the pros and cons of single-engine airplanes, of retractable landing gear, and other technical matters. He seemed quite impressed by Charlie's performance and even appeared to be a little envious of us.

As the end of our visit approached, the Shah took us down a corridor to the fabulous crystal ballroom of the palace, the walls of which are covered with thousands of tiny pieces of glass. When he turned on the lights of the many crystal candelabra, the twinkling and sparkling all about us was breath-taking.

From there we went to the garden to take some pictures and it was beside the pool that we said good-by, as informally, I think, as if we had been parting from acquaintances back home.

Tay and I had taken advantage of our visit at the palace to

mention a particular project we had in mind. Americans, I had remarked, would be interested to learn that the very best grade of caviar comes from Iran and not from Russia.

"Apparently," I said, "those big sturgeon don't like communist waters."

The Shah laughed.

"Yes," he replied. "They are capitalist fish—war mongers."

And His Majesty referred us to his Minister of Court for the special permits we would need to visit the southern coast of the Caspian Sea. To my surprise, this official turned out to be an old acquaintance of mine—Hussein Ala, who, a few years ago, had been the Iranian Ambassador to the United States, and I called on him at once. Mr. Ala was most helpful, and as a result, Tay and I, a few days later, went to the Caspian fishing center of Pahlevi just a few miles from the Russian border. We moved about under almost constant military supervision, for until the year before, and ever since 1876, these fisheries had been carried on by the Russians. Though the fisheries had now been national-ized by the Iranian Government, Russian sympathizers were still numerous in the vicinity of Pahlevi and because of that, as well as because we were the first Westerners to photograph the opera-tions, it was suggested that without military protection, our cam-eras, our exposed film, or even we ourselves might not be safe.

During our visit the fishing fleet was at sea and we saw nothing of it, but we did see sturgeon being caught in an enormous, 3000-foot net, and watched the caviar as it was processed, salted, graded, and refrigerated—the small black eggs of the lower grades, and the yellow caviar of higher quality. The rare "golden" caviar is not often found in quantity, and it is usually reserved for gifts to the Shah and to other people of importance. Because we are not caviar connoisseurs, the various grades made little difference to us. In fact, we are none too fond of the prized dish and it was with great reluctance that we tasted the endless samples. But politeness demanded that we do so, and by the end of the day we felt like sturgeon ourselves! That was when the Russian-

trained director spread an outdoor table with Vodka, wine, and—
for each of us—a large tin of those unwelcome eggs.

On Sunday, October 17, after our return from Pahlevi, Tay
and I made a sound film with His Imperial Majesty, the Shah. It
was done in the beautiful garden of his green Marble Palace, and
later that day, with Charlie carefully packed again, we took off
on our way east across northern Iran, bound first for Meshed,
the capital of the Iranian province of Khurasan, and then for
Afghanistan still farther to the east.

It is nearly 500 miles from Tehran to Meshed by the dirt road
we planned to follow, and we were determined to watch that
road carefully. It would not only be wise to be close to it in case
of trouble, but also Russian territory lies within fifty miles or so
of Meshed and we feared that without the road to follow we
might stray across the frontier.

Hoping to reach Meshed's gravel airstrip before dark, we
planned to take off by one o'clock in the afternoon, but we were
delayed. There were the usual pre-flight chores—weather reports,
flight plans, and the rest. There were customs and immigration
officials to satisfy. There were landing and housing fees to pay.
There was the fueling to be attended to and, because some of
this went slowly, it was two-fifteen before we taxied to the runway
and took to the air.

Tay, seeing the delay build up, prudently suggested postponing
our take-off until the following morning, but the sweat was in
my eyes, my temper was short, and I could not see canceling the
flight now and repeating the whole complicated process the next
day.

"Nuts!" I said. "We can still make it before dark. 'Weather'
forecast a tail wind from the ground up. Now, just relax."

By the time a slow climb-out had lifted us to 10,000 feet we
were nearly a hundred miles along our way, coming up on the
village of Samnan. The sky was cloudless and calm, the visibility
practically limitless. To our left the Elburz Mountains separated

the Caspian Sea from Iran's arid plateau. Twisting about in my
seat a bit I could still see Mount Demavend, and far off on our
right, where the horizon shimmered with a white glare, stretched
the desolate region of Dasht-i-Kavir, an utterly barren salt desert
as large as New Hampshire and Vermont combined.

A few days before, when I had shown my Tibet film at the
United States Information Service Library in Tehran, we had
met David Nalle, a United States vice-consul stationed at Meshed, and had told him that we would be flying his way.

"It's pretty dark by five at Meshed," he had said.

I had not thought much about it at the time, but his remark
came back to me now. It was three o'clock, and we still had the
better part of 400 miles to go.

The weather forecast had told us to expect a tail wind of
twenty-five miles per hour, but when we passed the town of
Damghan, some seventy-five miles beyond Samnan, a time-dis-
tance check with the computer told us that we were making
only our true speed of 150 miles per hour. In other words, there
was no tail wind at 10,000 feet and on that basis we would not
reach Meshed before five forty-five.

It is no wonder that I began to be impressed by what David
Nalle had said.

"We'll be O.K.," I thought. It might be cutting things a bit
fine, but we had landed at Tehran at six o'clock when we ended
our flight from Turkey. True enough, they had turned the runway
lights on, but there still had been light enough to see the ground
quite clearly.

This made me feel a little better. It wasn't until later that I
began to remember what two weeks in the fall can do to the
time of sunset, and I had quite forgotten to consider the loss of
sun time on a flight of three and a half hours to the east at 150
miles per hour.

I was bothered a bit, but the first real alarm did not come until
we were in the vicinity of Sabzawar, about 130 miles short of our
goal. It was there that I was struck by the long shadows below

us—long shadows that were cast by the sun as it neared the horizon.

I put Charlie into a gradual descent until we were within a thousand feet of the ground, for I did not want to lose touch with it as I had done over Turkey.

Fifty minutes to go.

"Well," I thought. "There'll be enough twilight to find the field. There's bound to be."

It was about then that Tay tactfully suggested that we land on the road and spend the night in our sleeping bags.

"It would be fun," she remarked.

But I had no desire to make my first road landing on the rutted and narrow road below, especially with our heavy load.

"We'll do that some other time," I replied, "when we're not so loaded. We'll make Meshed all right. Now, just don't worry about it."

And I went right ahead into a self-made trap.

The trap really began to close about the time we passed Nishapur, fifty miles or so short of Meshed. It was there I realized that a road landing would be extremely hazardous. The fast-gathering gloom was already hiding the pot holes. The time? It was thirteen-forty Greenwich Mean Time—five-ten local.

The American vice-consul had not been exaggerating when he said, "Pretty dark by five."

I still insisted to myself that there would be just enough light to find the airport. With our landing lights, that was all we would need. I would make a steep, full-flap approach, landing a third to halfway down the 5000-foot-long gravel strip. That couldn't fail to clear any wires, high trees, or stacks obstructing the approach, and we'd still have ample room to stop.

I kept a close eye on the road below and to the left, following every turn. There were several long straight stretches with the occasional splash of headlights which were now more apparent than the trucks or buses that threw them.

But now the trap snapped shut. Twenty-five miles south of

Meshed the road was supposed to turn ninety degrees north, for a straight run to our goal.

Maybe it did, but we could not see the turn in the gathering dark.

The Meshed beacon, which was classified in our facility information as "unreliable," proved to be just that. It was operating, but even this close our direction finder would not "home" on it. The little white needle just kept searching around the dial.

Well, I insisted to myself, we didn't need the beacon anyway. Or did we?

From our last-known position a few minutes back—if it was accurate—I figured that by turning to a heading of about five degrees we should soon bring up the lights of Meshed.

"What if the town hasn't heard of electricity?" I thought.

Tay was as quiet as a mouse, but her silence spoke volumes. She probably was wondering why I hadn't learned anything from my experience over Turkey.

I was thinking, now, about what to do if we couldn't find Meshed and had decided that our best bet would be to dead-reckon back to that straight section of dirt road. There I would hope to find the headlights of a truck which, with our landing lights, might get us down all right. It would be quite a gamble, yet far better than a blind stab at the black and unknown ground.

But now we began to see the lights of a city ahead.

Was it Meshed? Or had we erred in our navigation and made our way across the U.S.S.R. border to Ashkhabad or someplace else. Ashkhabad, of course, was 125 miles from Meshed, but the border wasn't. It was only forty-seven miles away—less than twenty minutes at 150 miles per hour! And if this was Russia, what kind of a welcome would we get?

We were approaching the scattered lights from the south, and I called Tehran on our high-frequency set. (I had been giving them our position every half hour.)

"Please stand by," came a voice—from Bahrein, of all places—

Bahrein, on the Persian Gulf. "You are blocking out an Air Force plane."

But I was not "standing by" for anybody but Tehran. Nor did I have time or inclination then to marvel at the fact that our light-plane, high-frequency transmitter was interfering with a station nearly 900 miles away, in a far-off land of pearls and oil.

The Tehran operator got my query, instructing me to hold on while he looked up Meshed in his airport directory.

Now, near the outskirts of the city, we saw two short rows of fires that looked promising, and the headlights of cars blinked on and off.

Tay was the first to see the vague, shadowy X of the field's two strips, and I blinked our landing lights.

"Tehran Control," I said into the microphone. "This is 2343 Charlie. We are over the Meshed airport now, about to land. Thank you very much for your help. Four Three Charlie out."

Tehran acknowledged and I circled the field, letting down slowly onto a wide base leg—onto the final approach with full flaps. Our landing lights were on and as we passed low over the cars I saw a man standing near one of them.

Our wheels touched a trifle sooner than I expected and we bounced into the air like a jumping bean. The last flare fell behind, for they had been strung along only the first hundred yards of the strip.

Now we bounced again and then were down to stay. Not a landing to brag about, but one we wouldn't soon forget.

Headlights bobbed up and down in the dust we had raised and, as Tay and I jumped out, the first car stopped beside our port wing and a man stepped to the ground.

"Glad you folks made it!" said the voice of the American consul.

I don't remember just what we replied, but we were glad we had made it, too.

XII. Among the Nomads
of Afghanistan

Meshed, the most impor-
tant city of northeastern Iran, is "the place of martyrdom" to the
Shi'ite sect of Moslems. In the year 819, Abul Hassan Ali, Al
Reza, the eighth "imam" of the Shi'ites, died in the nearby village
of Sunabad, a victim, the Shi'ites believe, of poison. A shrine
was erected to his memory in Meshed and this soon became the
most venerated spot in Iran, attracting pilgrims from all this portion of the Moslem world, and adding additional significance to
Meshed, which was already an important center of trade.

Unfortunately for Tay and me, our plans gave us little time
in the city, and we were unable to visit its mosques and shrines.
We much appreciated our Consulate's hospitality in putting us
up and in holding a reception for us on the evening of our arrival.
We were grateful, also, to the American members of Point Four
who later showed us something of their agricultural work with the
farmers of the area. But our excitement was so intense at the
prospect of flying into Afghanistan—long a forbidden land even
to visitors on foot—that Meshed figured in our minds as little
more than a new jumping-off place, and we soon found ourselves
in the air again.

A white ribbon of trail beneath us wound like a faint scar
southeast across the dry brown plain and over the occasional ridges

and mountains of red rock. Here and there by the side of the trail
we spotted the ruins of some old fort or caravanserai. Now and
then Charlie's shadow flitted over groups of travelers on the trail—
travelers who must have been conscious of the fact that such law
as existed in the country they were crossing rested, for the most
part, in the rifle that was slung over each man's shoulder or the
knife that was thrust into his belt.

The trail was the main road from Iran to Afghanistan, and it
would lead us, ultimately, to the Afghan capital of Kabul, which,
by the indirect route we would have to follow, was some 900 miles
ahead. There would be difficulties on the way, of course. For one
thing, Afghanistan is still a new land for travelers from the west.
For another, our American maps were none too accurate. And
for a third—though we did not know it at the time—we were
making the very first flight by private aircraft across this wild
country. It is no wonder that permission for our flight had neces-
sitated months of correspondence with the American Embassy at
Kabul and much work on their part.

The Embassy's first reply to us had warned that there were no
radio aids in Afghanistan, and that there would be no "search and
rescue" if we were forced down. There was not even any aviation
gasoline, a difficulty which had stymied us until, one day in
Beirut, we had a remarkable stroke of luck. We met the only man
in all the East who could solve that problem for us. He was an
American, Kochenderfer by name, who was the manager of Air
Jordan, a two-plane air line that once had had a contract to haul
Afghan Moslems to Mecca during the pilgrimage season. He said
that we were welcome to some tins of 100-octane gasoline he had
abandoned at a desert airstrip near Kandahar, an Afghan city
which is within a hundred miles of the Baluchistan border, about
halfway from the Iranian frontier to Kabul.

Here was a near miracle, for without Kochenderfer's generous
offer, Tay and I and Charlie would have had to fly east by way
of the normal air-line route, following the shores of the Persian
Gulf and the Arabian Sea to Karachi, and we would have missed

one of the most colorful experiences of our year-long journey. Charlie just did not have the range to fly from Iran to Kabul and then on to Pakistan without refueling.

It was 600 miles, or a trifle less, from Meshed to Kandahar. For 200 miles, we followed the trail that led southeast and east to the ancient Afghan walled city of Herat. From there we headed south for an hour or so, before turning east once more for another 225 miles, and finally reaching the Kandahar airstrip. We had been in the air a little more than four hours from Meshed but we had been guided by a series of trails and roads that a caravan could not have traveled in a month.

Time was when Kandahar was the largest city in Afghanistan, but that is true no longer. It is now far surpassed by Kabul, the capital, but even yet this lesser city is the center of an irrigated region in which orchards and vineyards are unusually luxuriant. And because of several colossal dams that have been built in southern Afghanistan through American aid, it is likely that Kandahar, in the years ahead, will regain at least some of the importance it has lost.

This old city, incidentally, was chosen for the headquarters of the Morrison-Knudsen Company, the American construction firm that has built the new dams, and burly Dan Butler, the company's administrative officer in Kandahar, helped locate the tins of the Air Jordan 100-octane gasoline that Mr. Kochenderfer, in Beirut, had told us we might have. The fact that we actually found it intact still strikes me as a minor miracle. Why those tins of gasoline had not been taken over by Afghan bus drivers is more than I will ever know.

Dan Butler, having located our gasoline for us, also put us up for the night at the Morrison-Knudsen camp—an unexpected treat that was doubly welcome because of the camp's supply of American beer and ice cream.

It was the next morning that we took off on the last leg of our journey to Kabul. We were flying now above the number-one highway of a country that until recent years was forbidden to all outsiders because of its strategic location between Russia and British India. But centuries before Britain came to be a power in Asia, this land had been one of the crossroads of the East. Because it is a gateway to India, Afghanistan, since ancient times, has been churned into dust by one marching army after another—Scythian, Greek, Persian, Tartar, Mongol, Durani—and Alexander the Great himself, nearly twenty-three hundred years ago, not only entered Afghanistan from Persia by much the same route we had taken, but also followed the very road above which we were flying now on our way to Kabul.

As we penetrated more and more deeply into this mountainous portion of Central Asia, the barren earth kept rising until at an altitude of 9000 feet, we were barely skimming the trail. We were over the beginnings of the Central Asian highlands, which culminate in the mighty peaks of the Hindu Kush, the Karakoram, and the Himalayas beyond which, 600 miles or more east of where we now were, lay the elevated and wind-swept plains of Tibet.

The road below us was usually without a sign of life, but after a time we were surprised to see in the distance what almost appeared to be another army of invasion—a great column that was miles in length. As we sped closer, however, we saw that this was not an army. Instead, it was a migration—a great movement of nomads with their flocks of sheep and goats, and their heavily laden camels. Here was a scene that seemed to have been lifted from the distant past—something not unlike what had existed here even before the time of Alexander—for these were people on their autumn migration from the mountains of Afghanistan to their winter grazing grounds in the Indus Valley across the frontier of neighboring Pakistan. We were tempted to land on the trail and join them, but we knew better. These nomadic people might have considered us and our belongings a gift from Allah.

They all looked up, a few waved, and, so far as we could see, there was only one unfriendly act. One man hurled a rock at us.

We were glad he did not fire his rifle, for at 500 feet we would have been a handsome target.

The nomads and their animals disappeared behind us and before long, through a pass in the mountain wall ahead, we caught the glitter of sunlight on windows—Kabul!

Zooming through that pass, up each side of which an ancient, crumbling defense wall ran, we made a fast, low circle over the city in a gesture of salute before searching out the grass airstrip a few miles to the north.

Having landed, we were cordially greeted by several members of the American Embassy staff, who expressed their relief to know that we had not "gone missing." Also on hand were representatives of the Afghan Government, one of whom—His Excellency Abdul Wahab Tarzi—was especially interested in us because he remembered my father's visit to Kabul thirty-four years earlier. It is no wonder that he recalled that visit, for Dad had arrived after a journey through the Khyber Pass in a Buick touring car that must have been one of the first autos ever to reach Kabul. In his book *Beyond Khyber Pass*, my father wrote that the car practically had to leap from boulder to boulder, and that "on our entire journey from the Khyber Pass to Kabul and return we averaged a puncture an hour."

Kabul, which is located at the foot of a bare and rocky ridge on the western side of Kabul Valley, is hemmed in by mountains and, except to the north, has no room to expand. For ages it has been the key to northern India, and it also commands the passes from the north through the Hindu Kush, as well as the pass from the west through which we had flown.

It is most definitely a city of the East, its narrow streets crowded with camels, veiled women, and what appeared to be turbaned descendants of Genghis Khan. Within high adobe walls were lovely gardens shaded by fruit trees. Time was when the roads leading to Kabul were all but impossible for wheeled vehicles, but that is true no longer.

Throughout our visit in the city one thought was foremost in our minds—to find some way of joining, at least for a few days, one of those bands of migrating tribesmen. We talked the idea over with Charles Little, who, as chargé d'affaires, was for the time in charge of our Embassy, and I broached the subject when I was received by the Afghan Prime Minister, Sardar Mohammed Daoud. At first I was doubtful of getting permission but, to my surprise, the Prime Minister liked the idea.

With that much accomplished, we were soon on our way, carrying, as interpreter, a young government official named Amin. Our destination—the town of Khost—was within a thirty-mile strip along the Pakistan border that is normally forbidden to foreigners because of the tension between the two countries—tension which, since our return to America, has verged on war. The trouble has been over the question of an independent state for some seven million Pushtu tribesmen who live in Pakistan just east of the frontier in a belt of land that parallels the border for a thousand miles, from the Hindu Kush Mountains in the north to the Arabian Sea.

Pakistan has claimed and governed this whole region ever since Pakistanian self-rule was established, but Afghanistan—itself a Pushtu state—has been insisting that its brothers be permitted to establish their own sovereign state. Pakistan's loss, of course, would be Afghanistan's gain, so it is not surprising that trouble has developed, or that the Russians, with their genius for creating difficulties, have egged on the Afghans.

When Tay and I, with Amin, our interpreter, climbed away from Kabul one morning in October, we were bound for a region which foreigners are rarely permitted to visit because of the trigger-happy tribesmen whose allegiance is so questionable, though perhaps the government was willing to have us run the risk of proving that this frontier region was not so wild and dangerous as is commonly believed.

We followed the road south for some sixty or seventy miles to the town of Gardez, turning eastward there and climbing to 11,000 feet in order to cross a range of mountains which, by way of a series of gorges, dropped steeply down on the other side to a 3000-foot tableland. Winding through one of these gorges was a caravan of tribesmen with their camels, donkeys, and flocks of sheep and goats—nomads such as those for whom we were looking.

Twenty miles east of the mountains we found Khost, with a landing area that had no boundary markers or runways. It lay beside a fort about which we had been told, and someone had thoughtfully lighted a heavily smoking fire to show us the direction of the wind.

I landed carefully and taxied toward the fort, where a group of officers and others awaited us, while in the distance soldiers were holding back swarms of villagers and tribesmen who had hurried to the field. One officer, who spoke a little English, told us that ours was the first plane to arrive in a year and that it was fortunate he had been advised of our coming, otherwise we might have cracked up in one of the ditches or pot holes that his soldiers barely had time to fill.

We got Charlie tied down just as a jeep station wagon arrived in a swirl of dust with the local administrator—the governor of the prefecture of Khost, Abdul Rahman. He was a middle-aged man dressed in nondescript Western clothes, and he drove us to his two-story residence a few miles away. There, over a cup of tea and through our interpreter, we outlined our intentions.

The governor seemed ill at ease as I suggested hiring horses and pack animals and striking out along the river until we came upon a nomad encampment. In fact, he frowned on our idea, and we were thankful later that he did, for back in Kabul we were told that at that very moment Russian agents were active among some of the tribes of that area.

Instead of accepting the suggestion we had made, the governor sent out an aide to locate a trustworthy band—if "trustworthy" is the right word for people who are so independent that they wander back and forth between Afghanistan and Pakistan, owing allegiance to neither, and who are loosely organized into tribes that are often at each other's throats. They even unite occasionally against the Kabul government. Their exact numbers are unknown, but one estimate was two million, which, in a nation of only twelve million, is quite a sizable minority, especially as they are indomitable fighters. Even the long arm of Great Britain in its heyday on this frontier was never able to subjugate them.

The result of Governor Abdul Rahman's scouting was that we were ultimately sent by jeep some thirty miles west of Khost, where we alighted at the entrance to a gorge and were greeted without excessive cordiality by scores of tribesmen in robes and turbans, with bandoleers of cartridges across their chests and rifles over their shoulders. Nearby was their camp of the moment, a cluster of black tents set up in a dry stream bed.

Amin, our interpreter, suggested apprehensively that we enter the camp and try to make friends, for in the end their acceptance of us depended upon the impression we made. So Amin and I marched forward, Tay bringing up the rear, as was proper and fitting in a land where women are mothers and servants, period.

We walked up to a group of elderly men who rose as we neared the tent before which they had been sitting. They had an air about them of "Who the devil are these funny people?" but they shook hands with us, voicing loud "*salaam a laicums.*" The eldest, in his bearded seventies, beckoned us into his tent, and his women, when we entered, hurried to spread rugs for us to sit on. The tent, I noticed, was made of the same black hair as the tents of the Sahara, but its arrangement was different. A rectangular area open to the sky was surrounded by four curtains hanging to the ground from poles. In the heat of the summer, no doubt, the tent was closed overhead and opened at the sides.

Our bearded host, who spoke for the group while everyone stared at us, was a colorful character. His face was round and genial, and his teeth were stained. He wore a dusty white turban, a faded, ankle-length robe, and leather sandals that showed some mileage. Speaking in Pushtu through our interpreter, he said that

Allah had directed us to his tent, and that he was happy—that we were a feast for his eyes.

I replied by saying that we hoped his journey had not been too arduous, and that his tribe had had a prosperous summer. And had he seen our plane as we had come over the mountains?

"Yes," he replied. "We were just coming through the pass. You were higher than the birds."

From this we knew that the long procession of animals and people we had seen in one of the gorges was this very band.

We came to the point slowly, as one must in the East. I explained that we had heard much of the tribes of Afghanistan, and that we admired their determined struggles for independence. We hoped, I added, that we might pass some days with his band so that we might tell the people of America how they live. Would it be possible?

Without a moment's hesitation our elderly host replied that Allah had surely guided our footsteps—that he and his people would be happy to have us whether for a day, a month, or a year. Whatever was theirs was ours. Allah and they would be our protectors.

Such Moslem expressions of welcome have a very genuine meaning, but, like many in the English language, they should not be taken too literally. Still, his welcome was reassuring, so we picked a vacant area of gravel—which was already generously sprinkled with goat dung—and unrolled a tent we had borrowed in Kabul. It was a wonder we ever got it up, for we were surrounded on every side by helpers, but once it had been erected, rugs were brought for us and spread before the entrance and everyone crowded around to see what we would do next.

Women poked their heads into the tent and offered their rough and calloused hands to Tay in welcome, smiling and saying in Pushtu, "May Allah bless your tent." They were dumfounded by our Primus kerosene stove—the first they had seen—when Tay heated a can of soup.

While she prepared our supper—which consisted only of that

can of soup and some flat strips of Afghan bread—I continued my conversation with the bearded one. His name, he told me, was Safy, and that of another elderly leader was Gulbehar. With the help of Amin, I learned that we were with two clans—one of the Dowlat-Zai, and the other of the Taghar tribe. They numbered sixteen tents—about one hundred and twenty people. The tribes were large aggregations of people, the Dowlat-Zai alone numbering, roughly, about 11,000.

The fall migration was under way, and already they had come more than halfway to their winter pasture on the frontier, in a valley known to them as "Black Water." With their flocks of sheep and goats, and with more than a hundred camels, they had already traveled more than sixty miles from their high summer pastures above the valley of the Shiniz River, west of the town of Gardez, and they would return there in the spring. Their migration, each way, takes about a month, with the necessary stops to graze their animals.

When I asked Safy how long his people had been making these annual migrations in search of grass, he specifically named eight generations, but he admitted that beyond that the past was shrouded in mist, for there are no written records.

The wealth of these nomads is measured in livestock—principally in camels—upon which they are taxed by the Kabul government.

"Ah!" I thought. "Taxes. Here is something we have in common."

Gulbehar, the other leader, said that they were called upon to pay ten afghanis—about twenty-five cents—for each camel, and two afghanis for each donkey, goat, and sheep, though there was no tax on horses.

"Where do you get the tax money?" I asked.

"From the sale of some of our milk and wool," Safy replied. "We also barter these products for salt, sugar, tea, and some of our clothing."

The two tribes represented by this group, I learned, were increasing in numbers, the average now being between five and ten people per tent. And, though there are no doctors among them, their health is better than it formerly was.

"How about tribal warfare?" I asked.

"Not like it used to be," I was told. "Everything is peaceful now."

"Why, then," I asked, "do your men carry rifles and daggers?"

Safy smiled and explained that both families and herds need protection, for everything they own goes on these migrations. The rifles, Gulbehar added, were captured from the Pakistanis in 1942 while the British still ruled India.

"Do any of your children," I asked, "ever give up this life for the village or the city?"

"Never," was the answer. But I was told that above anything else, they want land of their own on which to settle, so that they might have permanent homes. They had heard of the government's scheme for settling destitute nomads on new tracts of irrigated land about to be opened up in the Helmand Valley west of Kandahar where, before the coming of irrigation, there had been little but shifting sand. That was where the American firm of Morrison-Knudsen was at work on their enormous dams—a project which the Kabul government hopes will eventually provide enough cultivable land for the country's many nomads, thereby eliminating the constant threat to the government their restless status poses, and also removing the feared possibility that Pakistan (if the drive for an independent Pushtunistan fails) will gain the allegiance of these sturdy warriors.

Just before dark, but after our meager dinner of soup and unleavened bread, Safy came to our tent with something wrapped in cloth. It was a dozen eggs, which were most welcome. We hard-boiled some of them then and there against the danger of breakage, and kept a few for soft-boiling the following morning.

The nomads were planning, Safy told us, to move on at the first light of dawn, for it was twelve miles to the next water and the animals must get there in time to spend the afternoon grazing.

Would five o'clock be too early for us? If so, we could probably catch up with them by midmorning. I replied that whenever they were ready, we would be, but that we would need a pack animal or two to carry our gear. These, he said, could be supplied.

With nothing better to do, and with the next day's early start in mind, we blew up our air mattresses, slid into our sleeping bags, and were dead to the world by eight o'clock. So were the surrounding tribesmen, except for a few men talking by a fire and a ring of young warriors posted around the camp as guards.

The peace of the night was frequently shattered by barking dogs. About midnight, when the rising wind set our tent to flapping noisily, one dog circled around us yapping madly until Amin, who slept across our doorway, and I drove him off with a shower of rocks. These nomad dogs are a vicious lot, their job being to protect their master's tents, which they do so conscientiously that we had been warned not to walk about during the night.

"The dogs are cruel," said Safy.

We knew our friends would need no more than an hour to eat their morning bread and curds, to pack their camels and donkeys, and to begin their march. We meant to rise at four so as to be ready when they were, but it was not until five that we awoke to the gurgling growls of unwilling camels being loaded. Some were already leaving, as we could see when they passed between us and the faintly lighted eastern sky.

We had slept fully clothed, so dressing was no problem, and I had no need to shave. We didn't even want to wash, for the only available water was in a muddy ditch that the animals had been using. So we used the emergency supply we carried in our two canteens, wondering what we would do when that was all gone, and soon had our breakfast of soft-boiled eggs, Nescafé, and a melon the governor had given us.

While we were eating, someone came for the rugs and tent poles they had let us borrow the evening before, and we paid the price for oversleeping when the tent collapsed around us.

Safy and several others came up with two donkeys and a horse, and, when we began fumbling awkwardly with our tent and other belongings, two or three nomad experts, with a few mutterings and laughs, swept up everything like magic, stowed it efficiently on the animals, and we were off, though we were a good hour behind those who had been the first to leave.

"Boy!" I thought. "You don't begin to know a trail until you walk it. Just look at that dust!"

The people and the animals that had preceded us had churned the trail into deep dust. Our shoes sank almost out of sight, and a suffocating cloud of dust enveloped us, but after a time we caught up with the rear guard—women and children walking in little groups—donkeys and camels shuffling along.

Once under way, the camels—all of them dromedaries with single humps—stopped grumbling and accepted their fate. They were moving forward silently now, some with babies and chickens lashed securely on their loads of blankets, tents, poles, and cooking pots. The babies accepted it all without concern. They were wrapped in blankets against the morning chill, and as they bobbed to and fro in rhythm with their mounts, some of them nibbled crusts of bread or sucked on corncobs. One camel appeared to be carrying only a pile of blankets, though closer inspection revealed two tiny hands sticking out of a carefully contrived fold.

Farther ahead, a wizened old woman sat cross-legged under a great black shawl on one of the camels. The old and the sick, as well as the very young, get first-class passage on these migrations. Two lambs that were too small to walk so far, thrust their heads out of the rear of one camel's load, and a tiny puppy, precariously balanced on all fours and in danger of falling overboard, was on top of another, while a rooster, obviously experienced and unperturbed, squatted silently beside the puppy. But a little later, hearing a great squawking and fluttering, we saw a white hen with a string tied around one leg, as she dangled upside down between the hind legs of a camel, protesting vigorously until someone came up and tossed her back on the load again.

We plodded on, mile after mile. Where we were, everything was dust, but farther away were green slopes and pine-covered mountains. Far, far away to the north, the snowy summits of the Hindu Kush stood against the sky. We passed through a tiny village of mud huts. Village dogs snarled at nomad dogs. Village children taunted the children of the caravan, and everyone looked at us—the two *feringi*—wondering, perhaps, whether we were white slaves or just plain crazy.

As we passed through settled areas, the women and little girls fanned out on either flank, scouring the already harvested fields for anything that might burn in that evening's campfires—dry twigs, strips of bark, wood from tree stumps, and certain kinds of sun-dried dung—all of which they thrust into their upturned aprons.

For three hours we plodded along, turning down occasional offers to trade places with the elders who rode small but sound-looking horses. But eventually we had to give in, and I must say that half an hour in a saddle was welcome for, foolishly, I was wearing a new pair of boots.

Since women scarcely rate at all in that nomad society, a tiny donkey was thrust under Tay just as she was about to collapse, and her toes, as she rode, actually trailed in the dust. She was surrounded by women who not only kept her miniature mount going by pounding him on the rump but also periodically came to her assistance when she threatened to fall off.

"I was having great difficulty holding my feet off the ground," she wrote later. "Some of my solicitous friends noticed this and came to my rescue by tying my legs up with rags that were none too clean.

"The only way I could stay on the donkey was to hold onto some of my friends, but now that they had me 'hog-tied,' they began feeding me crumpled bits of walnut—a great delicacy to them—but I knew that the nuts had been cracked on the road under someone's heel. It was this that made me decide that I had

had enough, and I climbed off the poor donkey and went back to Lowell and the other men."

We still had miles to go, with the road getting dustier and the sun hotter, but we were finally both given horses to ride. We sat on several layers of comfortable blankets, with crude leather stirrups for our feet, and about twelve-thirty we turned off into a field. We had reached the end of the road for that day.

Asked to pick our camp site first, we chose a grassy knoll, though everyone else, to our surprise, chose a bare and rocky area just below us. Once our tent had been pitched we had to get water, but there was no beautiful, cool mountain stream anywhere about. There was only a small irrigation ditch in which the children were already wading and two thirsty camels were standing. A woman, too, was scrubbing her blackened pots in the same mudhole. Because it was necessary, Tay washed our cooking utensils there, too, before filling a pot with water and putting it on the Primus stove to boil. And we boiled it thoroughly, though no amount of boiling could get rid of the mud. But then, what is a little mud?

For lunch we had peanut butter, Afghan bread, and tea, and then Tay spent an hour or more boiling pots of water to refill our canteens. The women still found the Primus stove fascinating, but, "How I must puzzle them," said Tay, "by cooking just plain water."

"All the men," Tay wrote in describing our experience with these people, "have long hair, bound up in turbans, and most of them are clean-shaven and very handsome, with sharp, even features beneath a perpetual suntan. For the most part they look strong and healthy. The hard-working, far-walking women look worn and haggard at an early age, their long, dark hair usually in disarray, their full-length dresses shabby and dull. But there were a few exceptions. Some of the wealthier women wore dresses of many bright colors, lavishly decorated with silver jewelry. One girl had a ring on each finger, while others wore jangling bunches of silver bracelets and anklets, or had silver coins sewn to their dresses and capes. Chief Safy's wife wore a beautiful half-moon silver necklace that was encrusted with pieces of turquoise and lapis lazuli, and among the older women it was not uncommon to find one with a silver ornament fastened at one side of her nose.

"Some of the youngest girls were very pretty, but given a few more years of life on the trail and they, too, will look old for their age. No beauty parlors for them; no facials to hold off the ravages of sun, wind, and dust. In fact, they hardly ever have a bath, and, between childbearing and their heavy work, there is nothing to keep them young."

We had boiled potatoes and tomatoes for dinner that evening—both gifts from the governor of Khost—and we also had corned-beef hash and canned fruit that we had brought with us from Kabul. Then we sat on rugs inside the tent, talking with visitors until we both almost fell asleep, though it was only six-thirty. That day on the trail had been a hard one for us, and we would be rising at four-thirty the next morning.

Chief Safy offered to delay the start, "Since you aren't accustomed to our early hours," but I felt that we should fall in with their regular schedule. Our guests left, and when we went outside to brush our teeth, we saw why they had pitched their tents well clear of the grassy knoll we had chosen. We were literally surrounded by sheep and goats which were munching their evening meal. In fact, some of them even stuck their heads into the tent, and we went to sleep to the sound of their grinding teeth, often within a couple of feet of our ears.

We were awakened the next morning by complaining camels, braying donkeys, baaing sheep, and the voices of our nomad friends, and were shocked to find that it was five-thirty. The encampment was already packed and many animals were on their way. Apparently our friends had thought it impolite to waken us, although we had asked them to.

Tay had taken off her slacks and blouse the night before, for it was warm, but she was sorry now, and she tried to dress in "the privacy" of her sleeping bag while those who still remained in camp—men and women, too—stood around and stared. This was not mere impolite inquisitiveness. It was serious interest. After all, none of these nomads had ever seen a Western woman before.

We were late, of course, in taking the trail, but we made it at last, and the dust, fortunately, was not so bad as it had been the day before. The day's march was much less, too—only about two hours—so we were soon in camp again.

I asked Chief Safy to let me photograph his wife as she performed her household tasks, and when she shyly consented, she began "to put her house in order." But when it came time to go to the spring for water, another woman appeared. We were confused, until Safy explained that she was his second wife. We had not thought of that possibility. While polygamy is accepted by these people, only the wealthiest can afford the luxury of more than one wife, and our friend, the chief, was among the few rich enough to do so in our particular camp.

We followed the second wife while she filled her goatskin bag with water from a narrow and very muddy irrigation ditch, and once we were back in camp, we were shocked when she let the children drink the dirty liquid. It seemed obvious that among these people, those who did not die in infancy developed certain powerful immunities. How, otherwise, is it possible for them to remain alive?

It seemed to us that they lived on a near starvation diet, their meals consisting mainly of bread, curds, and, occasionally, rice. The bread, we thought, was delicious. The dough, rolled flat on a copper dish, was baked on an iron skillet over the fire, and the taste could hardly be improved upon, but we wondered where these people found enough energy for the hard lives they led. It troubled us to see the children scrape out our empty food cans, and they actually fought over our leftovers—melon rind, bits of tomato, and moldy bread.

When we went to put up our tent this time we found it already raised—and in the center of camp. It was a demonstration of the friendliness of these people, but we asked their leave to move it, for their fierce dogs were all around us there, and it was frequently necessary to hold the mangy curs off with rocks. On one occasion three dogs came for me with their teeth bared, and I was rescued just in time.

The nomads had camped that day near a level stretch of land —about two hundred yards long—that was good enough, I thought, for a landing strip. I walked over the area, accompanied by some of our friends, picking up the larger rocks, and, having satisfied myself that Charlie could land there safely, I told Chief Safy to look for me after a while, and with Amin I set off on a half hour's hike to Khost, toward which the nomads had been moving since we had joined them, in order to pick up the airplane. I had asked Safy to take good care of Tay, and he took my request seriously.

"I went into the tent for a little privacy," Tay told me later, "and the chief posted a guard just outside. He brought along a rug and a water jug, and his authoritative yells kept everyone at a distance. He even threw stones at chickens that came too close."

In an hour and a half, Amin and I were back over camp in Charlie, but everyone was so excited that it was difficult to clear them off the strip. Tay later remarked that two young shepherd boys were so intent on watching Charlie that they had to be driven off with switches.

Everyone was even more excited than I realized at the time, but I managed to land all right—that is, on the second attempt—and even taxied up near camp and shut off the engine before I found the plane surrounded, with all the nomads standing and staring until a few pressed close and shook hands with me.

I let Safy and Gulbehar sit in the plane, but I watched the crowd lest, unintentionally, they do some damage. Most were content merely to look at their first airplane, but a few could not resist touching the shiny metal, though they did so gently—almost reverently—as though Charlie were the most fragile thing in the world.

We pushed the plane right into camp beside our tent while the tethered dogs barked their heads off. The chiefs assigned guards, and the people backed off to one side where many of them sat until dark, just staring at this strange contrivance from the West.

After dinner I turned on the plane's radio, picking up programs from Kabul, Karachi, and New Delhi, and bringing in beautiful symphonic music from Moscow.

"I'm sure," Tay wrote later, "that there wasn't much sleep in camp that night. We could hear animated conversation around every campfire, and I believe that the guards by the airplane talked all night long.

"The camp noises began earlier than usual the next morning, for the march was to be an extra long one across a waterless expanse to the Pakistan border. We had hoped they would wait until the sun came up, but we could not detain them. Hundreds of other nomads would soon be pouring down from the mountains behind us, and our friends did not want to share their meager sources of water. From my sleeping bag inside our tent, I watched the camp break up, and I was sorry, in spite of the difficulties, that we weren't going at least a little farther with them.

"Safy and some of the other men who had horses stayed behind to see us off, though, as usual, they were in a great hurry, so we packed and were ready to take off by seven-thirty. There were no crowds to worry about now. Except for the few who had remained, the whole area was deserted.

"We said good-by and climbed aboard. The take-off was bumpy but easy, and just after we were airborne we saw the whole caravan only a few miles away, all strung out and in imperceptible motion."

We circled once over our friends below and then turned toward the west, climbing to 11,000 feet to cross the range that lay there. The few days we had spent with that band of Pushtu nomads had opened our eyes. For generations, these people have been said to be quarrelsome, unfriendly, and distrustful, but we had not found them so. A few days before we had come to them as strangers, but when we left, they and we were friends.

XIII. *Hunza—the Land That Stands on End*

Returning from our visit to the nomads, we flew back to Kandahar, where we had refueled on our way from Iran. There we filmed a story of nomad land settlement in a newly irrigated area of the Helmand Valley—a story that pleased the officials of the Kabul government, for they saw that we were now turning from the old to the new, and that it was not our intention merely to hold up the nomads and say, "This is Afghanistan."

The old, of course, still dominates most of the ancient country. It is a land without railroads or air lines. Even its highways are crude, and old ideas are still widespread. But such backwardness as exists, I believe, is traceable less to internal inertia than to external influences. The dead-hand policies of Great Britain and Russia have been strong in this remote region until no more than a few years ago, and Aghanistan has only recently begun to catch up with the times.

At the time of our visit, the Morrison-Knudsen firm, under contract to the Afghan Government, had just completed two enormous dams on the Arghandab and Helmand rivers north and west of Kandahar. In connection with these, they had also constructed a vast network of irrigation canals in the Registan Desert to the south. Hundreds of nomad families, like those that made up Safy's band, had already settled on that reclaimed waste and were living, for the very first time, in villages of mud-brick houses, and with land of their own.

It was a family in the village of Chah-i-Angir—the "Well of the Figs"—that Tay and I chose for our picture. We filmed scenes around their home, showed the father and son plowing their field with oxen, and showed the little boy at school. While we were there, too, we saw more families arriving with their camels and goats, gladly accepting this new way of life, and giving up the bitterly hard and insecure existence of the nomad. But perhaps most impressive of all was the way the hard-bitten American contractors had transformed illiterate shepherds and camel drivers who had no mechanical background whatever, into successful operators of enormous bulldozers and draglines, even to the point where the Americans were only supervisors.

It was not easy to break away from the hospitality, the hot showers, and the American "chow" of Morrison-Knudsen, but if we were ever to get home, we had to push on. So loaded once more and staggering under the added weight of gifts of American canned fruit juice, Charlie took off on November 8 and we set a course to the southeast.

Karachi, the capital of Pakistan, was our immediate destination, but flying southeast until we reached the mountains west of Quetta, we changed our course to the south and for two hours flew over the Registan Desert and the mountains of Baluchistan—wild, Godforsaken regions of sand and rock where we saw no signs of man, and where a forced landing might well have been our last. But Charlie, judging by the way the engine hummed, might have been flying over the beaches of Florida. The weather was fine, the flight was easy, and we raised Karachi Control several hundred miles out.

Karachi, like Cairo, was a place we would have skipped had it not been necessary to land there for political reasons—that is, to explain our purposes and to seek permission to visit remote, "off-limits" regions. Before leaving home, Tay and I had called on

Laurie Shaffi, the Pakistan Consul General in New York, and had told him of our plans to visit his country. He had been most considerate in giving us information, but we had not dreamed of the lengths to which he would go in making us feel at home once we got there.

Coming straight from the Afghan desert, where we had been associating with hard-boiled American dam builders, we were dressed, when we landed at the Karachi airport, in soiled blue jeans and "beat-up" flying jackets. But to our embarrassment, we were met by a dignified representative of Prime Minister Moham- med Ali who certainly must have had his doubts when he told us that we were to be the guests of his government. Then, despite our blue jeans, he drove us in an official limousine to the Prime Minister's guest house.

A week before, we had been guests of Pushtu nomads. Now we were guests of the Prime Minister of Pakistan. It left us a bit breathless, but, fortunately, we had time to "slick up" before meet- ing the jolly and young-looking Prime Minister and his charming wife number-one, Begum Ali.

Before becoming head of the Pakistan Government, Moham- med Ali had been as he now again is, Ambassador to the United States, and he had a genuine fondness for our country. During lunch at his residence he talked about his experiences in America, and referred to them often during our visit in Karachi. On one occasion, when we interviewed him with our camera and our recorder on his miniature golf course, where he was trying out a telescopic putter given him by President Eisenhower, I took the liberty of saying that Americans were glad to have Pakistan on their side in the "cold war."

"It is *we* who are glad," the Prime Minister replied, "to have you on *our* side."

It was shortly after that interview that we were on our way once more—this time to Pakistan's wild, strategic northwest. With the blessings of our host, the Prime Minister, we were bound for "the land that stands on end"—the fabled Hunza Valley among the Karakoram Mountains, where Pakistan faces Russian Turkestan, Chinese Turkestan, and Indian Kashmir, with Afghanistan close by. We were going to fly Charlie to a new Pakistani Air Force strip deep in the Karakorams at Gilgit, there to exchange our wings for pack animals that would take us on to our goal. We understood that this was the first time permission had ever been granted to any private airplane to fly into the Karakorams, and we were excited at the prospect of another "first."

The initial leg of the flight—from Karachi to Rawalpindi—was tame. We flew north northeast for a hundred miles or so to the bend in the Indus River, and then followed that lazily curving stream and its tributary, the Chenab, to the airport at Multan. Here we found that the two airport runways were made entirely of bricks—millions of them—all laid as neatly as on the best suburban terrace in America!

We refueled at Multan, and from there followed river and railroad to Rawalpindi, where we landed just before dark at the military field of Chaklala. And here we bumped into a Civil Aviation representative whose nose was out of joint because he had had no word from Karachi of our arrival or our plans for flying farther north. As a matter of fact, he said that it was absolutely impossible for us to fly into the Karakorams because they were in a highly sensitive military area. Furthermore, he told us, flying among their peaks in a single-engine plane was just too dangerous.

It was with our hearts in our boots that we called on the local government officials and told them our story. They listened and wired Karachi, and Karachi replied with a wire that was sent directly to the Civil Aviation chap at the airport—a wire that may have said, for all we know, "They're mad, but let them go."

On the morning of our take-off, Tay and I called on the air force weather office at the airport. The morning reports were in from Gilgit and intermediate stations, and they looked okay—a little high cloud, good visibility, and light wind.

"I wouldn't go if I were you," said the Pakistani meteorological officer, "but there's no reason for my stopping you. It looks all right, but go soon because more clouds are rolling in from the west."

We took off a little before nine o'clock in the morning on the second day after our arrival, somewhat troubled because the field could not produce any maps against which we could check the accuracy of the ones we had. We were troubled, too, about the difficulties we might face in our navigation, though none materialized. We soon learned that there was no question about losing our way, for we followed what is perhaps the most prominent gorge on earth, and found colossal 20,000-foot mountains placed like snowy sky markers along the route we took.

We were flying with a much lighter load than usual, for we had left behind the heavy recorder and camera, as well as a couple of suitcases, and we climbed away from the Chaklala field on a heading of 340 degrees over hills that rose to four or five thousand feet within ten miles. We leveled off at 7500 feet and with a power setting of twenty-one inches of manifold pressure and 2100 rpm, Charlie gave us an indicated speed of 135 miles an hour. Far off on our right we caught a glimpse of a snowy summit that rose behind a line of lesser peaks—a solitary mountaintop with a short cloud streamer stretching from it to the cast like a wind sock in a stiff breeze. We do not know, but it may have been mighty Nanga Parbat, and if so, the distance between us was 130 miles.

The town of Haripur was soon below us, and a few miles beyond, the Indus River flowed out of the gorge that we were to follow. Several minutes passed before we were in a position to look directly into that stupendous ravine. Then we were in it, though at 7500 feet it was miles in width—nothing like what it would soon become.

On our right, sparsely wooded slopes culminated in a north–south ridge of about 9000 feet. Barely visible over the top from time to time were some snow-covered 17,000-foot peaks farther to the east. The air was smooth, and high clouds were visible to the north and west, but except for a bit of high cirrus, the sky was clear to the northeast and east. Still, it was apparent that a change

was due in the area. A little later, in fact, some 19,000-foot mountains to the west had their heads hidden in gray mist.

We were glad to see that the water in the Indus was low, and
that far beneath us gravel bars here and there lined the river.
Some of them were large enough, perhaps, for us to land on in a
pinch. The river's altitude is well under 4000 feet most of the way
to Gilgit, and even there it is only 4600, so altitude, at least, would
be no problem in landing on or in subsequently taking off from
any of these bars.

Farther along, the great walls of gray rock closed in more and
more, rising higher, too. The Indus frequently bent nearly double,
and one needed little imagination to grasp some understanding
of the enormous period of time and effort that the river had ex-
pended in cutting its way through these gigantic mountains.

As the gorge closed in, the air grew so turbulent that we had
to secure our cameras. I added power and climbed to 11,000 feet
so as to free our wings of the drafts of rising and descending air,
and in the process we not only reached smoother air but also prof-
ited by our greatly increased panorama. To the right we looked
up a broad valley where a barely discernible track led through
several villages, with glistening peaks and glaciers lying beyond.

The Indus turned to the east when we were 145 miles from
Chaklala, the gorge broadened, and there, sixty miles ahead,
towered the immense mass of Nanga Parbat. High cirrus clouds
concealed the mountain's summit, but the ice and snow of its
lesser peaks shone against a patch of blue. Nanga Parbat—26,660
feet high—the mountain that has killed more climbers than any
other. What a sight that was out of Tay's window, with 22,000
feet of rock and ice rising steeply from the river, and with one of
its hanging glaciers just beyond our wing tip as we banked steeply
and turned north again to follow the course of the Indus.

Now the gorge was closing in fast. Through the windshield a
few miles ahead lay the main range of the Karakoram, which, a
hundred miles or so to the east, includes K-2—Mount Godwin
Austen—28,250 feet high and second in all the world only to

Mount Everest. K-2 itself was hidden by intervening peaks, but there ahead of us was the Rakaposhi group reaching up to 25,550 feet and forming the south wall of the Hunza Valley beyond.

Hunza, the northernmost state in Pakistan, had been one of my objectives ever since I crossed the Himalayas to Tibet with my father in 1949. For, like Tibet, Hunza is also "out of this world." Others have visited it, but not many, and all along our way through Africa and the Middle East, Tay and I had been heading for the region we were approaching now.

Ahead of us was a fork in the river—the confluence of the Gilgit River with the Indus, the latter coming down to this point from the barren, sky-high plains of Tibet farther to the east, while the lesser Gilgit River flowed down from the northwest. And it was northwestward, up this smaller valley, that our route now led us, while just to starboard rose an ugly 20,000-foot peak shaped like a deformed tooth. We rounded a bend, and there was the town of Gilgit at the head of a canyon, with trees, terraced fields, and an airstrip to the east.

The landing gave us the creeps, for a base leg headed us directly toward an abrupt 9000-foot mountain wall which, when we turned to the runway, seemed only a few yards away. Then, at the bottom of our landing approach, we dragged in over a sheer rock ledge and onto the strip with a 16,000-foot mountain rising steeply from the other end of it. Not much room for a "go around" at Gilgit!

There to greet us was the Political Agent's secretary, the Agent himself being under the weather with a cold. Also awaiting us were a major of the Northern Scouts, the airport controller, and others. We tied Charlie down to cement blocks and were driven in a jeep through Gilgit to the Political Agent's house, where we were shown to a dimly lighted but comfortable room with a tiny fireplace. After tea had been served, our host—Mohammed Jan—came from his bed and, despite his cold, joined us for our second breakfast—porridge, eggs, and *chapatties* cooked in clarified butter, or *ghee*.

Mohammed Jan proved to be a "five by five" type, and even with his cold he was a jolly rolypoly. He wanted to know all about our flight and seemed amazed that we had come alone and in so small a plane as his friends had told him Charlie was.

"I knew your plane was smaller than a Dakota (a DC-3)," he said, "but not so tiny as this! How is it possible? Don't the air pockets frighten you? And how can you go so high?"

Before hitting the trail to Hunza, we flew back to Rawalpindi for Tay's sister, Frances Pryor—now Mrs. Robert Haws—who had accepted our cabled invitation to join us on one last fling before getting married. She had flown out from New York but if she had really known what this Karakoram Valley would be like in winter I doubt if she would have boarded the Pan American clipper at all.

On the first of December we got under way from Gilgit, at first by car (the P.A.'s jeep) which would take us to where the walking and horseback riding would begin. The Political Agent's driver was at the wheel. Frances was on his left, halfway out of the jeep, while Tay and I were on his right. I had never thought four could possibly ride in the front seat of a jeep, but we had to, for behind us was a mountain of baggage and supplies, and sitting on top of it all was the P.A.'s cook, whom we had borrowed for the trip.

We were bound for Chalt, about thirty miles farther into the mountains, and at first the road ran over gravel and sand, winding among strewn boulders. But when we came to the Hunza River the trail climbed away from the water. Barely wide enough for the jeep, it zigged and zagged upward at an incredibly steep angle, traversing shear walls that rose above it into obscurity, and that sometimes dropped almost straight off on the right to the muddy rapids of the river hundreds of feet below. Riding on the outside, I held my breath when the wheels came within six inches of the edge of the road and the view was almost straight down.

These traverses had been hewn right out of the rock, and any vehicle longer or broader than a jeep could not have managed them. Sometimes, in fact, the trail had been partly built out from the cliff for a little way on props let into the abrupt rock face, and from where I sat on the right side of the crowded vehicle I sometimes found myself looking down from the edge of an overhang!

At Chalt the going became too tough even for a jeep, and we switched to shaggy little ponies like those of Tibet, but not before we had lunch with Mir Shoukat Ali Ghazi Millet, C.B.E., the ruler of the little region known as Nagar. Over an excellent lunch of tender mutton and steaming rice, the thirty-one-year-old Mir, who spoke perfect English learned at a British school in Srinagar, told us that Chalt is the winter capital of Nagar and does not belong to Hunza as a number of travelers have mistakenly believed. And it is the winter capital because it is the warmest spot in his tiny state, and also because wood for the fireplace is a little more plentiful there.

Hunza and Nagar, he told us, are sister states lying on opposite sides of the Hunza River. Founded about five hundred years ago by two Persian princes, they formerly fought almost constantly, but now, though they both retain their political individuality, they are united through the marriage of their ruling families. Each state numbers about twenty thousand people, and both are Moslem. Oddly enough, however, the people of Nagar are Orthodox Moslems of the Sunni sect and they frown upon the gay ways of their brothers across the river who are Ismailis—followers of the Agha Khan—who love their wine.

It was after two o'clock when we left Chalt on ponies the Mir provided, and Tay's sister, Frances, who, as a horsewoman, has jumped her hunter at many Madison Square Garden horse shows, could hardly wait to mount. But she was unaccustomed to so small a pony, and as she threw her leg over his back she went right over herself. Even the porters laughed, and one of them took the reins, convinced, no doubt, that she had never ridden a horse before.

We had three guides, and our western-style saddles were cushioned with blankets. An extra pony carried about 200 pounds of our stuff, and a sad-faced donkey, which had to be constantly coaxed and herded along the trail, carried five gallons of kerosene, my portable recorder, and a bag of oranges and odds and ends.

The porters were jolly, picturesque fellows in their great white cloaks of coarse wool, their beretlike caps of the same wool, and their red-stained mustaches. They were full of smiles and the picture of health, but none of them knew English, and their language, which is called "Burushaki," was unlike anything I had ever heard before.

Our way led through a part of the village of Chalt, but we soon went down to the river and crossed it by way of a shallow ford. Then, on the Hunza side, the trail climbed steeply in switchbacks up an enormous scree slope until we were some 500 feet above the river. There it leveled off and headed east, at first four or five feet wide, but soon narrowing to half of that where it made its way over occasional galleries built out from the valley wall. There were no guard rails, of course, to keep men or animals from falling off. Pack animals, we were told, were frequent victims, and people occasionally fall off, too. We dismounted and walked across these *rafiqs*, and the girls were often terrified. In fact, I wasn't too happy about them either, for it is not pleasant when you can touch the rock wall with one hand while looking down hundreds of feet on the other side of so narrow a trail. It far surpassed in sheer terror the Himalayan trail my father and I had followed five years earlier from northern India to Lhasa.

We dropped down to the river again and crossed it on a swaying suspension bridge. Only two animals were allowed on the bridge at a time, and when we reached the farther side I understood why. Neither end of the bridge quite touched the ground. It was truly a suspension bridge hanging in the air. I watched one of the pack ponies coming off the bridge, and he paused, his head lowered and his ears intently forward, waiting for the bridge to reach one extreme in its sideways swaying before he nimbly hopped to the ground.

We had been told by the Mir that we would make this stage of our journey in "only four hours," but at five-thirty, when I asked by pointing to my watch and holding first one finger, then two, and three, how much longer we would be, one of the porters replied with two fingers, and I realized that the Mir's estimate did not apply to those who never trotted.

We passed a large boulder with mileages painted on it, indicating that we had come eight miles from Chalt and had eleven to go to reach Minapin, which was our goal for that day. From this it did not take much figuring to see that two extra miles had slipped in—another hour at our pace.

We passed through a little village that had all but gone to sleep and continued on our way in the gathering dusk, but total darkness never came, for the quarter moon always made it possible to see the trail. On we went up 500 feet or more and down again— along a level stretch and then up once more. Then we entered a somewhat larger village, though there were no sounds or lights. Everyone was inside, possibly asleep, and only one dog barked in the distance.

"Minapin?" I asked our headman.

"Gulmit, Sahib," he replied. "Minapin *panj* mile—five miles."

Our porters went into a huddle, apparently about making camp there instead of going on. But it seemed to me there was no choice between bedding down on some stone floor without any dinner, and going on to the bungalow in Minapin where fire, food, and cots were waiting.

"Minapin," I insisted. "Minapin." And I told the girls we would be there by eight o'clock.

But now the cook came up and motioned me to follow him. He. led the way to a two-story wooden house that had glass windows and a porch. It was unlit and the door was locked, but after a while female voices spoke to us from above. The cook replied but seemed to make no progress, so I spoke up.

"We are three tired travelers," I explained, "looking for shelter for the night. Won't you please let us in?"

Perhaps the foreign language succeeded where the cook had failed. At any rate, a light showed behind the door as it was opened by a man who seemed to be the janitor, and we were shown into a huge room with bare floors, dusty chairs, and dozens of pictures on the wall—a room that had apparently been closed for the winter, its owner having left for warmer climes.

In no time a fire was burning in the small fireplace, the chairs had been put aside, and beautiful carpets covered the cold floor. Our baggage was brought in, and after an hour or so our cook brought us some of our canned vegetable soup, some bread, and a tin of cheese. For dessert we had Nagar walnuts, almonds, grapes, and apples. And so to bed, the three of us in sleeping bags reinforced by blankets, on air mattresses that were spread on the floor.

We were up at seven and on the trail again by nine, though it took us more than two hours to cover the five miles to the bungalow at Minapin. There we had some soup and boiled potatoes, paid off our men from Chalt—three rupees, or about a dollar, per man. And at one o'clock we were once more on our way, with a new batch of porters and ponies, with the town of Nagar, the capital, seventeen miles ahead, though it was raining lightly now.

"We felt we were walking in another world," Tay wrote in describing this stage of our journey. "Absolute silence all around us, and rocky slopes that disappeared into a thick white mist not far above our heads. We knew it was snowing on the mountain slopes above us, and it was so still that I imagined I could hear the snowflakes falling.

"The rain soon stopped and we began to catch glimpses of the mountains all around us. One moment we would see billowing clouds, and the next we would see a patch of deep blue sky, with a spectacular peak of rock and new-fallen snow outlined against it.

"Late that afternoon, when we rounded a curve in the rock wall, a long column of 18,000-foot mountains stood ahead of us. The wide, terraced valley beneath them and across the river from us was Hunza. We could even make out the white palace of the ruler high on a hilltop, outlined against the brown rock of the mountain backdrop. And while we were admiring the view, the clouds above parted, showing us snow-specked rock pinnacles that rose fantastically high. They were the 25,000-foot summits beyond Hunza, unnamed on the map. The sun was setting behind us now. We knew because it turned the vanishing clouds a salmon pink, but it left the white peaks and the deep blue sky untouched.

"The magnificence left me breathless, and so did the glimpse of the trail ahead—a thin line across a mountainside of scree. I was shaking with fear before we reached it, for the trail was barely wide enough to stand on.

"Halfway across, some small stones hopped across the trail from the steep slope above. I looked up and saw rocks and boulders heading our way fast. Frances and most of the caravan were safe far ahead, but one old porter with a horse was behind Lowell and me, and they were blocking our retreat—or so I thought. But both porter and horse turned with lightning speed, which was a tremendous feat on that narrow trail, and we followed them back to the safety of a large rock outcrop and watched the stream of stones and boulders ahead of us."

The slide, luckily, was not a major one, and after peace had returned to the steep talus slope, we went on again. Just before dark there was another halt at a tiny village, this time for a discussion among our porters. Again we had the prospect of night travel ahead, and the men did not like it. We had left the valley of the Hunza River and were traveling, now, through the narrower valley of the Nagar River itself.

In bad weather I do not believe we could have made it to Nagar capital, but as it was, the moonlit beauty of the mountains inspired all of us, except the shaggy little mountain-bred ponies who had the sense to recognize bedtime. On and on, until it almost seemed that we were destined to spend the rest of our lives crawling along an endless precipice. When, at last, the Mir's palace appeared, faint and silvery, ahead and above us, we were almost too far gone to comprehend its meaning. Twenty-two miles we had come that day—more than ten hours through the Karakoram —walking almost the entire distance. So it was not just the Mir's little palace that we now saw before us. It was Shangri-La.

We were warmly greeted in that moon-drenched house an hour later by the Mir's eight-year-old son, Barket Ali, who, despite his complete ignorance of English, listened intently to our account as we tried to warm our hands before his fire. The prince wore Western dress—woolen pants and a corduroy jacket —and with excellent manners he smiled and nodded each time we spoke to him. Only cigarettes were served us before the fire, but dinner was announced shortly, and we followed the little fellow through a dark hallway to the dining room that was as cold, it seemed to me, as a deep freeze. Tay was so cold that she visibly shook, and even the little prince's teeth rattled a time or two. "Hardy people," I thought. "Worse even than the British when it comes to unheated homes."

But we soon learned the reason. Firewood is the only source of heat, and there is hardly any timber in the valley.

We slept that night at a nearby dak bungalow and though a small fire was burning in the fireplace we crept into our sleeping bags fully dressed. We were wearing long flannel underwear, sweaters, and heavy socks, but it grew so cold during the night that we were glad to have some blankets to pull over the sleeping bags.

We spent the following day at Nagar, part of the time with seventy-year-old Wazir Sarwar, the Deputy Prime Minister. He was over six feet tall and was full of energy despite his years. He spoke no English, but I succeeded in learning the local names of some of the more prominent peaks that were within view. Then Frances, Tay, and I went for a walk with him. He took us through a number of stone hut settlements, but no activities whatever were in progress. It almost appeared that the people had gone into semi-hibernation for the winter. He also took us to a vantage point where we could see two of the nearby glaciers and had a tremendous view of the upper Nagar Valley and its mountains— many of them still unmapped. Terraced fields showed their contours under new-fallen snow, still I was surprised at the warmth and dryness of the air. There was no sun, but the great peaks apparently catch whatever moisture blows this way, and little snow falls at these lower elevations. If that were not so, avalanches would wipe out many of the settlements on the valley slopes.

It was the next day—December 4—when we started back over the trail that had led us to Nagar. We were bound downstream now, to the junction of this side valley with the Hunza River Valley, and there, we planned to cross the Hunza to its other side on our way to Baltit, the capital of Hunza.

It was about nine o'clock when we rode across the Mir's polo ground, went down the hill through his private orchard, and started back along the Hunza trail. It seemed far less terrifying in daylight than we had thought it to be in the moonlight two nights earlier, but steeply above us great pinnacles of rock and ice rose to 20,000 feet or more against the deep blue sky.

We had not gone far along the way when the sound of drums and piping behind us announced the coming of royalty. The Mir's family was on its way to join the Mir in Chalt for the winter.

We stepped aside with our cameras leveled and let them pass, exchanging waves as they rounded a bend and disappeared ahead —three children bundled up and riding in the arms of servants; the Rani of Nagar herself, her face hidden beneath a heavy brown veil; two unveiled servant women, and then more men and pack animals.

At the village where we had deliberated continuing to Nagar on our way in, we exchanged our Nagar porters and ponies for a group of porters from Hunza, and after the usual arguments over rates of payment, we scrambled down a steep and narrow goat trail to the valley floor. There, with three thin logs for a bridge, we crossed the boiling Nagar River, coming only a little way farther on, to a much more terrifying bridge over the Hunza. It stretched across the river from one rock wall to the other, three feet wide and about 300 feet long, and it consisted of nothing but thin planks supported by cables and spaced wide enough apart— almost like railroad ties—to afford a continual view of the rushing green and white water a hundred feet below. And as we crossed, the whole fragile affair bounced up and down like a badly adjusted trampoline.

Once on the other side, we climbed steeply to a little village that was perched at the edge of a cliff. A crowd watched eagerly to see what sort of travelers were coming their way, for few ever come from Nagar, the traditional route through the Karakoram lying on the Hunza side.

Ponies were waiting for us there, and we gladly mounted, turning across the village's polo ground and up a slope so steep that we had to dismount again. But our journey was short. From the top of the slope we could see the Mir of Hunza's new palace, which was our destination, and before long we were greeted by a boy carrying a cloth-covered platter.

As we breathlessly approached, he opened the cloth, and there lay a pile of apples—a wonderfully pleasant welcome for travelers as weary as we. And the warm sunshine that greeted us on Hunza's southward-facing slopes further warmed our spirits as we trudged up to the palace.

There we found a letter from the Mir—a letter addressed to "My beloved guests, Karimabad, Hunza."

My dear friend [it read],

I hope you will be kind enough to excuse the trouble in my house during my absence which is not suitable to civilized personality like you I afraid, but I have given orders to my attendants and the Agent to look after you as my guests during your stay in my House.

I hope you both and your companion will feel this poor home like at home, and you can ask anything you need which will be a great pleasure to me and my wife.

I and my wife and the children are looking forward to see you in my House on our return, I am cutting short my stay and will reach Hunza on 15th December '54.

With kindest regards, yours sincerely,
Colonel H.H. The Ruler of Hunza

The Mir's new palace was a three-story, gabled building of

wood and granite. His aid showed us our upstairs quarters and brought us an armful of wood—about enough for half an hour, we thought, but we learned that it was for a whole day in fuel-scarce Hunza, where the precious, life-giving apricot trees have to be cut for firewood, and the constant choice these people face is "More fire? Or more food?"

We found the Karakorams so cold in early December that we weren't out of our heavy clothes once in our two weeks there, and we took off our heavy jackets only when we crawled into our sleeping bags, which we rolled out on the floor before our little fire. We wore every bit of clothing we could find—including our fur caps—even when we ate our meals in the unheated palace dining room. There was a thermometer on the wall of the dining room, and I once read it at thirty-two degrees.

The morning after our arrival on the Hunza side of the valley, Tay woke me up with a nudge in the ribs, and when I opened my eyes she gave me the startling news that she was going to have a baby. She had to repeat the statement before its meaning really sank in, for it was the last thing I expected to hear. In fact, I would have been dumfounded even back home, for after nearly five years of wanting children and having none, I had given up thinking I would ever become a father.

I was naturally thrilled by Tay's announcement but, just as naturally, I was alarmed at the position that confronted her. We were in one of the most remote regions in all the world—far from our kind of civilization and from the medical facilities upon which we of the West depend. We were in the world's most rugged corner, and on one of the world's most treacherous mountain trails. No wonder I was frightened!

"What do we do now?" I asked after expressing my joy. None of us knew anything about the care of expectant mothers, though Tay now recalled having heard that they should not ride horse-back.

"Great!" I thought. "Then how do we get her out of here?"
Our plans for meeting the Mir—for camera-hunting the rare

Ovis poli, which are the handsome bighorn sheep that live high
up in this portion of the world—for doing a film study of these
people—all were shattered by Tay's announcement and by the
pressing problem of getting her safely out of the mountains.

It took two agonizing days to contact the Pakistani doctor in
Gilgit over a primitive, battery-operated telephone. One had to
shout in order to make the phone whisper at the other end, but
finally I thought I had his instructions. Tay was to stay in bed
until she felt well enough to start the journey back, and then she
was to ride out on horseback, but by slow stages.

A pregnant woman on horseback! And on that breath-taking
mountain trail! It didn't sound good to me, and I vividly recalled
another desperate bit of mountain transport when, five years
before, my father had been thrown from a horse in Tibet, breaking
his leg in eight places. We had had to carry him in a litter for
nearly three weeks, and we barely made it.

Tay spent most of the next three days in her sleeping bag before the fireplace—reading, eating her meals, and dreaming of
being at home. And then, with many misgivings, we started out
on the first stage, which was to take us ten miles over the trail to
the village of Aliabad.

"I felt ready for anything," Tay wrote later in describing this
portion of our journey. "We had a crystal-clear day for our departure. The snow-covered giants, white plumes trailing from their
peaks, encircled us. The sky was a deep, deep blue.

"Many townspeople lined the trail as we left, saluting, mur-
muring gracious farewells, reaching up to shake our hands, and
we stuffed our pockets with gifts of almonds and apricots.

"The ride that day was short—two hours along the valley floor.
We were going to divide those two twenty-mile hikes into four
days, and I planned to ride most of the way. Of course, I was
aware of every jolt, thought it was the bumpiest ride I'd ever had
on a horse, and that it would never end!

"We spent that night at a young Pakistani doctor's home—the
only medical man in the two valleys, and he was just back from

Above — Our joy at being the first to reach Kabul — capital of Afghanistan — by private plane is unmistakable. And there to greet us are His Excellency Abdul Wahab Tarzi, wearing the black karakul hat, and a young official named Amin.   *Below* — Afghan nomads, passing through settled land on their autumn migration to the warmer climes of neighboring Pakistan. The rifle is for self-defense in this tribal country. In the background a nomad boy rides a laden camel.

Above — Safy, turbaned leader of those sixteen nomad tents, entertains the children with a melancholy tune on a shepherd's flute. *Below* — "Open House!" Nomad women and children gather round our tent to see what Tay is up to.

Above—Nomad children marvel at Tay's dishwashing antics — a reminder that children everywhere are filled with boundless curiosity. A camel strolls away after drinking its fill at the stream beside Tay. *Left*—A nomad elder joins us for breakfast of Afghan village bread and eggs boiled over our Primus stove. Charlie, whom I had landed on a camel track the previous evening, waits to whisk us back to Kabul. *Below*—Nomad camels look with haughty contempt upon Morrison-Knudsen's monumental irrigation works in the desert west of Kandahar.

Above—Bill Crosson of Morrison-Knudsen instructs an Afghan colleague in the operation of an enormous dragline. We were astonished at the way Bill and other American constructionists had transformed illiterate camel drivers into operators of such complex equipment.   *Below*—Making a bit of history, with the first flight by a private plane into the Karakorams of northwestern Pakistan. As we twisted through the gorges of the Indus River we were hemmed in on all sides by stunning but savage peaks of more than 20,000 feet.

On our way into the Hunza Valley, on the Nagar side, Tay gingerly negotiates the world's most dangerous trail, barely wide enough in places to stand with both feet together.

Right—Naibullah Beg, dressed for school in his very best suit. But hooky seems the intention of his little companion, who holds a stick for playing polo on foot. *Below*— At the chilly capital of Nagar, where Tay has an audience with the Mir's youngest son, held by a palace servant. Great icy peaks thrust into the distant sky, far beyond carefully terraced fields.

Left—Aboard the Arab dhow *Faras* at the Persian Gulf port of Dibai. The dhow's captain faces the camera, and Persian-style wind towers rise above many of the town's earthen homes. Attached to the port side aft of the nearest dhow is a *zuli*—the sole plumbing on these antique vessels. *Below*—The dhow's crew had a feast in my honor before I left them in Dibai. At "the captain's table"—rice, boiled fish, and onions—all eaten with the right hand only. Interpreter Ahmed Hassan is on the extreme left. Next to him is a freed slave.

Above—The King of Saudi Arabia—His Majesty, Saud Al Saud—with members of the royal family at his palace in Riyadh. His Majesty is a central figure in the Moslem world, ruler of desert tribes, and king of oil, which pays him annually about a quarter of a billion dollars. *Below*— Aramco's "G-8" rolling among the dunes of the Empty Quarter on enormous sand tires, looking for signs of still more oil. The double-deck trailer is the sleeper.

Above—The city of Shibam in the Wadi Hadhramaut, where skyscrapers of sun-dried brick have been in vogue since the time of the Queen of Sheba. People still live in these eight-story buildings, although without benefit of elevators.   *Left*—Charlie arrives in New York after flying the Atlantic, dismantled, in a Pan American cargo DC-6.

two years with the Army in Baluchistan. He was a charming host and served us some of Hunza's famous apricot wine, but we had to sleep that night dormitory style, three beds in a row in the doctor's 'hospital.'

"We were off early the following morning to cover the next ten miles along what is surely one of the most dangerous trails on earth. The path was often cut into sheer rock walls, upon which galleries were frequently built out over thin air. To me nothing could be worse, for I kept thinking of the German mountain climber killed here a few months before, and of the many Hunzakuts lost along this trail each year.

"We reached the end of our march at noon and I breathed a sigh of relief. We were halfway out now, and there was an attractive bungalow in which we spent the rest of the day and the night. From its porch we had a magnificent view of Rakaposhi, 25,550 feet, the highest mountain of Hunza and Nagar—unclimbed and with tremendous snow slopes and rock faces, and also with a great white plume streaming from its summit. 'Bright Smoke,' the Hunzakuts call it.

"Our third day on the trail was the longest, and it almost didn't go well. About an hour's ride along the way we climbed over a steep slope and saw a cloud of dust rolling over the trail far ahead of us. An avalanche!

"No one said anything, but we wondered if the path had been swept away and, if it had, whether we could go any farther. We all thought of the possibility of prolonged delay—weeks, perhaps, while the trail was being rebuilt. But when we went ahead we found that the slide had not been a great one, and though the trail was covered with loose dirt and stones, it was still intact.

"In another hour we had reached our next stopping place, and the following day we rode into Chalt about noon. Here was the end of the trail for the ponies. Only a short jeep ride now lay ahead.

"The Mir of Nagar greeted us like old friends. In fact he gave my sister, who was to be married two months later, a handsome mountain-fox pelt for a wedding present.

"The trip from Chalt to Karachi seemed a swift dream compared with those days on the Hunza trail. And at Karachi, Frances left us, to hurry home for Christmas, while we, on December 20, took off in Charlie for a holiday in the Persian Gulf, on the island of Bahrein."

XIV. *By Dhow Across the Persian Gulf*

I N 1952 TAY AND I HAD FLOWN
from Bahrein to Karachi in a British jet air liner—a two-hour trip
at 35,000 feet—and we barely had time to get comfortably settled
in our seats and to eat an elaborate breakfast. Now we were going
to fly from Karachi to Bahrein in Charlie, and that would take
two days. Furthermore, we would not be flying at an altitude of
seven miles. Our altitude would vary—perhaps from 200 feet to
7000—depending upon the sights along the way, and the strength
of the prevailing "westerly" at various altitudes.

From the high-flying British Comet, the land below had been
little more than a blur of white lumpy sand—the water only an
unbroken expanse of blue. Sharja and Jiwani had merely been
names used by the pilot to report his position. But in Charlie we
would stop at both those places, and the flight would be almost
entirely new to us.

We took off from Karachi on the morning of December 20 with
Jiwani, 350 miles ahead, for our first stop. This remote emergency
airfield in western Pakistan overlooks the Arabian Sea from the
tip of a peninsula that is only twenty miles from the Iranian
border, and it was the only field in the first 800 miles of our flight
where we could get gas.

Flying northwest from Karachi for fifty miles or so, we turned west at 2000 feet, along the wild Baluchistan coast. Sandy beaches and desert unfolded beneath us while off to our right jagged, stony mountains rose higher than we were flying. We had flown over many mountain ranges on our journey, but none so bleak as these.

We now and then swooped low over the rolling sand dunes to look at small villages that had been invisible from the jet air liner, and sometimes we saw fishing nets drying in the sun, and fleets of small, lateen-rigged dhows on the blue water nearby.

We passed over the little fishing settlement of Gwadar and flew on for another thirty miles to Jiwani, where we circled the small sand strip while the tower operator told us in halting English to come right on in. There was no traffic—aerial or otherwise—to worry about here.

While a bushy, black-bearded Shell representative refueled Charlie, we had a cup of tea with the tower operators—a big occasion for them, for few planes find it necessary to land at Jiwani. They told us that they "thought" the weather was good over the Persian Gulf, but in case we encountered fog or low clouds, we could return to Jiwani even after dark.

"My house is over that way," one of them said. "Just circle it a few times, and give me fifteen minutes to get to the airfield. I'll start the generator and turn on the emergency lights."

That was good enough for us, and we were off the ground again at three-thirty on a two-hour flight along the southern coast of Iran to the mouth of the Persian Gulf. This narrow entrance had been of great importance to pirates in the old days, and to nations as history progressed, but it was nowhere near narrow enough for Tay, who hates flying over open water on only one engine. But Charlie did not let us down, and we watched the Trucial Oman coast looming closer and closer, and then crossed the mountainous peninsula—skirting an 8000-foot peak—to its flat, sandy western shore.

For the first time in months we heard crisp British voices through our headphones—R.A.F. planes landing at their Sharja air base. We joined in the conversation and were quickly cleared to land on a long hard-sand runway at a field that had been used by our Air Transport Command during World War II.

When Charlie had been taken care of, we asked the field commander where we might spend the night and were taken to a kind of picture-book fortress nearby, where there were living quarters for the British personnel and guest rooms for occasional passers-by as well.

The high walls, the lookout towers with their searchlights, and the heavy iron entrance door weren't there just for atmosphere. And though the fort had been built during the pirate days of the nineteenth century, it is not maintained merely as a monument to the battles of the past. It has protected British lives in very recent years, for Trucial Oman still has occasional wars between its local Sheiks, and foreigners never know just when they may need protection from rampaging Omani Bedouins.

The next morning we took time out to wander through the town of Sharja—a picturesque Sindbad the Sailor seaport. Low, clay houses with ornately carved teak doors lined sand streets that led down to the turquoise-blue water of the Persian Gulf, and a long, flat sand bar a few hundred yards offshore made a small, sheltered cove for anchored Arab dhows. On the other side of town we saw donkeys and camels plodding out into the desert, carrying oil drums and jerry cans on their way to collect water at an oasis five miles away—the town's only supply. Not only is drinking water scarce, but also the people must pay the local Sheik for it, for he owns all the land in Sharja and levies all the taxes. In fact, we ourselves contributed to his income by arriving in Charlie, for he even collects landing fees.

Later in the day we took off for Bahrein, flying the roundabout route over the desert coast line instead of hopping straight across 200 miles of open water as the air liners do. We flew over myriads of reefs, shoals, and islands which offer almost perfect shelter for pirates even yet, and we also passed the towns of Dibai and Abu Dhabi, two sheikdoms that are frequently at war with each other.

In two and a half hours we were over the Qatar Peninsula, a giant finger of sand that stretches from the Saudi Arabian desert out into the Persian Gulf. We could see several man-made seaports, as well as storage tanks and derricks which now mark this oil-rich land, and far to the north, black smoke was rising into the sky—the Bahrein Petroleum Company's flares of burning gas.

Christmas is a day to spend at home, but since that was impossible for us in 1954, we could think of no more perfect way to spend it than with Aunt Leila and Uncle Max Thornburg (to whom we are not related, but are very close friends) on their own island off the larger island of Bahrein.

In the 1930s Uncle Max came out to Bahrein for the Standard Oil Company of California, and he was largely responsible for developing the oil fields and the refinery there. The Sheik of Bahrein—the father of the present ruler—was so grateful that he presented Uncle Max with an island, giving it to him and his son, Russell, in perpetuity. The island was merely a low strip of sand and sea shells, three quarters of a mile long and several hundred yards wide, about a mile off the western shore of Bahrein. It had no fresh water, and no vegetation of any kind, but Uncle Max saw possibilities in it and in fifteen years he and Aunt Leila transformed it into a veritable paradise.

They drilled several wells, found an unlimited supply of fresh water, and were able to grow a wealth of vegetation—casuarina trees, oleanders, hibiscus, date palms, cocoanut palms, and even grass for a lovely lawn. They grow many kinds of flowers and vegetables and have built a beautiful modern home, with a guest house and a swimming pool. In fact, they have made an almost ideal island Shangri-La out of a barren sand bar, and we were naturally delighted at the prospect of a holiday there.

The Thornburgs met us at Bahrein's international airport, and we drove to the far side of the main island where we transferred to a launch. A short, pleasant ride and we were "home" on Umm a' Sabaan—"Mother of Sea Shells."

Christmas can be wonderful anywhere in the world—even in a Moslem land on the Persian Gulf. It is the spirit, of course, that counts. And where could the spirit of Christmas have been more evident than on Umm a' Sabaan? Besides the Thornburgs themselves, there were four Thornburg grandchildren and, to round out the family party, my father and mother arrived by plane from New York.

Our Christmas tree was a casuarina pine, appropriately decorated. Presents weren't lacking, of course, though most of them had a Middle East flavor, and Christmas dinner was just what it would have been at home—turkey, cranberry sauce, and everything else that belongs on the table at such a time.

Two or three days later, having looked the little island over carefully, I decided that Charlie could land on its uncultivated southern half. It took a good deal of work to clear the "strip" of blocks of solidified sea shells, to flatten the humps and fill in the holes, but in three days it was done. I even set up bushel baskets for boundary markers, and knew that the Thornburg flag, which differs from the flag of Bahrein only in that a gold shell is superimposed on the red field, would serve in place of a wind sock as it flew from its tall flagpole.

Tay and I went over to Bahrein for Charlie, but everyone else—including the houseboys, the gardeners, the boatmen and the dogs—waited excitedly on Umm a' Sabaan. The flight from the international airfield was a short one, and when we arrived we circled low over the water, approaching the narrow strip from just above the waves, and landing easily. Then we parked Charlie among the oleanders and turned to other matters.

We swam, both in the pool and in the Persian Gulf, though the waters of the gulf, to our surprise, were cold. We fished and spent hours by the fire in Uncle Max's library, where he has what is undoubtedly the most complete private collection of books on the Middle East—about four thousand volumes all told. And—most fun of all—we sailed in the waters about the island in the Thornburgs' small dhow.

I had long since read Alan Villiers's book on sailing on trading dhows in these Eastern seas, and the Thornburgs' dhow renewed my interest in these ancient and interesting craft. As a result, I decided to hitch a ride on one of the large "freighter" dhows for a week or so, just to see what life with the descendants of Sindbad would be like.

Such craft are almost always crowded, of course. There is no such thing as privacy, and since women, when they are aboard, are relegated to the dark, dank, odoriferous holds throughout the voyage, Tay elected to stay behind. But here, I thought, was an opportunity that might not come again, so I set about finding a vessel that was soon to sail and that would take me aboard as a passenger.

I found her before long, too—a large "jalboot," which is one of some fourteen types of dhows. Her name was *Faras*, which is Arabic for horse, and she had been built here on the island of Bahrein twenty-five years before—built of Malabar teak, with a little African wood thrown in. All her life Mohammed Abdul Lattif had been her captain—her *nakhoda*—and as jalboots go she was a big one, with a carrying capacity of five hundred bags of sugar—about fifty tons. She measured thirty-two "forearms" at the waterline and her beam was ten and a half. In other words, her waterline length was about fifty feet, and her beam about fifteen. She was completely decked, and the headroom below was all of eight feet. Fully laden, her draft was about six feet and under sail she might make as much as six knots, depending on the wind. And, most remarkable of all to me, she had been equipped with a light Diesel auxiliary engine.

The *nakhoda*, unfortunately, spoke no English, but when I learned that he was about to sail for the Trucial Coast—sometimes called the "Pirate Coast"—of Oman, where, at Sharja, I could get a plane back to Bahrein, I went to work on him through an interpreter and ultimately persuaded him to take me along, and Ahmed Hassan, the interpreter, too, for my smattering of Arabic wouldn't enable me to make much headway with the *Faras's* Moslem crew.

The voyage was short by the standards of these hardy sailors who not infrequently sail to India or down the coast of Africa. Leaving Bahrein, we would sail around the tip of the peninsula of Qatar and down its eastern coast to the port of Doha—about 120 miles. And from there we would sail eastward to the Pirate Coast port of Dibai—some 360 miles in all, a mere two hours and a half in Charlie but three days, perhaps, and possibly more in *Faras.*

My accommodations were first class, if anyone's were, though there were no private staterooms. In fact, there were no staterooms at all, and the space that was particularly reserved for me was on a narrow deck that was raised several feet above the main deck near the stern, and built across the dhow from rail to rail. Here, with the *nakhoda* and three or four others of the elect, I had just enough space to unroll my sleeping bag, while overhead were two longitudinal poles and three or four lateral ones over which a rolled-up awning could be spread in stormy weather.

Sailing from Bahrein under power, we made our way to Doha, the capital of Qatar. There we added sixty-three home-going Omani laborers to our passenger list before sailing once more— still under power—for Trucial Oman and the port of Dibai.

Let no one imagine that life aboard a Persian Gulf dhow is in any way comparable to life aboard any other kind of ship that sails the seven seas, for it is not. I recall, for instance, being awakened early in the morning when we were more or less midway from Doha to Dibai. Above the sound of the wind in the rigging I sleepily heard a high thin voice—the unmistakable whine of the muezzin as he called the faithful to their morning prayers.

> *"Assolotu Khairum Ninan-Nawm.*
> *Allohu Akbar.*
> *La ilaha illa Allah,*
> *Mohammed Rasul Allah."*

I opened my eyes, and there on the deck stood the *nakhoda*, silhouetted against the first rosy flush of the eastern sky beyond our bow. It was he—Mohammed Abdul Lattif—who was giving the call to prayers. He started every day like this, as did every other dhow captain, whether here in the Persian Gulf, or in the Arabian Sea off the Malabar Coast of India, or far down the coast of Africa with a cargo of salt and Tigris-Euphrates dates. And the words he used said:

> *"Prayer is better than sleep.*
> *Allah is Great.*
> *There is no god but Allah,*
> *Mohammed is his Prophet."*

I propped myself up on an elbow in my sleeping bag, which fit snugly across the section of the poop deck that I shared with Ahmed Hassan, my slightly English-speaking interpreter. From that vantage point I could take in the full length of the dhow from its square, overhanging stern, past the single and forward-raking teakwood mast, to the stubby upswept bow.

Although the *nakhoda's* call did not apply to me, the one infidel among a shipload of Moslems, and though the sun had not yet risen, I felt that it would be discourteous to sleep longer, so I slid out of my sleeping bag and pulled on my shoes and jacket against the midwinter chill. Then, I am afraid, I cheated a bit, for I opened one of the few cans of orange juice in my rucksack and, with my back turned, so that none of the praying Moslems would see me, I drank it, taking, as well, an anti-dysentery pill as a safeguard against the ship's food and water.

I had had some doubts about this voyage, short though it might be. For one thing, I was not certain about the risks that a Westerner might face in sailing with men who, in large part, make their own laws—who still are much given to carrying contraband —even, sometimes, slaves—and some of whom now and again engage in piracy, though on a scale that is far less than it was a century ago. Even the food and water, as my use of an anti-dysentery pill suggests, offered possibilities of danger to a Westerner with few immunities to Eastern germs. And, too, I knew this voyage across the Persian Gulf would be a very real test for a bit of advice given me years ago by a much-traveled uncle who had said, "Don't carry a gun. Arm yourself with a smile."

So far, I had managed all right, but the other passengers—mostly Omani laborers returning home from Saudi Arabia—had stared at me constantly since they had come aboard, and had stared sometimes, I felt, with hostility in their eyes. As a matter of fact, even the *nakhoda* and his crew treated me with great reserve. Perhaps they thought I was a spy for the British. This possibility, ever since I had thought of it, had worried me. After all, they could do what they pleased with me, for I would be aboard for at least another day.

Still, I had taken the risk in the hope of filming life aboard one of the vessels of the largest sailing fleet still left on earth—on a picturesque dhow such as those that have sailed the Indian Ocean between Arabia, India, and Africa since at least a thousand years before the Portuguese first rounded Africa and discovered the sea route from Europe to India. A pillar erected by Vasco da Gama on his great voyage of discovery stands to this day on the coast of Africa at the little Kenya Colony port of Malindi where he obtained a pilot—an Indian, perhaps, but possibly a Persian Gulf forebear of the *nakhoda* of the *Faras*—who took him directly to Calicut. And—or at least so the story goes—his voyage would have been more successful than it was but for the jealousy of Mohammedan traders—from the Persian Gulf, probably—who feared for their own trade and consequently incited the Hindus against the newcomers from Europe.

That was history now, of course, and had no effect on me as our elderly captain—he was sixty and looked older—still knelt on his small prayer mat in front of the Negro helmsman. He was facing the stern where I sat—facing toward Mecca, that is—and, in completing his prayers, was giving praise to the Lord of Daybreak for deliverance from the perils of the night.

These morning rites took much longer than one might expect, for every good Moslem must perform his ablutions before prayer, and the ship's plumbing facilities were of the simplest. There was nothing but the *zuli,* a crescent-shaped box slung over the portside aft, where it dangled a few feet above the sea. It was about three feet in diameter and two feet high, and it bulged away from the hull for a couple of feet, but the only thing that kept its squatting occupant from falling into the sea were two slender slats across the open bottom.

I watched one graybeard climb into that box, where he unwound his turban, pulled up his robe, and then washed himself with cold sea water scooped up in a tin can on the end of a string, but much time elapsed before the six members of the crew and the passengers had all done the same. In fact, the sun rose while some of the faithful were still waiting for their turn in the *zuli,* and while others were still praying. The crew, however, had long since fulfilled their morning obligations, and the *nakhoda* now gave an order, as a Western sailor would say, "to heave the lead."

The second in command, whose title was *sekooni*—meaning, I believe, "the one who steers"—whirled the lead in a quick vertical circle and hurled it into the sea well forward of the bow. The light line followed, and when we came abreast of the point at which the lead had reached the bottom he took in the slack of the line and pulled it up in double arm-length loops.

"Tissah!" he called, as the lead came out of the water. "Nine!" Nine times his full reach, in other words, or about fifty-four feet.

The *nakhoda* gave a slight change in heading to the freed slave who steered with the aid of an ancient liquid compass in a box before the helm, for in the shallow Persian Gulf, which, despite its 90,000 square miles of area, has an average depth of only ninety feet, experienced captains can tell their position with remarkable accuracy merely by sounding.

All night long the dhow's Diesel had been rumbling steadily. Without any measurable breeze, the great lateen sail had not been raised. But now, as the sun came up, a steady breeze from the north set in. The *nakhoda* was quick to notice it, and he ordered the sail set to supplement the engine. His crew went to work at once on the patched and badly worn canvas, lashing it to the spliced and ponderous lateen yard, whose length actually exceeded the length of the dhow. The *nakhoda* himself tied the final knot—the one that would rise the highest and take the greatest strain.

When all was ready, the sailors began hoisting away on the main halyard, inching the heavy yard and the great sail up the mast. They chanted as they labored, and not even my Arab interpreter fully understood their words, though the gist of it, as I got it from him, seemed to be that "Our ship is bound for 'Bandar Oman.' Yo-ho-ho! Let the wind blow!"

Again and again they sang, and at the end of each verse the tackle creaked and creaked again as they heaved together.

With the sun up and the sail set, it was time for breakfast. Hamed, a member of the crew, doubled as cook, for little time or attention is given to the preparation of food on an Arab dhow. I went forward to watch him, climbing among and over the crowded passengers, most of whom were eating thin sheets of bread they had brought with them, only a few willing to pay the extra rupee—about thirty cents—for the luxury of sharing the ship's rations.

For a galley the sailor-cook had a movable box about three feet by four. Stones lined the bottom, and on these a wood fire was kindled. A blackened teakettle and a few grimy cooking implements were ready for use, and over the fire *chapatties* were frying in a pan greased with *ghee*. Made of wheat flour, and not unlike oversize flapjacks, these were the fare at "the captain's table" both for breakfast and for dinner. Hot off the fire, they were very good, too, and filling.

The "captain's table" was a circular straw mat on the deck forward of the wheel and the compass. Eight of us sat on this, with the platter of *chapatties* in the middle, and we each tore off a piece of the topmost cake with the fingers of the right hand. It is terrible manners in this part of the world to touch food with the left hand, which is reserved for other things.

After the *chapatties* had disappeared, the sailor-cook returned with four tiny cups in one hand, and a brass samovar in the other. Into the cups he poured cardamom-flavored coffee, offering the first to me and the second to the *nakhoda*. I had long since become an advocate of the Arab's coffee and think that there is none better. It is strong, of course, but you never get more than a few swallows at a time.

I held out my demitasse-size cup for another filling, tossed that down, and also had a third. But then I returned the cup with a wiggle of my hand. Anyone failing to wiggle his cup would have it refilled until the samovar ran dry, but I have never seen an Arab, no matter how tired or thirsty, take more than three cups. To do so would be an unthinkable breach of etiquette.

The cups got a quick flushing in sea water before coming back with another drink—something new to me. It was a hot, milk-colored drink called *zengebeel*, made in part, I was told, of a potent spice from India.

"Protection against the cold," said my interpreter. And he was right. It seemed to kindle a fire in my stomach.

With breakfast over, one of our literate passengers—a Persian—began to read aloud from the Koran, the Moslem Bible, and everyone fell silent as they listened to the sacred words. But a little later, through my interpreter, I had a chance to talk to the *nakhoda* about dhows and the sea.

Most of his business, he told me, consisted of the transshipment of goods landed from steamers at Bahrein, and he usually sailed to Qatar, the Trucial Coast, and the lesser Persian, or Iranian, ports. On this voyage the dhow's two holds carried crates of Singer Sewing Machines, bags of flour, some electrical equipment, and many round baskets of Basra dates. Probably equally profitable, however, were our passengers, the passage to Dibai costing them ten Indian rupees each—roughly three dollars.

"How much do you pay your crew?" I asked the *nakhoda,* and the bearded skipper explained the profit-sharing system of dhow mariners. Operating costs—for fuel, wood, food, and so on—are first deducted, and one half of the remainder goes to the ship—that is, to the owner. And of the other half, three shares go to the *nakhoda,* two to the engineer, one and a half to the *sekooni,* and one to each of the other sailors.

This looks like good business for the owner, especially when, as in the present case, he is also the *nakhoda.*

That the engineer's share was next to the captain's indicated the importance nowadays of auxiliary power, and I asked the *nakhoda* if he thought sails would be completely replaced by engines.

"No," he replied. "We can't trust engines."

He pointed to a distant island on the horizon to starboard—the desolate island of Seer—and told me how an overcrowded dhow had counted too heavily on its Diesel and had been compelled to abandon forty passengers there when the engine broke down and both water and rations ran short.

"What if ours quits?" I asked.

"I always carry one month's food and water," he replied, "for each five days at sea. We would make it under sail alone."

But I doubted his estimate of the ship's supplies, for most of our passengers had come aboard unexpectedly at Doha. If anything happened, I thought, the fate of the ship's human cargo would probably be up to Allah, "the all merciful." If Allah arranged for such an island as Seer to be nearby, the passengers would probably be put off, and if they were not rescued, that, too, would be "the will of Allah," and so much the worse for them. I learned later, incidentally, that several of those who had been marooned on Seer had failed to survive, but local laws did not cover such matters, and nothing was done about it.

"What about piracy nowadays?" I asked, and the *nakhoda* replied that the most recent case involved the taking of a "boom"—that is, a dhow somewhat larger than a jalboot. It occurred off

Sharja on the Trucial Coast, and though the pirates were ultimately caught by the British, it was not until they had sailed 1500 miles—clear around the bottom of the Arabian peninsula to the Hadhramaut.

The most piratical waters these days, according to the *nakhoda,* are those along the Arabian Sea coast of Iran—no doubt because this coast line is not under Great Britain's control. And this suggests that piracy would quickly return on a much broader scale to the Persian Gulf were the British to pull out.

Off and on through the morning we were escorted by schools of porpoises, one group of six swimming for a long time, and occasionally leaping from the sea, just forward of the bow. Directly above them, on the bowsprit, lay Saleh, the engineer, sound asleep and unaware of the playful mammals below him. It seemed incredible that anyone could sleep on so precarious a perch, the bowsprit being round and no more than eight inches in diameter, and why he did not fall into the sea I'll never know.

Prayers were offered again at midday, after which we of "the captain's table" had our main meal of rice, a little boiled fish, some bits of onion, and sweet and sticky dates. While we were eating, a quarrel that threatened to grow ugly broke out between two of the passengers—an Omani and a Bedouin.

"You call yourself a man?" roared the Bedouin. "I should tear out your beard and throw it into the sea!"

The trouble had started when the Omani had inadvertently knocked over a part of a pile of cargo onto the Bedouin, and the insults that were exchanged appeared to be leading to a free-for-all. The *nakhoda,* sensing this, leaped between the two.

"Are you no better than goats," he demanded, "to quarrel like that? Neither one of you is a man if you don't settle your dispute calmly. Come now. Don't disgrace my honorable dhow."

The quarrel was grumblingly brought to an end, and this was not the only time the *nakhoda* had to use his wits in handling his crowded craft. He was inclined to ask nothing of his passengers except that they keep out of the crew's way, cause no trouble, and pay their fares, yet, oddly enough, he had permitted all those passengers to come aboard without collecting their fares in advance. Only now, on the afternoon of the last day of our voyage, did he and the *sekooni* begin to demand payment.

The two of them went about the crowded deck, collecting ten rupees from each passenger and writing down the names as the payments were made. Several turbaned Omanis resisted, but in the end, the *nakhoda's* scorching vituperation—and the glowering of the crew—brought forth the fares.

One of the Bedouin passengers was a striking figure—tall, thin, and dressed in a travel-worn gown. He also wore a tan kaffa that was bound around his head with two black cloth rings, or agals. Because of his black beard, his long face appeared even longer than it actually was, and his skin was yellowish brown in color and almost waxen in appearance. I had caught his eye and smiled at him a number of times during the voyage, and now I beckoned to him, hoping he would come up to my raised section of the deck for a visit.

He came courteously, and through Ahmed Hassan, we talked about the voyage. At last I asked him where he came from. He pointed toward the mountains of Oman that were now faintly visible in the distance and explained that he lived on the other side of them, and beyond the Buraimi Oasis, in a little Sheikdom of about fifteen thousand people. He told me that an American doctor from Muscat visits that area several times a year, but that no British ever come.

"Has an airplane ever been there?" I asked, thinking that Tay and I might find it interesting to drop in.

He replied that no plane had ever landed in the Sheikdom. Sometimes, he said, they flew over, and if they "had no wheels"—that is, if the wheels were retracted—they were believed to be American. But any planes "with wheels hanging down"—with fixed landing gear, in other words—were thought to be British. And at such planes, he added, his people always shoot.

That certainly let Charlie out, but why, I asked, did they have it in for the British?

His Sheikdom, he explained, had been caught in a quarrel between Saudi Arabia on one side, and Muscat and the British on the other. Muscat claimed his Sheikdom, and the British sup- ported that claim. But his Sheik, he explained, wants to stay with King Saud.

He told me proudly that his village had much water and good land.

"Why, then," I asked, "have you gone away?"

He had been to Saudi Arabia, he said, to call on King Saud for his annual gift. Any man of his village who calls on the King in Riyadh, he told me, is given a gift by the King. Presented once a year, the gift may be of one, two, or three thousand Saudi rials—that is, from three hundred to nine hundred dollars. My Bedouin friend assured me that as soon as he reached home, his brother would set off for the King's court in order to profit also by this munificence.

"King Saud is very good to my people," he added, and I could only agree. "Every year he gives my Sheik forty thousand rials, and each of his four sons ten thousand. And he has given my Sheik two cars—the only ones in the Sheikdom. We like you Americans because you made King Saud rich enough to give us fine gifts. The British give us nothing."

His remarks were most illuminating and, among other things, explained how unpopular the British have become over the boundary disputes of the Buraimi area of the Arabian peninsula.

But now, quite suddenly, the Bedouin fell silent. Then, after a time, he asked Ahmed, the interpreter, if he was sure I was not British. Ahmed assured him that I was not, but that failed to satisfy him, and he got up from where he had been sitting beside me and returned to the main deck. Obviously he was troubled, and after a time he came back and asked Ahmed to swear to Allah that I was not British.

When I realized how disturbed he was, I got out my American

passport. He could not read it, of course, but he may have noticed that the color was different from that of a British passport, and Ahmed read the words "The United States of America," which were printed on it. I was glad to see that this reassured him, especially when I told him that we Americans had ourselves once fought the British for our independence.

By sunset we could make out the coast line, and I asked the *nakhoda* if he would go into Dibai that evening. He replied that there would not be enough water in the inlet before morning, and that we would anchor outside.

We had our evening meal of *chapatties,* and when darkness had fallen, Ahmed, the *sekooni,* began to use a flashlight, flashing it intermittently ahead. As a result, a small dhow ultimately appeared and, with its sail furled and its engine running very slowly, the two vessels came together. The smaller dhow made fast to our starboard side, and our *sekooni* leaped onto its deck and greeted its Arab skipper with a warm embrace and a kiss on each cheek.

I asked my interpreter what it was all about and he told me that we were getting a pilot to show us into the harbor. But when I replied that it was odd that our experienced *nakhoda,* who knew every port in the gulf, should need a pilot, the interpreter let me in on the real purpose of the rendezvous. The other dhow, he explained, had come out to bid on six drums of kerosene that our crew had brought from Bahrein as a little venture of their own, the sale of kerosene in Dibai being a monopoly.

The discussion between our *sekooni* and the other chap was over price—fifty rupees bid for each fifty-five-gallon drum, and sixty asked. The deal was eventually closed at fifty-five rupees, though those drums had cost our sailors only twenty-two apiece—a very profitable bit of smuggling, I thought.

What other items were smuggled ashore I could only imagine. Two prosperous-looking merchants who had been passengers on our dhow went aboard the smaller craft with some mysterious trunks, and were landed, I suppose, under cover of the darkness.

During the night, too, while we lay at anchor offshore and I tried to get some sleep, other boats occasionally came alongside. Now and then, when I opened my eyes, I saw turbaned newcomers as they clambered aboard and talked with the members of our crew. I understood nothing of what they were discussing, but the frequent recurrence of the word "rupee" gave me a broad hint.

The next morning we entered Dibai's inlet with the tide—an inlet so narrow that from the air it appears to be no more than a creek, its green waters penetrating the desert like a fishhook with a stem four miles long and with the barb touching the open gulf.

Dibai itself numbers about twenty thousand people and lies on both sides of the "creek." It is an unplanned conglomeration of one-story mud-brick houses, many of which have Persian "wind towers" another story high. These catch any wind that may blow, funneling it into the living quarters below—a form of air conditioning thousands of years old. The town is one of the native ports of the Trucial Coast, and it probably has not changed much in appearance since it was a center of slave running and piracy generations ago. But now piracy is rare, though smuggling, as I had seen, is common. Still, our *nakhoda* and his crew were perfectly at ease when I joined them at a coffeehouse over glasses of sugary sweet tea and a pull on a bubbling *hookah*.

In a few hours I would be on my way to the R.A.F. base at nearby Sharja and would begin a short flight back to Bahrein. My erstwhile shipmates, however, had now completed another successful voyage. Allah had guided them safely across the gulf, and their business—illegal as well as legal—had been profitable.

When I told the *nakhoda* how sorry I was to leave him, I felt honored and deeply touched by his reply.

"You have treated us like men," Ahmed Hassan interpreted him as saying, "and it is as if you are one of us. We will miss you."

I left them, marveling at the way they had responded to my sincerely friendly approach. It was further proof that peoples everywhere, whether in the jungles of the Congo, in yak-hair tents on the roof of the world, in age-old sailing vessels on the Persian Gulf, or even in New York, are all the same at heart. Even here on the Pirate Coast of Oman, the smile had won again.

XV. Into the Empty Quarter
of Arabia

E̲VEN BEFORE I LEFT UMM A'
Sabaan for the Persian Gulf voyage on the dhow, Tay and I had
decided soon to begin our journey home. Our plan was to fly back
to Europe, perhaps selling our plane in Cairo, for the Cessna
Company's offer to repurchase it had now expired. We still hoped
to be able some time to fly on through India, southeast Asia, and
Indonesia, and on to Australia, too, but Africa and the Middle
East were enough for one jaunt. Anyway, the most important
thing for us just now was the baby that was on its way. On that
account alone the time had come to wind up our globe-trotting
and return home. Before beginning so extensive a journey, however, it was obvious that Tay should see a medical specialist, and
luckily the Arabian American Oil Company—Aramco—had a
hospital at the nearby town of Dhahran which was staffed with a
highly competent group of American doctors.

Dhahran lies on the Arabian mainland only twenty miles from
Bahrein—no flight at all for Charlie—but it is in Saudi Arabia,
where the government is exceedingly strict in its control of visitors. Max Thornburg therefore passed the word along to friends
in Aramco, asking that they obtain the necessary permission for
us to enter the country. We were cleared, but it took a week, and

all that time we almost held our breath on Umm a' Sabaan, wondering if we would be permitted also to bring Charlie.

Permission for both of us, and for Charlie as well, came at
last, but we did not fully appreciate our fantastically good fortune.
It was not until later that we were told that ours was the first
private plane, other than those of the oil company, to land in
Saudi Arabia, and that permission had come all the way from His
Majesty, King Saud, himself. We were helped, of course, by the
fact that Aramco had passed our request on, but we might very
well have been turned down if it had not been for my father's
visit to His Majesty's court a few weeks earlier while he was
circling the globe in filming a new production for Cinerama.

Unaware of all this, of course, we said good-by to Aunt Leila
and Uncle Max and took off from the homemade airstrip on
Umm a' Sabaan. Even before we climbed aboard Charlie we
could see in the distance the smoke of the huge Aramco refinery
at Ras Tanura, and by the time we reached 3000 feet, the buildings of Dhahran, not very far south of the refinery, stood out
clearly against the desert beyond. In no time we were circling the
town, marveling at how much it looked like a town in the United
States—rows of homes laid out precisely, with lawns and hedges,
paved streets, sidewalks, large office buildings, and so on. Dhahran is so American, in fact, that it even has a supermarket, a
beauty parlor, a movie theater, and a golf course, and most of
Aramco's seven thousand American employees live there—many
with their families—in company houses. The only difference is
the setting—the yellow sand that stretches away on all sides, and
the bright blue Persian Gulf a few miles to the east. And yet, now
that I come to think of it, that is not the only difference. Another
is that there is not so much as a can of beer in Dhahran, for by
royal decree—which is based on the Koran—alcoholic beverages
are out. You won't find any pickled infidels—or Moslems either—
in Saudi Arabia.

Between Dhahran and the Persian Gulf is one of America's
Strategic Air Command bases, also serving as Arabian head-

quarters for Aramco's air fleet, one of the largest company-owned fleets in the world. And this was where we landed, and where we rolled Charlie into the Aramco hangar before making our way to town.

Aramco put us up at Steineke Hall, which is as fine as any hotel in America, and an appointment was made for Tay to see Dr. Brown, one of the two obstetricians at the company hospital. How busy he and his colleague were, is suggested by the fact that one hundred and sixty-eight American babies were born in Dhahran in 1954. His report, in Tay's case, was that she was coming along fine, but he strongly advised her not to get out of touch with competent medical help from then on. In other words, no more Hunzas—no more migrations. In fact, Dr. Brown didn't think much of the idea of her flying in a single-engine plane, for he was concerned over the possibility of a hard knock in the event of a forced landing.

Our confidence in Charlie was such that we didn't worry about that, but we were compelled to consider his advice about not getting too far off the beaten path. So—and even this was going out on a limb—we planned to fly back to Sharja near the entrance to the Persian Gulf, there to cut across the Oman "thumb" to the Gulf of Oman. Then, following the shore of the gulf to Muscat, we would continue to Aden by way of the coast of Arabia, refueling at the Royal Air Force bases on the offshore island of Masira, and at the mainland ports of Salala and Mukalla. Then, crossing the Red Sea to Asmara again, we would fly on to Cairo as we had done before. If we failed to sell Charlie there, we would fly along the North African coast, returning to France by way of Spain. And in Europe, we knew, selling the plane would be a cinch, and we should be able to recover its cost at least.

But first, we sent word to Riyadh, the capital of Saudi Arabia, hoping to be able to make arrangements to meet King Saud Al Saud, one of the few absolute rulers on earth. Ordinarily, one would no more expect to be received by His Majesty than by the rulers of the Kremlin in Stalin's time, but my father had been received not long before, and, perhaps because of the impression he had made, a message arrived in the King's name, and both Tay and I were invited to come to Riyadh. We were delighted, of course, but Tay's bad luck caught up with her. At almost that very moment she came down with an attack of grippe, making it impossible for her to fly the 240 miles inland to Riyadh, so I took off alone.

Actually, the distance I flew was more than 300 miles, for instead of cutting directly across the desert, I followed the railroad Aramco completed for the King in 1951—the only one in Saudi Arabia since Colonel Lawrence knocked out the Hejaz Railway in 1917. This recently completed line is single-tracked, and it links the desert capital of Riyadh with Dhahran and the Persian Gulf, and though its route inland is indirect, it seemed wiser to follow it than to strike out by compass for a pinprick on the map so far across the empty sands. By following the railroad I would be sure, if Charlie and I were forced down, of being able to flag the first train—or so I thought. The fact was, as I learned when I reached Riyadh, that the trains weren't running. The tracks, strangely enough, had been knocked out by floods! Floods, I repeat, and in the desert!

The "iron beam" led me to the south over some of the world's most enormous oil fields, the total extent of which is not yet precisely known. And yet, all I could see, as Charlie took me over these fantastic natural reservoirs of petroleum, was an endless expanse of wind-blown sand.

I flew over Hofuf, Arabia's largest oasis, and the home, it is said, of more than two hundred thousand Moslems. A little farther on, the railroad bent from south to west and the sand below abruptly changed its color from white to orange. This was the eastern edge of the Dahana, a belt of sand stained by iron oxide, and varying in width from fifteen miles to fifty as it curves for 800 miles north and south through the Arabian peninsula.

Farther on, the sea of sand came to an end and barren hills of rock rose from the desert—the foothills of the Tuwaiq Mountains.

At last I made out Riyadh, a tight cluster of earthen-colored buildings—hard to distinguish against the late-afternoon sun. And a few miles to the north I could see the gravel airfield used by the King's Convair, and by the planes of the Saudi Arabian Airlines.

Taking my instructions from the English-speaking tower operator, I put Charlie down on the northerly heading strip and taxied back to a new terminal building where I was met by a serious-faced official in a brown, gold-braided Saudi robe that came down to his ankles. He was the King's secretary, Sheik Abdullah Bulkhair.

"Welcome to Riyadh," he said as I stepped from the plane. "We expected you sooner and were afraid you had lost your way across the desert."

I apologized for having caused any concern, explaining that Charlie was not as fast as a Convair, and also that I had taken an extra half hour to follow the railroad.

Sheik Abdullah beckoned me into a royal limousine before I could even see to having Charlie staked down. But it was better, I thought, to let the plane blow away than to offend His Majesty's right-hand man. Still, I wondered what the hurry was all about as the big new Lincoln started off with a rush and, with the Sheik and me in the back seat, careened madly along the rough gravel road to the city. I had long since learned that Arabs drive with the accelerator on the floor board, but this, it seemed to me, was more than usually extreme, though I soon learned the reason.

"His Majesty," the Sheik remarked, "has invited you to dine with him. We'll just make it."

"Praise be to Allah," I thought, "that I put on my best suit instead of my usual khakis."

That had been Tay's idea, and it was a good one, for I was to be given no opportunity to change.

Suddenly, though its speed was no less, the shiny new Lincoln began riding as a Lincoln should, and I looked out the window to see that the gravel had turned to pavement. We were on the final mile of the highway to the palace, and were rolling along a four-lane road that was divided in the best U.S. style by a strip of trees, grass, and flowers. And though there was very little traffic, and I saw no crossroads, traffic lights were spaced along it. The contrast between the red sands of the Dahana and this Riyadh turnpike left me breathless.

The highway, which had been very recently completed, led us directly to His Majesty's new palace, a two-story structure that extended in all directions. But what impressed me most as we drove up in the half light of evening was the lavish and spectacular display of electricity.

Over the entrance and all along the edge of the palace roof were brilliant rows of neon lights. Sheik Abdullah Bulkhair hurried me past the Bedouin guards and into a long, carpeted hallway. Several members of the royal family and a group of officials, all of whom were dressed as the King's secretary was, were standing before a door, with a dozen armed Bedouin guards nearby. Clearly, it would not be well to roam about the palace without an escort, but as the Sheik and I approached, the door opened and we, as well as the waiting group, all filed into the royal dining hall.

I had imagined that the King's meals would be spread on the floor—a richly carpeted floor, perhaps—and that everyone would eat with the fingers of the right hand in true Arab fashion. So it was with some surprise that I saw a great banquet table arranged in the form of a squared-off U, with the places set in Western-fashion with silver and china. It was about as it would have been at the Waldorf-Astoria, which, no doubt, was what the King intended.

Flowers decorated the table, fluorescent lights were brightly reflected by the enormous mirrors that lined the walls, and my first impression was that I was back in America, though I had little time to think. The Sheik, without a pause, was leading me between the two arms of the U-shaped table toward the closed end where a solitary figure sat on the table's farther side, with square patterns of yellow daisies, as well as an enormous pink rose and two miniature Saudi Arabian flags, on the table before him. He was broad-shouldered and erect in his brown and gold trimmed *aba*. He wore thick-lensed dark glasses, and his white headdress was held in place by two broad agals that were made of braided gold thread.

It was His Majesty, King Saud Al Saud.

As we approached, he half rose to shake my hand across the table. Then, before I could say anything, Sheik Abdullah motioned me to sit to the right of the King but at the base of the inside of the U, which meant that I had to turn to the right in my chair each time I faced the King.

The Sheik, who didn't sit down, acted as interpreter, and through him the King asked about my flight from Dhahran. In replying I also told him how greatly I appreciated the honor of being in his presence, and thanked him for letting me come. He asked about my father; I said that he was probably in India at the moment. I also found an opportunity to explain why Tay had not come with me, and His Majesty remarked that his wives would be disappointed not to have the company of my wife at their dinner in the harem.

When I mentioned the beauty of the desert, and referred to a few patches of water I had seen on my way to Riyadh, King Saud said that the rains, which had been widespread, had also been so heavy as to surpass anything previously known in some sections of his kingdom.

It was at this point in the conversation that a young Arab entered. He took a position to the right of His Majesty about ten feet away, and began reading the news of the world in Arabic. All conversation ceased while the King listened, but the meal went on. Orange juice and soup were served. Mutton, potatoes, and spinach followed, together with lettuce and tomato salad. Then came boiled chicken and rice with almonds, and the dessert was Jell-O, as well as oranges, bananas, and apples. And all of this was served by waiters in spotless, white, Western-style uni-

forms. I even heard that Aramco had imported a Western chef
for the King, though I naturally did not see him.

When the King rose, everyone instantly got to his feet. The
meal was over, whether or not any of those present had finished
eating. I noticed that as His Majesty walked toward his private
doorway, a tray of toothpicks was held toward him, and I noticed,
too, that he took one.

The rest of us left the room as we had entered, making our
way through several anterooms and past a detachment of the
royal guard into a huge parlor. The only furniture consisted of
chairs and sofas placed around the sides of the room, the central
area being without furniture, though the floor was entirely covered with exquisite Persian rugs. Many chandeliers hung from
the ceiling, and at the far end of the room were several especially
impressive chairs.

I was invited by my guide and mentor, the Sheik, to sit just
to the left of the grandest chair of all, but everyone stood until
His Majesty entered.

King Saud took the elegant, overstuffed chair next to mine,
and coffee was served at once. It tasted just as the coffee had
tasted aboard the Persian Gulf dhow, but now it was served in
fragile little porcelain cups by a young African who moved, I
thought, with remarkable speed and dexterity.

This was the moment, Sheik Abdullah told me, to discuss any
business with His Majesty, and the secretary dropped on one
knee before the King in order to act as interpreter. Taking advantage of the opportunity, I apologized for the request I was about
to make and explained the purpose of the year-long flight Tay
and I were making. It was only then that I asked His Majesty if
he would consent to being photographed as the Shah of Persia,
the Prime Minister of Pakistan, and others had done?

The King replied that he was frightfully busy but that he hoped
he could find a few minutes for my camera the next morning.
One or two others in the room then spoke to him, but in a few
minutes a smoking vase of incense was passed. It went around the

room twice before the King rose, shook hands with me, and the evening was over.

I spent the night at a half-finished hotel, and at noon the following day Sheik Abdullah Bulkhair took me back to the royal palace, saying that if I was lucky I might be able to film His Majesty on his way through the garden to lunch.

I set my tripod and camera up in the garden, and after a long wait we heard the honking of automobile horns and the roar of racing motors at the palace gates. A few moments later in walked King Saud with a great following of relatives and officials. His Majesty came directly toward the camera, paused for a moment at just the right distance, smiling and talking to Sheik Abdullah. Then, to my great pleasure, he asked me if I would care to share another meal with him.

I shall always count it an honor to have had two meals with the King of Saudi Arabia in twenty-four hours, but even more surprising was His Majesty's permission to take his photograph— both in movies and stills—while he was eating. Nor will I ever forget how, when I closed in for a final shot, His Majesty spoke his first and only English to me.

"Just one more?" he said.

My mind was full of my experiences in Riyadh when Charlie and I headed back for Dhahran that afternoon—directly across the desert this time. And I was also admiring my new gold wrist watch, bearing the King's green seal of two crossed swords beneath a date palm. The watch, together with a Saudi gown and headdress, had been a gift of His Majesty.

With Charlie headed east and with the sun at my back I could plainly see the Dahana miles away—that great strip of red sand that extends south for nearly a thousand miles, far into the Rub' al Khali—the "Abode of Emptiness" or the "Empty Quarter." I wished I could head Charlie south above the Dahana and into this almost unknown region, "the largest continuous body of sand in the world"—a vast expanse about the size of Texas where not even the Bedouin or his camel can find a living.

Until recently, the Rub' al Khali, which occupies most of south central Arabia, had been penetrated by only three Westerners— all British explorers who made separate dashes across this unequaled desert. The first of these was Bertram Thomas who penetrated this desolate region in 1931. In 1932 he was followed by H. St. John Philby, and in 1948 by Wilfred Thesiger. But now Aramco's geologists were beginning to roam the Rub' al Khali almost at will in search of oil. I wished I could join them for a while—to see something of this phase of development in the Middle East and to set foot in one of the few remaining regions of our planet still marked "unexplored" on the map.

Back in Dhahran I took the idea up with Jack Reed, Aramco's head of exploration, and he not only said "Yes," but also added that this was a good excuse for him to get away from his Dhahran office. He would personally take me into the Empty Quarter.

Kissing Tay good-by again, and leaving Charlie in the Aramco hangar, I took off with Jack Reed and Brock Powers, Aramco's thirty-year-old head geologist. We were flying in one of Aramco's single-engine Beavers which was outfitted with huge desert tires, and Cotton McGinty, a towheaded ex-Marine fighter pilot and regular desert fox, was at the controls.

Cotton's first target was a tiny drilling camp called Ubaila, 325 miles south at twenty-two degrees North Latitude, and forty-nine degrees East Longitude, and as we flew into this northern portion of the Empty Quarter Jack Reed explained that Aramco really hoped it would not find any oil there, for the problem of getting it out would be terrific. Anyway, the pools of oil already found are enough for years. They are exploring the Empty Quarter, he said, because Aramco must return a portion of its huge concession area to the Saudi Arabian Government each year. Not wishing to give up productive regions, they are compelled to explore all the land that lies within the limits of their concession. Even so, he added, they are looking only for the largest oil-bearing structures. Smaller ones—even some that would look huge elsewhere—are not worth developing because of the cost involved.

Cotton McGinty flew us directly to Ubaila as if it had been a magnet, and as we landed on its oiled sand strip I noticed sections of red fence along each side. In the United States such structures would be called "snow fences," but they are "sand fences" in Arabia, and those at Ubaila were there to keep the wind-blown sand from accumulating on the airstrip.

We stopped only long enough to have lunch with the eight Americans who, with their Arab helpers, run a deep-test drilling rig, and for Cotton to refuel the plane. Then we were off again, flying deeper into the Empty Quarter. Our course was to the southeast and in the next hour and a half the shimmering sand gradually changed from yellow to pink.

Cotton was searching for a two-man tent outpost in a region of sand formations that Jack Reed called "incredible." He was very nearly right, too. In a vast area of reddish-orange sand, centuries of wind had piled up huge hills that were hundreds of feet high—in some cases more than a thousand. A veritable mountain range of orange-colored sand ran from northeast to southwest, and between the sand mountains were grayish plains, hard, absolutely flat, and sometimes miles across. It was as if some gigantic Middle Eastern jinni from the *Arabian Nights* had swept up millions of tons of the desert's sands into these enormous heaps.

While Cotton searched for tire tracks that would lead us to the tiny camp, I filmed this most amazing mountain range. After a search of more than half an hour, we spotted a steel tower rising from a summit—the Shoran station operated by an American and a Canadian who, together with their Saudi guards and helpers, were the sole inhabitants of that corner of the Rub' al Khali.

Cotton put the Beaver down on a level area that had been marked off with oil drums for landing, and in a few minutes a red Powerwagon drove up. At the wheel was Aramco's Charlie Felds. His feet were bare, he wore no shirt, his khaki pants were rolled halfway to his knees, and the tan he had acquired suggested that he had lived in the Empty Quarter for quite a spell. He was glad to have visitors, of course, but what really made his face light up was Cotton McGinty's announcement that he had brought a dozen steaks from Dhahran.

We climbed into the truck for the drive across the plain to the gently inclined base of an orange sand mountain where two white tents were pitched. There we met Charlie's companion, John LeGrande, a Canadian whose bushy beard made him look much older than his twenty-six years.

These two young men and their Shoran station played a vital part in the high-altitude aerial survey that was then being conducted in the Rub' al Khali. LeGrande was the technician, and his station, working in conjunction with another somewhere in the desert, could "pin point" with remarkable accuracy—within a radius, apparently, that was to be measured in feet—the position of the photographic plane—a B-17—each time its crew took a picture.

We were taken up the mountain in the powerful four-wheel drive Dodge Powerwagon to the steel tower and radar station. With the car's big oversize tires churning up a miniature sandstorm, the powerful vehicle gathered frightening speed on the gentler slopes in order to carry to the tops of the steeper ones, and we had to hang on to keep from sailing into the air when the car leaped over the occasional sharp cornices.

These mountains of sand forever reflect the force of their maker, the wind. Graceful ripples, delicate ridges, and an infinite number of symmetrical patterns mark them, and they are forever changing, for under the urging of the wind they never cease moving. Their steepest slopes, we were told, were called "slip faces," and on these the sand was pitched so steeply as always to be on the verge of sliding, like snow on the steep slopes of timberless mountains. We all walked out onto one of these slip faces, and the sand, to a depth of a few inches, began to slide beneath our feet. It did not move rapidly as powder snow sometimes does, but very, very slowly. And as the movement began I heard a deep, faint droning sound that seemed to come from far away—a sound such as that of a squadron of propeller-driven bombers flying in the distance and at a great altitude.

What I heard were the "singing sands" of Arabia—first reported by Bertram Thomas, the English explorer who made his pioneering dash by camel across the Empty Quarter in 1931. This phenomenon of the Great Desert seems to be caused by the sliding of one layer of sand over another, a movement which creates so plain a vibration that I could feel it through my shoes.

We four newcomers helped John LeGrande and Charlie Felds polish off some of those fresh steaks at our evening meal, and then we spread our sleeping bags on the sand and fell asleep with the huge constellation of Orion overhead. Not since I had been high on the Mountains of the Moon had I seen the night sky shine so brightly.

After breakfast the next morning, we waved good-by to the sole inhabitants of these sand mountains, and Cotton headed the Beaver for one of Aramco's mobile units—G-8—that was just about at the dead center of the Empty Quarter, some 250 miles west.

The flight was tame enough until Cotton reached his estimated time of arrival. Ideally, of course, he should have been able, by then, to see the big white trailers, but there was nothing except rolling sand in every direction. Up to that point Cotton had been flying a compass heading, correcting for wind drift by watching the plane's track over the desert. There had been no check points, so he had been compelled to estimate his ground speed by watching the desert slip by—a method at which he was expert. But now, not having found the mobile unit, he flew beyond his estimated time of arrival long enough to know that the big trailers were not ahead of us and then, instead of searching about aimlessly, he began a search pattern that was as methodical as if he were searching for an aircraft carrier at sea.

First he turned ninety degrees to the left and held that course for fifteen minutes, and he would have completed a rectangular "box pattern" eventually and then taken off for Ubaila and its

beacon if the target had not been sighted. Cotton McGinty is
not one to continue a search until his gas is too low to make it
to some safe base. And in this case, he was still on the first leg of
his search pattern when he spotted truck tracks in the sand.

He called G-8 on the radio and was told, when he described
the direction of the tracks, that we were probably south of camp,
so for twenty minutes we followed the tracks to the northeast.
Still no G-8 was in sight, so he radioed again and was told,
apologetically, that truck tracks running in the direction he had
described also lay to the north of the camp. He reversed his
course, therefore, and another twenty-five minutes brought us to
the trailer camp.

We landed next to the camp on a smooth section of yellow
sand, the Beaver's oversize tires making such a landing easy, and
a red Dodge sedan rolled up. It was "Red" Caudill who stepped
out—a bantam of a man in his late thirties, freckled, redheaded,
wisecracking, and the foreman of G-8 and another mobile unit
—G-9—that was operating hundreds of miles away. Red hails from
Oklahoma and was just the man to ride herd on two outfits in
the Empty Quarter, keeping them at work and well supplied.

G-8's task was to drill down through the sand and then through
thousands of feet of rock, bringing up sample cores and plotting
their depth. It was a part of the task of mapping the desert's
sub-surface and of locating any possible oil-producing structures.
But Red's "string," as he called it, was to move that afternoon
to a new location some eighty miles to the southwest, and this
would give me a chance to film a move across the Great Sands.
So I joined the men of G-8 while Jack Reed, Brock Powers, and
Cotton McGinty flew on to where G-9 was working in the desert.

By the time Red Caudill had his string ready to roll that afternoon, the drilling rig had already vanished over the dunes, getting a head start because it moved so slowly behind its caterpillar
tractor. What remained were four long white trailers—one the
office, another the kitchen, a third equipped with washbasins and
showers, and the fourth a double-decked sleeping trailer. All of

these were on enormous, low-pressure dual tires, and in addition to these ponderous vehicles, there were a water-tank truck, a couple of Powerwagons and sedans equipped and geared especially for sand, and a few other support vehicles.

With two trailers behind each of two huge Kenworth trucks, G-8 rolled off to the south—as remarkable a caravan as the desert ever saw.

Bill Reiss, the unit's geologist, led the way in a sedan, and I rode with Red Caudill in another, though he kept off to one side of the string where he could keep an eye on it. The Kenworths were in the hands of turbaned Saudis who set Red to cursing when they took sand gullies and drifts so fast as to rock an occasional wheel off the ground. When that happened, Red stopped the guilty driver and told him off in good pigeon Arabic.

To keep his outfit in order, Red had to run circles around it, roaring along at forty and fifty miles an hour over the trackless desert. He had to watch his compass, too, and the lay of the land, and in the midst of this he had a radio call to make to Dhahran. And all the time he had to keep his car from rocketing off the dunes or rolling down one of the many unexpected slip faces he approached. What a ride!

Worst of all, it seemed to me, was when Red, at fifty miles an hour, would turn around in his seat to check the tuning of the transmitter which was strapped in place on the left rear seat. At such times his eyes would be off the sand ahead for what seemed long periods to me, and he often turned back and spun the wheel in the nick of time to miss some hummock or hole in the sand.

Late in the afternoon Red called a halt on a gravelly plain where blowing sand had polished the stones and pebbles until they glistened. There was just enough time before sunset for the Saudi helpers to gather wood for their cooking fires, though they had to roam widely over the desert to find enough dead and scattered bushes.

While camp was being set, I hiked out to the highest nearby

dune, and from its top I had a view of countless miles of rolling sand. I was away from the sounds of camp, and all I could hear was the faint whistle of fine sand as it blew over the crests of the dunes.

When I returned supper was ready—American steaks cooked in an old oil drum over a fire of desert wood, vegetables from the kitchen trailer's deep freeze, milk, and ice cream with frozen strawberries. In a way, it seemed almost sacrilegious to eat such a civilized meal in the Empty Quarter. A handful of dates and some camel's milk would have been more appropriate, though no such outfit as G-8 could ever have been taken into the desert on such fare.

I shared a tiny room that night with one of the four drillers— a "tool-pusher" named Burt. The room was in the upper half of the sleeping trailer, and I slept between clean sheets on a comfortable iron cot that had a rubber mattress. I was under blankets, too, for the desert can be cold in January.

The Saudi truck drivers and laborers, who slept in tents, as well as the cooks and the seven Americans, were all up long before sunrise. We still had some distance to go to our new camp site, but by midday we had reached it and the work of digging in began.

The new camp was set up rapidly, and when the drilling rig rolled in later that afternoon, two of the drillers supervised its positioning and erection by the Arabs. Under their direction, the derrick, pushed up on hydraulic jacks, rose to the perpendicular, which was about all of this complicated business that I could understand.

And now Jack Reed, Brock Powers, and Cotton McGinty arrived in the Beaver, landing on the sand where Red Caudill had run his sedan up and down to make a track. The plane then taxied right into camp, its three passengers climbing down and excitedly showing us some flint arrowheads and pieces of petrified wood they had found where G-9 was working, and where they said they would take me the following morning.

Morning dawned on the windy side, the anemometer on top of the office trailer registering gusts up to thirty miles an hour, and all around the camp the blowing sand, most of which fortunately rose only a few inches above the ground, drifted across the desert in what looked like streamers of smoke. Aloft in the Beaver visibility was poor. There was enough sand in the air to blot out the horizon, but Cotton McGinty readily found G-9. The string was working in the southwest corner of the Rub' al Khali not far from the Yemen border, and we were soon driving a G-9 Dodge fifteen miles farther south to a new Aramco discovery.

At the southern end of a gravelly plain were the petrified stumps and fragments of a forest that had stood there perhaps a million years ago. The petrified wood had a reddish color, and tons of it lay in the vicinity. But even more fascinating to me were the flint arrowheads and spearheads that were scattered about. How old they are, or who their makers were, no one knows.

Hans Helley, G-9's geologist, thought that perhaps the plain was once a lake bed, and that inhabitants of this land that is now no longer inhabited then sometimes made their camps beside the water. Sitting before their tents, they may have made these arrowheads and spearheads, discarding the imperfect ones and losing others, thus making it possible for us to find them, even though the lake has been gone for ages and the forest that once stood on its shores has been petrified.

Who dwelt in this land before it became the desolate waste we call the Empty Quarter? What kind of land could it have been when forests thrived where we found only desolation?

These are questions that anyone who sees this portion of the world must ask. But no one knows the answers. The Rub' al Khali has guarded its secrets well.

XVI. *Homeward Bound*

Only a few hours after my Aramco friends and I had been trying to reconstruct the prehistoric past of a portion of the Empty Quarter, we were back in Dhahran and I was showing Tay the flint arrowheads and bits of petrified wood I had collected. She was rather envious of my experience in the Rub' al Khali, and when our conversation turned to a discussion of our coming flight to Cairo and our return home, I made a suggestion.

"Why not fly across the Rub' al Khali," I asked, "to Salala on the Arabian Sea Coast of Oman? We already have permission to land there, and it will save us from flying the whole southeastern coast of the Arabian peninsula."

We measured the distance on our maps. From Dhahran to Salala, which sits on the southeastern coast of the peninsula about midway between the mouth of the Red Sea and the entrance to the Persian Gulf, was 700 miles, most of which would be over the vast and impressive desolation of the Empty Quarter—a daring undertaking for so small a single-engine airplane as ours—a plane with just enough range to make it, and with almost no reserve to fall back on in case we met adverse conditions.

Tay was inclined to turn the idea down completely, and I didn't blame her. But then I suggested that we might land on the narrow

oiled desert airstrip at Ubaila. This Aramco station was just about
halfway, and we could spend the night there, refueling and taking off the next morning for Salala.

With that plan in mind, Tay consented, and on the afternoon
of February 14 we took off on what was to be a kind of climax
to our year-long flight to adventure—the first flight by a small
privately owned airplane across the Empty Quarter.

Armed with our exit permits—for leaving Saudi Arabia is no
less difficult than entering—and with our other preparations carefully made, we took to the air at two-fifteen and pointed Charlie's
nose toward a corner of the globe that, until recently, has been less
known than almost any other. Our flight charts, except for a few
notations the oil company had penciled in for us, were a complete
blank, showing only symbols of sand and gravel, and the superimposed lines of latitude and longitude.

We leveled off at 4000 feet, skirted a half-moon Persian Gulf
bay, and flew southeast on a course that paralleled the coast, and
with the island of Bahrein looming large a few miles away on
our left. Holding this course to a point roughly ten miles from
where the western coast of the Qatar Peninsula joins the mainland, I turned the plane onto a course that led us directly south.
This, I hoped, would intersect tire tracks on the desert that the
oil company had told me led straight to Ubaila.

The flight ahead was a thrilling one to me, though Tay still
had misgivings. She even began thinking about the possibility of
a rough forced landing on the desert when, for a few anxious
moments, we thought we had gone too far and had missed the
tire tracks. But then we saw them plainly on the sand below,
and we turned a bit to the left to follow them to Ubaila.

I told Tay to keep her eye on them while I called Bahrein, but
the tracks grew fainter and she began pounding me on the shoulder, telling me to get off the radio and concentrate on the serious
business at hand.

Cotton McGinty had given me a few lessons in desert flying,
and I had worked out the search pattern I intended to use in

case of necessity. I knew perfectly well that our flight across the Empty Quarter had to be made with planned precision, and I began now to understand more clearly what that great flier, Harold Gatty, had meant when he had told me on one occasion that "adventure is the result of bad planning."

I did not need to use my search plan just now, however, for we picked up the faint tire tracks again and in another fifteen minutes we passed a group of tents beside which rose a tall, thin tower that I recognized as a Shoran station—the mate to the one I had earlier visited in Cotton McGinty's Beaver. This being our first definite "fix," I radioed back to Dhahran, giving our time and altitude over the station, and repeating our estimated time of arrival at Ubaila.

We were still following the tire tracks, but they became fainter until they vanished altogether. As far as the eye could see—fifty miles, perhaps—the ocean of yellow sand spread in every direction. I still held accurately to the course the tracks had been following up to the time they disappeared, and suddenly I made out a tiny dark splotch on the yellow sand—a camel trough of which we had been told. It was a strange check point but a welcome one, for it told us not only that we were on course but also that Ubaila, with its big camp and its tall derrick, was 110 miles ahead. And because so prominent an installation would be visible for all of twenty miles, we could expect to pick it up in about another thirty-five minutes.

There had been no sign of life at the camel trough, but not far beyond it we could see sections of an oil line that had been laid across the sand to guide Arab drivers who refuse to put their faith in such magical things as compasses. The oil line ultimately disappeared beneath the drifting sand, and we were strictly on the compass again, but after some time Tay leaned forward in her seat.

"Look!" she cried. "There's a car."

And there, sure enough, was a red Dodge sedan bowling over the desert in the direction we were flying. A little later, too, we spotted a couple of abandoned oil drums which, small as they were from 4000 feet, stood out boldly against the sand.

The big derrick did not show up on the horizon just when we thought it should, but it appeared quite suddenly at last. It was dead ahead and we both jumped with relief when we saw it. I estimated the camp to be twenty-five miles away, and it must have been just about that, for it took us ten more minutes to get there.

"HZAP, HZAP," I called on the company frequency. "This is Cessna Four Three Charlie. Over."

A voice replied and I reported that we were within sight and would be there in ten minutes.

"How's the wind down there?" I asked, for I was worrying a little about landing in a heavy cross wind.

"Wind from the north," came the reply, "at eight miles an hour."

Just to show off a bit, I let Charlie roar around the rig and the camp buildings at a thousand feet. Then I came in for a landing on the narrow oiled sand strip, which, as we approached, seemed to be no more than a slot between two dunes, with snow fences on each side.

We taxied back to the wind sock and a cache of gasoline drums, where a couple of drillers were waiting for us, and as we stepped to the ground we noticed a third person—a third person who made us look again, for it was a girl! She was Emily Drewey, whose husband worked the big Ubaila drilling rig, and Aramco, following their established policy, had flown her down for a visit with him. However, Ubaila was the only desert station to which wives were allowed to come, the others being too rugged and too limited in accommodations.

Ubaila, I suspect, is one of the most amazing American "towns" in all the world—a cluster of three long, narrow, white wooden houses in a row. Off to one side were several storehouses and machine shops, as well as some cars and trucks, a Diesel power plant, a water tank painted with aluminum paint, and, a little way off, the small structures that are occupied by the Arab workers. All of these faced the typical American deep-well oil derrick, which, like such derricks elsewhere, was surrounded by sections of pipe and equipment.

What surprised us most were tiny beds of green grass in front of the three houses, some blossoming oleander, and a trellis covered with a green vine, all of which, as well as a six-foot-deep swimming pool, were made possible by a well Aramco had drilled, and from which a pump was drawing water that flowed steadily into the swimming pool through two six-inch pipes.

We had not planned on taking a swim in the Empty Quarter, but we did. And, incidentally, one of the men pointed out that their swimming hole had "the largest beach on earth."

At dinner that evening we had soup, a tender steak at least an inch thick, eggplant, beans, potatoes, iced tea, and ice cream. And, just to top it all off, cherry pie! After dinner, too, we joined the dozen or so Americans at Ubaila in watching *Dial M for Murder*, which was then a late Hollywood production.

In the morning, after a breakfast of cereal and flapjacks, we went across to the derrick where, with my motion picture camera, a Saudi driller and I climbed some hundreds of feet up the vertical ladder. From the top of the derrick I filmed the camp and also pointed the camera straight down for a view of the drilling floor. With the drill probing more than 13,000 feet into the sub-strata, the outfit was still at work, though with what results we were not told.

While we were there, Cotton McGinty and his Aramco Beaver arrived on another of his rounds in the Empty Quarter. And when he refueled his plane, he also refueled ours before coming to camp and giving me all the dope he could on the flight that lay ahead—a more hazardous one than that of the previous day.

The distance from Ubaila to Salala, on the Indian Ocean coast, was just under 500 miles.

"About sixty miles east of here," Cotton told me as he indicated a position on his own well-worn and heavily penciled map, "there's a big white finger of sand running north–south."

He traced out its contours and exact position with his finger.

"That is just about halfway," he went on, "to an airstrip we used to use on a big gravel plain. It's called Tumaisha, and you'll see a lot of truck tracks, and there ought to be some oil drums there, marking out the strip."

He marked this information on my map, and I noticed that our course would take us right over the tip of that finger of white sand, giving us an excellent check on our ground speed and wind drift. Cotton also confirmed the exact location of the Shoran station among the sand mountains almost exactly 200 miles from Ubaila.

With the first two check points he had given us, it should not be impossible to locate the Shoran station, and from there to Salala would be a matter of flying almost due south for 220 miles, picking up still another check point in the coastal range of the Oman. Barring a sudden sandstorm or engine failure, nothing should prevent us from spending the night in Salala, though those two possibilities were not to be discounted. We knew that we would be pretty much on our own from Ubaila to Salala, and it was with real excitement that we took off.

Charlie, I must say, was well prepared for this adventure. While he had been waiting in the Aramco hangar in Dhahran, the company mechanics had given him a thorough going-over. The engine got a routine, one-hundred-hour inspection. There were new spark plugs. The points had been cleaned. The magnetos had been checked for proper timing, and all lines and fittings had been checked for tightness. A leak in the right brake had been repaired. The radios had all been checked. And, as a final touch, Charlie's aluminum skin, which had become dull and clouded in the salty atmosphere of Bahrein, had been polished until it sparkled.

We took off from Ubaila at one-ten and immediately turned to a heading of 116 degrees as we began our slow climb to 3000 feet. Although it was the fifteenth of February, a heat haze made the horizon indistinct, but if all went well, we should reach Salala by four-ten.

Never before had I been more careful to keep an exact compass heading, but updrafts of hot air from the desert made flying rough, so we climbed to 4000 feet. About an hour from our take-off we passed the abandoned airstrip of Tumaisha, and I radioed Ubaila, giving our time over the strip. It was Cotton McGinty who replied, and I also reported that we were changing our heading to 146 degrees, which included a five-degree correction to the left for wind drift.

The air was still rough, so up we went to 6000 feet, where it was as smooth as silk, and within another ten minutes we sighted the great mountains of sand I had seen before. They looked, Tay said, just like the top of a bowl of stiffly beaten egg whites. Only their color, which was a deep pink orange, and their astonishing height seemed different.

We did not see the Shoran station but passed over tire tracks leading to it. After flying for a half hour over the sand mountains, which appeared in the afternoon sun like burnished gold when we looked out of Tay's window but deep red—almost maroon— out of mine, we passed over a flat gravel plain and came to yellow sand once more.

Now we saw tire tracks again—many of them, running roughly east and west. Unable to guess what story they had to tell, I radioed Cotton McGinty, and he said that the tracks we reported had probably been made by the Oman Border Patrol, and that they marked what Oman held to be its border with Saudi Arabia, though the border, as we knew, was in dispute because of the possible presence of oil beneath that portion of the desert.

The visibility was unrestricted now, and the horizon must have been a hundred miles away. We were flying due south, on the last lap to Salala, and before long the coastal range, our destination just beyond, began to rise above the southern horizon. About this time we heard, over our earphones, Aramco's main station in Dhahran as it made its afternoon round of calls to the various camps in the Empty Quarter. When it was Ubaila's turn, we faintly heard Cotton McGinty as he reported our progress. It was a heart-warming experience to know that if anything went wrong and we were forced down, "Desert Fox" McGinty was well informed on every detail of our course southward, and that in his Beaver he would almost surely be able to find us.

Now we began to see the ocean beyond the summits of the coastal range. Then we were above the range itself and could see the beautiful band of green that stretches from the foothills to the sea. And there, too, was the town of Salala at the water's edge, and just inland from it were the two gravel runways and the few buildings of the little British air base.

Though the distance to Ubaila was far for our radio—more than 400 miles—I called in order to report that we were within sight of our destination, and "Many, many thanks," I added, "for all your help." I could vaguely hear someone replying, but the signal was too faint. I repeated my message again, and this time one of Aramco's mobile units—either G-8 or G-9—answered from the southwest corner of the great desert.

"Cotton says so long," they told me, "and have a good trip home."

So Charlie had conquered the world's most forbidding desert— the Rub' al Khali—the Abode of Emptiness—the Empty Quarter. It was another record for our small airplane, and Charlie, if he has the feelings with which we sometimes credit him, must have been as proud as we were when we settled into our landing at Salala.

We were met by the young British commanding officer of the airfield—a field, incidentally, that had been built and operated, or so we were told, by our Air Force during World War II as an intermediate stop on the way east to India and China. Now it is one of three skeletonized fields maintained by the R.A.F. along the coast of southern Arabia as a series of links between Bahrein and Sharja on the Persian Gulf and the important British base of Aden near the entrance to the Red Sea.

The C.O. invited us to spend the night at his quarters there at the field, but in a few minutes a man and a woman pulled up in a Land Rover.

"Here come the oil people to meet you," the C.O. remarked.

I put down the suitcase I had been unloading, and as I looked around the nose of the plane I was astonished to see a familiar face. For a moment I could not think of his name, but then I remembered that Fred Davies, chairman of the Board of Aramco, had told me that a man named Clayton was the headman for Cities Service at Salala. And now the familiar face, the small mustache, the prominent nose reminded me that I had met him in Turkey nearly eight years before—Ed Clayton, a dapper Southerner in the oil business.

I seized his hand, and he introduced us to his wife, Virginia, who was the only Western woman in those parts. They had seen us as we had been about to land and had rushed out to invite us to stay with them.

We were happy to accept, of course, and with the four of us crowding the front seat of their car, we drove off toward Salala, which despite its limited size, is the capital of Dhufar, the western-most province of the sultanate of Muscat and Oman.

Our zigzag course over the dirt streets of Salala brought us to the gateway of the Sultan's palace, which looks out on the sea, and toward several graceful dhows that rode at anchor just off-shore. We stopped to deliver our passports to the palace guard, so that they might be taken to His Highness, Sultan Said bin Taimur, and later in the day I petitioned His Highness for an audience.

"My wife and I," I wrote in the letter I sent to the Sultan, "are delighted to be in your fair land after flying over so much barren sand, and we wish to thank you for allowing us to land at Salala.

"We would be highly honored if we might have the opportunity of meeting you at your convenience while we are here."

The Sultan's reply, sent to Ed Clayton, was partly as follows:

"I am very busy with preparations for my departure on Saturday, the nineteenth of February. I will try to find time to see the Lowells before I leave should they be here during the next two days."

But "the Lowells" spent only one night in Salala, so the audience never came off.

We drove on from the palace for a mile or so along the beach to an encampment of half a dozen tents, in which the Claytons, as well as a Cities Service geologist, and a British doctor and two nurses lived. But what tents!

One was for guests, and it had been made most carefully and thoughtfully in Cairo. It was light green inside, and was handsomely furnished with oriental rugs, camel saddles, lamps with colorful shades, and so on. Set up on the fine white sand of the beach near a cocoanut grove, the cluster of tents provided comforts, and even luxuries, that were all the more surprising for their unexpected presence here in western Oman.

The beach, incidentally, was covered by incredible numbers of sand crabs. Averaging about six inches across, they lived in holes in the sand that were surrounded by cones of sand as high as twelve inches. What ugly creatures! Fortunately they were harmless, for one or two almost always found their way into the tents at night, there to climb up the tent walls near the electric lights, which seemed to attract them.

That evening, with one eye on the uninvited crabs in the tent, Tay and I talked with our hosts about the prospects of oil in Dhufar. Ed Clayton was highly optimistic, saying that they had found all sorts of geological indications.

"Maybe the whole Arabian peninsula," he added, "is an oil bed."

I had to admit that Salala might someday become another Dhahran, but at the moment, I knew, it was only an oil company's beachhead—a mere toe hold at the edge of a strange and little-known land.

We pushed on the following morning for Aden, flying southwest along the coast. The "beachhead" impression struck me again just west of Salala where, just behind the beach of a sheltered cove, the Cities Service drilling equipment and trucks were assembled—equipment that still had to be transported over the mountains to the edge of the Rub' al Khali.

The weather was fine, and flying along the coast was tame after the Empty Quarter. Here and there some of the coast line reminded us of the Costa Brava of Spain, though the rocks were often even more precipitous, rising abruptly, sometimes to almost 5000 feet.

Half an hour out of Salala we crossed into the Aden Protectorate—Great Britain being the protector—and as noon approached we landed at another R.A.F. airfield—Riyan, a few miles east of Mukalla. There we refueled, had soup and a sandwich at the R.A.F. mess, and took off again.

As we passed the picturesque port of Mukalla, the high black cliffs that rise so steeply behind it caught our attention. Mukalla's tall white buildings were tightly clustered back of the beach, and just offshore numbers of Arab dhows were riding at anchor. This was the coast of frankincense and myrrh, both of which are the resinous products of trees that grow in this portion of the world. In ancient times, as long ago as the twenty-eighth century B.C., Egyptian expeditions reached these hills, and the trade in frankincense continued for centuries, for it was important not only as a base for perfume and incense but also in embalming, which was a vital matter in the minds of the Egyptians. Myrrh, on the other hand, was used by the ancients as an ingredient in perfume and incense, as well as for a remedy. Even in Biblical times camel caravans carried it across the deserts to Mediterranean seaports where it was shipped to many ports of the ancient world. And even today the trade continues, though on a lessened scale, the principal uses for myrrh being in the manufacture of perfumes, dentifrices, and a tonic that is much in demand in the East.

Supported, in part, by this trade, a rich culture sprang up in a valley known as the Wadi Hadhramaut, and Tay and I, checking our maps as we flew along the coast, thought of flying inland for a glimpse of this region. Our gas tanks were full, and we knew we could do it and still reach Aden before dark with an ample fuel reserve. So, just beyond Mukalla, I turned Charlie toward the north and began reaching for altitude needed to cross the coastal mountains and the high plateau that lies behind them. But the land rose so steeply before us that we had to circle widely as we climbed to 8000 feet.

The air was clear, and it was not long before we spotted the Wadi Hadhramaut—a deep valley cut in the plateau. It reminded us somewhat of the Grand Canyon of Arizona, though it was broader and shallower—no more than 2000 feet deep, I believe. But when we dropped down into the valley and followed it from west to east, we found a most remarkable region beneath our wings.

Surrounded by green fields and date groves, and with multicolored cliffs on every side, we found one cluster of "skyscrapers" after another—skyscrapers that have been in vogue since before the days of Solomon and the Queen of Sheba.

We had read of these wonder cities but we still found it hard to believe our eyes as we flew over the strangely huddled skyscraper towns of Shibam, Saiun, and Tarim. Each of these tightly built communities was solidly filled with tall structures, constructed of sun-dried brick, and rising to the astonishing height of seven or eight stories.

Most incredible of all was Shibam. From a distance this crowded little city seemed to be an angular formation of rock rising abruptly from the valley floor almost like a butte. But as we flew closer we could see that it was a solid, rectangular mass of some six hundred mud-brick skyscrapers, and the whole of the city covered an area not much greater than a large city block in almost any American city.

Defense was the idea of those who built these cities—defense from raiding Bedouins. We had heard that the lower floors of the skyscrapers were used for storage, slaves, and servants, with the floors above set aside for family use. The uppermost, I suppose, would be reserved for the harems.

We wished that we could land and visit one of these fabulous communities, but that was impossible. We contented ourselves, instead, with a few aerial photographs before climbing out of the valley again and setting our course for Aden.

Aden is the British Gibraltar of this part of the world—a rapidly growing, increasingly modern city. There is industry there, and all the markings of civilization, Western style. We found the airfield paved, lighted, and equipped to play its part as one of the important air centers of the world. Charlie was quickly refueled and hangared, and we spent a comfortable night in a new, modern, air-conditioned hotel.

The next day we closed the circle by returning to Asmara, Eritrea, but this time we paused there only long enough to fill our tanks and check the weather. Then we flew 300 miles farther up the Red Sea coast to Port Sudan, where we spent the night in a European-style hotel, before flying on to Luxor.

The sky was cloudless all the way, and navigation could hardly have been easier. So long as Charlie's engine kept turning over faithfully, as it did, all was well, though a forced landing almost anywhere along the almost uninhabited Red Sea coast would have been highly undesirable.

Before leaving Dhahran we had made arrangements with Aramco to land at Jidda, the Arabian port of entry for Mecca—holy city of the Moslem world. We had originally planned to spend several days in Jidda, but we now decided not to cross the 150-mile width of the Red Sea, preferring to turn northwest to Luxor. It was only proper, of course, for us to report this change of plan, and I tried to raise the oil company's ground station by radio. I called again and again, but there was no answer, and just as I was about to give up, a faint voice came through the earphones. At first it was such a whisper that I could not understand what was being said, but by pressing the earphones tightly to my ears and listening intently, I recognized the voice of Red Caudill, foreman of Aramco's mobile units in the desert, G-8 and G-9. He was calling to say that he had picked up our message about not landing at Jidda.

For a short time I chatted with him, telling him that we were homeward bound, and urging him not to get lost in all that sand. Then his voice faded away into the Empty Quarter and we got out our smaller scale map to see how great the distance was between where Charlie was now flying and where Red's strings were at work in the Rub' al Khali. As nearly as I could figure, our voices had carried something more than 700 miles. Only once before had our small transmitter reached out so far, and that was on the evening Bahrein had heard us while we were trying to find Meshed in the dark.

It was on this otherwise uneventful flight, and for some unexplained reason, that we were reported missing. A newspaper report which we saw later said "Lowell Thomas, Jr., and his wife, unreported for six days on a flight over the Arabian peninsula, were located today on the Island of Sardinia in the Mediterranean . . . [There was concern] for their . . . safety after they failed to make routine checks on a flight from Aden . . . to Cairo. . . ." We have no way of knowing how this story originated. We never even came close to being lost or forced down, and we never reached the Island of Sardinia, either.

When we arrived at Luxor, 250 miles up the Nile from Cairo, the city was in the midst of a busy tourist season. It almost seemed that we were the only guests at the swank hotel who weren't members of some tour. Trouble awaited us at the Luxor Airport the morning after our arrival, too. The Egyptian control officer insisted on seeing Charlie's Certificate of Air Worthiness—the first time that particular document had ever been asked for.

And, worse luck, it had expired! I had visions of Charlie being grounded until an Egyptian mechanic could be flown to Luxor from Cairo—a week's delay, perhaps, and a colossal bill for us to pay. But then an idea occurred to me.

I went out to the plane and got out all the plane's papers *except* that troublesome certificate.

"Here you are," I said when I had returned to the control. "All the plane's papers. What you want is here somewhere. I've never seen it myself. You'll have to find it."

I held my breath. A week's time and hundreds of dollars hung in the balance. But as he studied paper after paper I began to see that he didn't really know just what he was looking for. He studied each paper carefully—the engine log, the last inspection report, and others, too.

"Is this it?" I asked, picking up the Weight and Balance Sheet.

The solemn control officer looked it over carefully and nodded. But he could find no dates on it, which puzzled him, and he asked me when it expired.

"Oh," I replied shamelessly. "Not for nearly a year. The airplane was just inspected by Aramco over in Saudi Arabia."

That much was true, certainly, and on the strength of what the oil company's people had done, no plane was ever more deserving of a Certificate of Air Worthiness. The trouble was that I had not thought to ask Aramco's mechanics to make out a new one.

The control officer nodded, as he returned the bundle of papers to me, and a few hours later we were in Cairo, where customs officers descended on our planeful of possessions with what seemed to me to be fire in their eyes. But we stopped them cold by saying that we didn't want to use our cameras or anything else. They could lock it all up in the customs house, and we would take it out of Egypt in a few days.

Cairo, of course, was also enjoying a booming tourist season, and it was three in the afternoon before we at last found ourselves riding up in the hotel elevator to our room. We had been up since before dawn and had had nothing to eat since sunrise. The flight had not been a short one, and we had been delayed at the airport. It is no wonder that Tay was half exhausted. But it startled me when she suddenly sank down to the floor of the elevator with her head between her knees as she tried to fight off her faintness.

A middle-aged American—a businessman, I imagine, who was probably fresh off a liner at Alexandria—was in the elevator with us, and he very kindly asked if my wife was all right.

I was concerned, naturally, but in my concern I imagine that I showed more confidence than I felt.

"Oh, she's fine," I replied. "She just hasn't eaten since six o'clock this morning."

I probably impressed him as being inordinately casual, for his brows went up.

"Why hasn't she eaten?" he asked icily.

Luckily the elevator reached our floor just then, and I didn't have to answer. Instead, I silently helped Tay out and down the hall.

A little later a platter of shiskabab and rice helped my co-pilot-navigator to feel better, though it was obvious that she deserved a rest before we began our dash for home. And, too, we had to find a buyer for Charlie, though now, having reached the point of selling him, the idea no longer appealed to us very strongly.

Since the expiration of the Certificate of Air Worthiness would be likely to scare off any interested parties, I set about getting a new one. We had heard of another Cessna in Cairo—a slower model than ours, owned by an American air-line captain, Bill Judd. I looked him up, anxious to talk about aviation in general, but also to enlist his aid in finding a licensed mechanic who could quickly make the necessary inspection and issue a new certificate.

Captain Judd, fortunately, knew just the man—an able Egyptian who helps keep four-engined Constellations flying—and I soon had the new certificate I needed. In the process, however, Tay and I changed our minds about parting with Charlie in Egypt. Instead, we decided to fly him back to Paris, which, since it was the actual starting place of our flight, seemed the ideal place for its ending, and Charlie's sale, too.

Before buzzing off again, Tay and I had several delightful visits with Bill Judd and his French wife, Colette, and I especially enjoyed introducing Captain Judd to Charlie. He was so impressed by our plane's performance that he sold his and, returning to the States a year later, he bought a new 180 which he proceeded to equip with extra gas tanks until it was little more than an aerial tanker. Then he undertook to fly it non-stop from New York to Rome, with the chance of going non-stop all the way to Cairo. He might very well have set a new distance record for a light airplane, too, had it not been for severe icing conditions and a few other complications over the Atlantic. Not merely once, but actually three times, his difficulties over the wintry North Atlantic culminated in complete loss of power, though he succeeded somehow in making it to Paris. It was an experience that I am glad Tay and I were not called upon to face.

When, at last, we took off from Cairo, our first destination was the Libyan port of Tobruk, a name that brings back memories of savage days during World War II. And on the way we would stop at Mersa Matruh, to clear Egyptian customs.

Our course from Cairo was across a pale yellow stretch of desert as we headed for El Alamein, where the tide of World War II began to flow in favor of the Allies. Long before we saw the town we began to spot twisted and rusted metal on the sand beneath us—grim reminders of the decisive battle in which the British defeated Rommel's Axis forces.

El Alamein itself looked like nothing but a tiny mud-brick town on the seashore, but inland a little way were many signs of the battle. I let Charlie descend to 500 feet, looking closely for some battle remnant that would make an impressive photograph, and found one, at last, when we located a knocked-out truck that lay tilted on its side in the sand. But as we circled and Tay began to shoot the movie camera, imagine our surprise to see an Arab in a white burnoose as he stepped from the truck's enclosed rear end, followed closely by what seemed to be his family.

How strange, we thought, are the workings of time. An instrument of war, abandoned in the Egyptian desert, had now become an Arab's home.

We climbed back to our cruising level, landing a little later at Mersa Matruh where, in short order, Charlie was refueled and we were cleared by customs to leave Egypt. Taking off once more, we followed the coast for about 200 miles to Tobruk where we landed at the small R.A.F. base of El Adem.

The R.A.F. was willing to put us up for the night, but the cockney non-com in operations seemed a bit distressed when we were assigned to the bachelor officers' quarters.

"But, Sergeant," he complained over the phone. "There's a lie-dy along!"

Whereupon the sergeant switched us to the "ladies' quarters."

The next day dawned with a sandstorm blowing off the Libyan Desert, so we sat tight, but the following morning we took off on what turned out to be the longest leg of our entire flight to adventure—750 miles. Our route lay directly to the southernmost point of the Gulf of Sirte, and from there over Sirte itself. Then we passed Tmed Hassan, Misurata, and Homs on our way to Tripoli.

Tripoli is one of Libya's two capitals, and we were tempted to linger, but both of us, by now, somewhat resembled the horse that is heading for the barn. We had been gone from home over a year and were eager to return, so the next morning found us in the air again. We passed directly over the ancient Carthaginian city of Sabratha and saw the columns of its great and well-preserved amphitheater gleaming pink in the sunshine. Then we turned north with the coast line, flying on for another 250 miles to Tunis where we landed in a cold rainstorm.

We wanted to return to France by the shortest route, which meant flying by way of Sardinia and Corsica, but the French airport officials in Tunis "pulled the book" on us when they pointed out that the regulations prohibited overwater flights by single-engine civil craft. Furthermore, we had no *ceintures de sauvetage*—no life preservers, that is, or Mae Wests in American parlance.

Compelled to resume our westerly course, but still hopeful of cutting across the Mediterranean without going all the way to Gibraltar, we borrowed the necessary *ceintures de sauvetage* and took off for Algiers. There we almost got clearance for the flight due north to Barcelona, flying by way of the Balearic Islands, but as we were taxiing out to the runway, radio instructions reached us that approval had been denied. We must return to operations. However, I persuaded them over the radio that we would fly on west to Oran instead, and they agreed to change our flight plan accordingly.

Tay was pleased with this change in our routing, but as we flew on toward the west I began to see that by turning out across the Mediterranean from a point about 110 miles west of Algiers we could save 600 miles or more. The alternative was to fly all the way to Ceuta, then across the strait to Gibraltar, returning to France by the same route we had taken to Morocco a year earlier.

To my surprise, Tay consented to this short cut, but before loosing our hold on the Algerian coast line we slipped into our Mae Wests and climbed Charlie to 8000 feet. At that elevation, should the engine fail, we would have eight minutes of forward gliding—about twelve miles—before hitting the water. And, too, this would give us time to radio our predicament and our approximate position, which might make all the difference in being rescued.

Out over the sea we turned, reaching for Spain. But no one, as yet, knew of this change in our plan. It seemed a good idea to report to somebody, so I called Algiers. There was no reply, and I called again and again. Still there was no answer, but before abandoning the idea I called on a frequency that is much used by U. S. Military Air Transport planes flying over North Africa.

"This is Cessna Four Three Charlie," I called blindly. "Calling any station. Four Three Charlie calling any station on 126.7 megacycles. Anybody reading Four Three Charlie please come in."

Back came a faint American voice.

"Four Three Charlie," it replied. "This is MATS Niner Seven. Go ahead."

I then asked MATS Niner Seven to please advise Algiers that we had left the African coast at such and such a point and time, and were on such and such a heading to Cartagena.

MATS Niner Seven replied that he would do so, but then he cheerily added a little postscript.

"Careful, Four Three Charlie," he said. "Don't get wet."

Neither Tay nor I cracked a smile over that bit of humor until we reached the Spanish coast forty minutes later. Then with the Mediterranean crossing behind us, we were able to laugh even though the weather along the Spanish coast was no better than it had been the year before.

Valencia, which was as far as the clouds would let us go, was shrouded in smog and light rain. We almost had to retreat, but at last we found the airport and landed, to the astonishment of the Spanish controllers who, no doubt, imagined that we had long since cracked up in Africa. They welcomed us royally, and there was a bit of elbow bending at the airport bar before we were given a lift into the city.

The weather was better the next morning, and we pushed on, passing Barcelona without a stop, and not coming down until the Costa Brava was far behind us and we had reached Toulouse. Here I ran into a difficulty over Charlie's *Carnet de Passage,* which, unhappily, the French officials saw had expired. And at the same time Tay ran into complications with customs, who insisted that the plane be completely unloaded. But at length everyone was satisfied, and early that afternoon we took off on the final flight of our aerial Odyssey—to Paris.

Most of our route was obscured by haze, but at 7000 feet we were in clean blue sky and were content to navigate by the radio compass alone. We knew we couldn't miss Paris, surrounded as it is by such a web of radio aids to navigation.

Glad not to have to keep our eyes on the towns, highways, railroads, and rivers below, Tay and I began to think of all the lands and peoples that we had come to know in the preceding twelve months. And what, we asked ourselves, did it all add up to, really? What had we learned from all these experiences?

A flood of answers came to mind, but it seemed to both of us that the most important lesson we had been taught is that the world is not a hostile place.

The old captain of the Arab dhow on which I had sailed, for example, had begun by being non-committal and uncommunicative. But when he saw that the Western stranger was willing to help hoist the sail or shift the cargo, and that I genuinely wanted to be friendly, he had thawed out completely.

Tay, too, had had a similar experience with the nomad women of the Jordan desert. We had been told that they might be surly, and they had actually been distant and standoffish until Tay had admired their babies. But then they had crowded around her, showing off their little ones and asking her to take their pictures.

Everywhere we had been, people had reacted to honesty with honesty. They had responded to friendliness with more friendliness—to little acts of kindness with larger acts of kindness. These are not merely Christian virtues. They are universal human traits, and we had found them everywhere.

In no time at all we were over the radio beacon at Chartres, only thirty miles from Toussus-le-Noble, the airport southwest of Paris where our journey had begun. Letting down into the layers of spring haze, we picked up the railroad that runs to Versailles. Then, at the right moment, we turned to a compass heading for the airport and at three fifty-seven Paris time on the afternoon of March 4, 1955, we came in for our last landing.

There to greet us was Jean Avot, who had done so much to start us off. He welcomed Tay with a bouquet of flowers and a kiss on each cheek. And there were flowers for Charlie, too—a wreath that was hung around his propeller. And they both deserved them, after some 50,000 miles over Africa and the Middle East.

I don't know whether Tay or I thought of it first. It is even possible that the idea came to both of us at the same moment— the idea that Charlie, after having served us so well, just couldn't be left behind. We both felt that he had become a part of the family, and we resolved to take him home, which we did.

When we boarded an overnight air liner for New York, Jean Avot had instructions to send Charlie after us, and a few weeks after we reached home, Tay and I drove to Idlewild Airport, on Long Island near New York. We were waiting there when a big, four-engined Pan American cargo clipper arrived from Europe. We watched it park and saw its loading doors as they were opened. Three handsome race horses were led out first, and then, inside and all dismantled, we saw Charlie. Carefully he was unloaded, and since then he has been put back together again. And he still continues to fly us around America.

But speaking of arrivals, the best of all was the arrival of our blue-eyed, brown-haired daughter, Anne, on August 10, 1955. She was by far the happiest result of our flight to adventure.